T0383277

BEHAVIOR
CHANGE
RESEARCH
AND THEORY

BEHAVIOR CHANGE RESEARCH AND THEORY

PSYCHOLOGICAL AND TECHNOLOGICAL PERSPECTIVES

Edited by

LINDA LITTLE
PaCT Lab, Department of Psychology, Faculty of Health and Life Sciences
Northumbria University, United Kingdom

ELIZABETH SILLENCE
PaCT Lab, Department of Psychology, Faculty of Health and Life Sciences
Northumbria University, United Kingdom

ADAM JOINSON
School of Management, University of Bath, Bath, United Kingdom

AMSTERDAM • BOSTON • HEIDELBERG • LONDON
NEW YORK • OXFORD • PARIS • SAN DIEGO
SAN FRANCISCO • SINGAPORE • SYDNEY • TOKYO

Academic Press is an imprint of Elsevier

Academic Press is an imprint of Elsevier
125 London Wall, London EC2Y 5AS, United Kingdom
525 B Street, Suite 1800, San Diego, CA 92101-4495, United States
50 Hampshire Street, 5th Floor, Cambridge, MA 02139, United States
The Boulevard, Langford Lane, Kidlington, Oxford OX5 1GB, United Kingdom

Library of Congress Cataloging-in-Publication Data
A catalog record for this book is available from the Library of Congress

British Library Cataloguing-in-Publication Data
A catalogue record for this book is available from the British Library

ISBN: 978-0-12-802690-8

For information on all Academic Press publications
visit our website at https://www.elsevier.com/

Working together
to grow libraries in
developing countries

www.elsevier.com • www.bookaid.org

Publisher: Nikki Levy
Acquisition Editor: Emily Ekle
Editorial Project Manager: Timothy Bennett
Production Project Manager: Caroline Johnson
Designer: Victoria Pearson

Typeset by Thomson Digital

Contents

4. Evaluating Mobile-Based Behavior Change Support Systems for Health and Well-Being

S. LANGRIAL, P. KARPPINEN, T. LEHTO, M. HARJUMAA, H. OINAS-KUKKONEN

5. Self-Affirmation Interventions to Change Health Behaviors

B. SCHÜZ, R. COOKE, N. SCHÜZ, G.M. VAN KONINGSBRUGGEN

6. Behavior Change Interventions for Cybersecurity

P. BRIGGS, D. JESKE, L. COVENTRY

7. Automatic Tracking of Behavior With Smartphones: Potential for Behavior Change Interventions

L. PIWEK, A. JOINSON

8. Intervening Online: Evaluating Methods, Assessing Outcomes, and Signposting Future Directions

E. SILLENCE, L. LITTLE, A. FIELDEN

9. BinCam: Evaluating Persuasion at Multiple Scales

R. COMBER, A. THIEME

Conclusion

A. JOINSON, E. SILLENCE, L. LITTLE

List of Contributors

C. Abraham Psychology Applied to Health (PAtH), University of Exeter Medical School, University of Exeter, Exeter, United Kingdom

T. Alahäivälä Department of Information Processing Science, University of Oulu, Oulu, Finland

P. Briggs Northumbria University, Newcastle upon Tyne, United Kingdom

R. Comber Open Lab, School of Computing Science, Newcastle University, Newcastle upon Tyne, United Kingdom

L.A. Condon School of Medicine, Nottingham University, Nottingham, United Kingdom

R. Cooke Aston University, Birmingham, United Kingdom

N.S. Coulson School of Medicine, Nottingham University, Nottingham, United Kingdom

L. Coventry Northumbria University, Newcastle upon Tyne, United Kingdom

S. Denford Psychology Applied to Health (PAtH), University of Exeter Medical School, University of Exeter, Exeter, United Kingdom

A. Fielden School of Psychology, Newcastle University, Newcastle upon Tyne, United Kingdom

M. Harjumaa VTT Technical Research Center of Finland, Oulu, Finland

D. Jeske Edinburgh Napier University, Edinburgh, United Kingdom

A. Joinson School of Management, University of Bath, Bath, United Kingdom

P. Karppinen Oulu Advanced Research on Software and Information Systems, Department of Information Processing Science, University of Oulu, Oulu, Finland

S. Langrial Oulu Advanced Research on Software and Information Systems, Department of Information Processing Science, University of Oulu, Oulu, Finland; Sur University College, Sur, Sultanate of Oman

T. Lehto Oulu Advanced Research on Software and Information Systems, Department of Information Processing Science, University of Oulu, Oulu, Finland

L. Little PaCT Lab, Department of Psychology, Faculty of Health and Life Sciences, Northumbria University, Newcastle, United Kingdom

M. Oduor Department of Information Processing Science, University of Oulu, Oulu, Finland

H. Oinas-Kukkonen Oulu Advanced Research on Software and Information Systems, Oulu, Finland

L. Piwek   School of Management, University of Bath, Bath, United Kingdom

B. Schüz   University of Tasmania, Hobart, TAS, Australia

N. Schüz   University of Tasmania, Hobart, TAS, Australia

E. Sillence   PaCT Lab, Department of Psychology, Faculty of Health and Life Sciences, Northumbria University, Newcastle, United Kingdom

A. Thieme   Open Lab, School of Computing Science, Newcastle University, Newcastle upon Tyne, United Kingdom

G.M. van Koningsbruggen   Vrije Universiteit Amsterdam, Amsterdam, The Netherlands

Digital Behavior Change

E. Sillence*, L. Little*, A. Joinson**

*PaCT Lab, Department of Psychology, Faculty of Health and Life Sciences, Northumbria University, Newcastle, United Kingdom; **School of Management, University of Bath, Bath, United Kingdom

DIGITAL BEHAVIOR CHANGE

This book is concerned with the planning, implementation, and evaluation of digital behavior change interventions. We define digital behavior change as a behavior change that makes use of technology to either (1) promote the delivery of the intervention, (2) enhance the environment through which the intervention occurs, or (3) encourage specific patterns of interaction that underpin the intervention.

BACKGROUND

Organizations, researchers, and professionals are increasingly interested in behavior change with the focus spreading beyond health behaviors to encompass issues such as energy consumption and security (Bell, Toth, Little, & Smith 2015; Blythe, Coventry, & Little, 2015). While the motivation for changing behavior is usually apparent and well documented, understanding how to bring about change is less clear cut. Psychologists, for example, utilize a wide range of behavior change techniques. Indeed a review of the literature by Michie, Johnston, Francis, Hardeman, and Eccles (2008) identified at least 137 individual techniques and concluded that a "one-size-fits-all" approach cannot be adopted within behavior change research. As Bell et al. (2015) suggest techniques should be selected based on an understanding of the specific antecedents of the behavior that is to be changed, and the approach tailored for this. Attention must also be given to the target population and their ability to access, understand, and process the information presented.

Behavior change techniques need to be evaluated in order to develop a clear scientific approach that is driven by theory and practice. Developing a clear behavior change science will in turn evidence the determinants of behavior best to target in interventions. Interventions that are driven by theoretical underpinning, evaluated, planned, and designed will create approaches that are cost effective and have long-term success in changing behavior.

Many researchers now recognize the role technology can play in shaping behavior change techniques (Lehto & Oinas-Kukkonen, 2015). For example, smartphones are easy to use and afford the opportunity to collect and record real-time behavioral data through mobile applications. Web-based delivery of intervention programs offers significant advantages in terms of resources and distribution (Griffiths, Lindenmeyer, Powell, Lowe, & Thorogood, 2006). The extent to which the technology plays a facilitating rather than a driving role in behavior change is, however, important (Patel, Asch, & Volpp, 2015) as is the notion that any use of technology in this context needs to focus on the end users themselves and be person-centered rather than technologically dictated (Yardley, Morrison, Bradbury, & Muller, 2015).

The chapters in this book attempt to capture the essence of "digital behavior change." The overarching goal of digital behavior change is alignment, put simply, that is the mapping of the target behavior with the affordances and opportunities provided by the technology. This process of identifying the behavior and possible technologies is one that has to be closely coupled. Rather than allowing the technology to determine the intervention, we need to begin with a strong sense of what it is that needs to change, and how technology supports that change through both the affordances of the technology, and the underpinning behavior change mechanism. Once the behavior has been identified it is possible to start thinking about the potential for technology. It may be that there is no appropriate and useful role for technology within any given context and the aim of this book is not to suggest that simply adding technology to any behavior change intervention will always be a good idea. Far from it, we suggest that successful digital behavior change requires the same detailed planning as specified in Abraham and Denford in Chapter 1. However, we also suggest that to maximize the return on a technology investment, interventions need to carefully consider how the technology used might support (or indeed work against) the underpinning change mechanisms. The goal of the remaining chapters in the book support this process by considering not only how technology can be used, but also why and when a specific technology might be best implemented as part of an intervention.

This book aims to offer practical guidance as to how to plan, implement, and evaluate behavior change interventions. The book encapsulates a number of different perspectives on behavior change including those from psychology, design, and software engineering and introduces key models and processes in relation to health and well-being, security, and environmental issues. Importantly, the theme of technology runs throughout the book, with authors highlighting current technology use, near future use, and suggesting directions for future work. Here we gain valuable insights into the ways in which technology can underpin the delivery of the intervention and assist with data recording and collection.

The book has been divided into three main areas: planning, intervention, and evaluation. This was done consciously to aid the reader in navigating to the most appropriate section. However, we are very aware of the importance of integrating all elements of a behavior change program, a point reiterated by the authors of Chapter 1. To these ends Chapters 1–4 discuss approaches to planning a behavior change intervention taking into account high level principles applicable across a range of contexts through to a number of specific worked examples of planning or takeaway guidelines and frameworks that could be used or adapted as appropriate.

In Chapter 1, Abraham and Denford outline the steps that can guide optimal planning of interventions to change behavior and guide the reader through an "intervention mapping approach." Chapter 2 presents a clear example of planning in action as it relates to a health intervention to optimize healthy dietary and exercise behaviors in adolescents. Chapters 3 and 4 take more of a computing science and design approach to planning interventions. Chapter 3 introduces the idea of persuasive system design approach (PSD) and outlines a number of software patterns as guides to developing interventions. Chapter 4 presents a planning framework for designing mobile applications for intervention. In the implementation section of the book we focus on three individual level interventions. In Chapter 5 the authors introduce self-affirmation and detail the literature on this psychological level intervention particularly within a health setting. In Chapter 6 the authors compare and contrast two different approaches to intervention within a security setting. Choice architecture and Protection Motivation Theory are reviewed in terms of guiding specific interventions in the security domain. While in Chapter 7, Piwek and Joinson take a more technological approach to intervention and focus on the use of wearable and mobile data collection and recording tools for facilitating behavior change.

Evaluation case studies in Chapters 8 and 9 provide a detailed account of how three digital behavior change interventions were evaluated. Health, energy consumption, and recycling behaviors are all considered and attention is paid to both the outcomes and the process of the intervention. The evaluation chapters highlight the different roles that technology can play in terms of delivering the intervention and collecting the resulting data. Finally the editors provide some concluding thoughts in which they propose a method for the alignment of behavioral change goals and the technology available.

References

Bell, B., Toth, N., Little, L., & Smith, M. A. (2015). Planning to save the planet: using an online intervention based on implementation intentions to change teen energy-saving behaviour. *Environment & Behavior.* Advance online publication.

Blythe, J. M., Coventry, L., & Little, L. (2015). Unpacking security policy compliance: the motivators and barriers of employees' security behaviors. In *Symposium on Usable Privacy and Security* (SOUPS), Vol. 22.

Griffiths, F., Lindenmeyer, A., Powell, J., Lowe, P., & Thorogood, M. (2006). Why are health care interventions delivered over the internet? A systematic review of the published literature. *Journal of Medical Internet Research, 8,* e10.

Lehto, T., & Oinas-Kukkonen, H. (2015). Explaining and predicting perceived effectiveness and use continuance intention of a behaviour change support system for weight loss. *Behaviour and Information Technology, 34*(2), 176–189.

Michie, S., Johnston, M., Francis, J., Hardeman, W., & Eccles, M. (2008). From theory to intervention: mapping theoretically derived behavioural determinants to behaviour change techniques. *Applied Psychology, 57*(4), 660–680.

Patel, M. S., Asch, D. A., & Volpp, K. G. (2015). Wearable devices as facilitators, not drivers, of health behavior change. *JAMA, 313*(5), 459–460.

Yardley, L., Morrison, L., Bradbury, K., & Muller, I. (2015). The person-based approach to intervention development: application to digital health-related behavior change interventions. *Journal of Medical Internet Research, 17*(1), e30.

CHAPTER

1

Planning Interventions to Change Behavior

C. Abraham, S. Denford

Psychology Applied to Health (PAtH), University of Exeter
Medical School, University of Exeter, Exeter, United Kingdom

OVERVIEW

In this chapter, we highlight the need for behavior change, and its potential impact on health and health expenditure. We discuss how change can be initiated, facilitated, and maintained, and introduce the "NUDGE" framework—a strategy tried and tested by both UK and US governments. We then use the Intervention Mapping (IM) approach to take the reader through the processes involved in optimal intervention design and evaluation. Drawing on the Information, Motivation, Behavioral skills (IMB) model, we introduce reflective and impulsive behavioral determinants that underpin behavior and behavior change. We end this chapter by explaining and emphasizing the need for evaluation of behavior change interventions in order to develop a science of behavior change.

INTRODUCTION

Population-level behavior change research has become especially topical because of the recognition that patterns of behavior shared across populations determine our health and well-being. More than 40 years ago, the Alameda County study of health-related behavior patterns followed 7000 people over 10 years and showed that sleep, exercise, alcohol consumption, and eating habits predicted mortality (Belloc & Breslow, 1972). Similarly, following 4886 individuals, Kvaavik, Batty, Ursin, Huxley, and Gale (2010) found that those who smoked, consumed less than 3 portions

Behavior Change Research and Theory. http://dx.doi.org/10.1016/B978-0-12-802690-8.00002-5

of fruits and vegetables daily, did less than 2 h of physical activity per week; and consumed more than 14 units of alcohol had an all-cause mortality risk equivalent to being 12 years older than those that did none of the above. Increasingly, eating and physical activity patterns are problematic across international populations (World Health Organization, 2015). In England, for example, more than 60% of the population is overweight or obese which, in turn, is associated with a range of health problems, including type 2 diabetes, coronary heart disease, hypertension, osteoarthritis, and particular cancers (Guh et al., 2009) that reduce life expectancy (Flegal, Kit, Orpana, & Graubard, 2013; Whitlock et al., 2009). This greatly increases health service costs. In the United Kingdom, for example, weight-related health problems are estimated to cost an additional £5 billion annually (Department of Health, 2013). Engaging people in their own self-management and behavior change is critical to health service management and to governance more generally.

CHANGE IS POSSIBLE

For most people, our reprogrammable brains (Maslin & Christensen, 2007), consisting of approximately 86 billion neurons has the capacity, over time, to rewrite the processes that direct what we think, what we feel, and what we do (Herculano-Houzel, 2009). We try new things and form new relationships. As we practice new behavioral routines over time we automatically reprogram our perceptions, our feelings, our thoughts, and our skills. So activities that at one time seem difficult or strange can become easy and everyday over time. The challenge for scientists working on behavior change is to model, explain, and then harness the cognitive, emotional, and behavioral dynamism of our regulatory control systems (Reynolds & Branscombe, 2015) and then to develop interventions that help people accelerate and consolidate behavior change processes (Denford et al., 2015).

We know too that interventions to change behavior patterns across groups can be effective. Reductions in smoking and unsafe sexual behavior, increases in physical activity, healthy diets, self-care, and health screening have all been observed following particular interventions (Denford, Taylor, Campbell, & Greaves, 2013; Greaves et al., 2011). The National Institute of Health and Care Excellence (NICE) of United Kingdom commissioned a review of reviews that included data on 103 systematic reviews of interventions targeting one of six behaviors (cigarette smoking, alcohol consumption, physical activity, healthy eating, drug use, and sexual risk taking) and, although the degree of effectiveness varied between populations and intervention characteristics, overall, interventions were found to be successful in changing behavior patterns (Jepson, Harris, Platt, & Tannahill, 2010; Johnson, Scott-Sheldon, & Carey, 2010).

This does not mean that behavior change intervention design is easy, or that interventions are usually effective. Careful modeling of relevant, modifiable processes that regulate behavior patterns (also referred to as "determinants of behavior") and subsequently, matched selection of specific change techniques known to be capable of modifying those processes is a prerequisite to success. Later we will describe an "IM" approach that can guide optimal planning.

CHANGING INDIVIDUALS OR CHANGING ENVIRONMENTS

Understanding how we can help people reprogram themselves is an important aspect of behavior change science and is the focus of this chapter but environmental changes may often provide more powerful levers of change. Changes in the physical, commercial, and social environment can prompt widespread behavior change without attempts to persuade or change individuals. Consider, for example, interventions designed to change obesity. At an individual level, an interventionist could target intrapersonal regulatory processes or psychological "determinants" of physical activity and eating behavior. If effective and widely applied such individual change could have population-wide effects (Laatikainen et al., 2007). By contrast, opening affordable community health and fitness centers, improving access to green spaces, providing lower cost healthy foods, restricting advertisements for fattening foods, taxing fattening foods all target the environment in which people make choices rather than choice mechanisms (see UK House of Lords, 2011 for a useful intervention typology). With large-scale complex problems—obesity prevention, for example—individual approaches are unlikely to be sufficient alone (Butland et al., 2007). This project recognizes the need for a whole system approach; targeting multiple processes, such as promoting healthy diets and redesigning the built environment to promote walking at the same time as tackling wider cultural factors to change societal attitudes around food and exercise.

Environmental change may include organizational change. Sometimes the structure, rules, and norms that constitute organizations are critical determinants of target behavior patterns. For example, Haslam et al. (2014) studied residents of care homes in which either (1) residents formed groups to redesign the home environment or (2) care staff redesigned the home environment for the residents or (3) there was no change. These researchers found that people in the residents-redesign condition showed significantly greater, clinically important increases in cognitive functioning and increased use of resident lounges (compared to the other two conditions), indicating that involvement in the redesign group changed residents' thinking and behavior. In this example, group and organizational processes, rather than intrapersonal processes, such as attitudes toward socializing with other residents, were critical to intervention effectiveness (Tarrant, Hagger, & Farrow, 2011).

Legislative change can also have important effects on behavior change and on health benefits. In the United Kingdom, for example, smoking in public places was banned in 2007 and it became illegal to sell tobacco to people below the age of 18 years. Evaluating a similar legislative change, Sargent, Shepard, and Glantz (2004) found that myocardial infarction admissions to a hospital in Montana, USA fell significantly over 6 months during a smoking ban in public places, while at the same time, surrounding areas (without a smoking ban) experienced nonsignificant increases.

Governments in the United Kingdom and United States draw on a range of influential approaches to facilitate behavior change. For example, the EAST framework stands for Easy, Attractive, Social, and Timely (Behavioural Insights, 2014). While not a comprehensive approach to behavior change, it is intended to be easy and accessible to be used by busy policy makers. Quite simply, the message is "if you want to encourage a behavior, make it Easy, Attractive, Social, and Timely. Similar sentiments are shared in the framework "NUDGE," and a very influential book demonstrates how NUDGEs can be used to change behavior (Thaler & Sunstein, 2008). Both US and UK governments set up teams to develop and evaluate NUDGE interventions. "NUDGE" is an unusual acronym because, for example, the "N" stands for incentives, that is, use of rewards or reinforcement to shape behavioral responses. Decades of work have shown that reinforcement, including use of financial incentives can change behavior patterns. For example, if people can be persuaded to deposit savings which they know they will subsequently lose if they fail to meet weight loss targets they lose more weight (Volpp et al., 2008). Similarly, if pregnant women are paid to abstain from smoking they are more successful. In one study smoking cessation follow up at 12 weeks postpartum found that 24% of those receiving financial incentives had been successful compared to only 3% in the control group (Heil et al., 2008). Governments cannot pay everyone to improve their health-related behavior patterns, so the key research question here is, can reinforcement-based interventions initiate psychological changes that bolster intrinsic motivation and, through practice, develop skills and habits that allow behavior change to be sustained, after incentives are removed. If so, such interventions have considerable potential but, if not, they are unlikely to have sustainable effects on public health. Further research is needed on the sustainability of incentive-based interventions but it seems unlikely that use of incentives is an effective way of motivating change in children (Kunz & Pfaff, 2002; Deci, Koestner, & Ryan, 1999).

The "D" in NUDGE stands for "default." This refers to the construction of systems that encourage the least-effort option. For example, when subscription to a service is automatically renewed or tax is automatically deducted. Such systems make it easier for people to act as required by removing the effort and costs of decision making and action. There is evidence that such default-opt-in, or assumed-consent, systems could benefit public health. For example, in relation to organ donation, Johnson and Goldstein (2003) have argued that opt-in systems impose physical, cognitive, and emotional costs on those wishing to donate organs and that these barriers reduce organ donation levels. They show that, in the United Kingdom, which uses an opt-in system, approximately 17% of people donate their organs after death while in a range of European countries employing assumed consent systems the figure is more than 99%. Similarly, Shepherd, O'Carroll, and Ferguson (2014) compared organ donation and transplant rates in 48 countries between 2000 and 2012. While deceased donor rates were higher in opt-out consent countries; the number of living donors was higher in opt-in countries. Of particular importance, the total number of both kidneys transplanted and livers transplanted were higher in opt-out countries (Shepherd et al., 2014). It is likely, therefore, that legislation in the United Kingdom could increase organ donation dramatically.

Use of reinforcement, including financial incentives, and the construction of default opt-in systems are quite distinct approaches toward encouraging population-level behavior change. So "NUDGEs" include a variety of intervention types drawing on a range of change techniques targeting different regulatory processes. Thaler and Sunstein (2008) characterize the interventions that they are interested in as altering "choice architecture ... without forbidding options or significantly changing economic incentives." They say that NUDGEs are "easy and cheap to avoid" and note that, "putting fruit at eye level counts as a nudge ... banning junk food does not." It is certainly possible to design interventions that use low value financial incentives but will they be effective? It is also possible to design easy default opt-in systems but, as with organ donation, many of these systems would require regulatory and legislative change (Marteau, Ogilvie, Martin, Suhrcke, & Kelly, 2011). Given the diverse range of interventions that could be characterized as NUDGEs, it is not helpful to ask whether NUDGEs per se are effective but, instead, to evaluate distinct types of environmental interventions. Some may work well in particular contexts, while others may not.

The term "choice architecture" implies that environments in which we make decisions and take action are preengineered by others. The options available, how these are presented, and what we see and think can be shaped by those who design the environment. Governments may prestructure choice architecture to promote public health as in the case of assumed consent donation policies. Commercial organizations can structure how we see options as we browse online and decide which products are highlighted in television programs, films, and on clothes worn by sporting celebrities. Retailers can structure how goods are presented in shops and restaurants. Similarly, of course, health professionals could likewise design their waiting rooms and consulting rooms to structure our thoughts and actions. Effective structuring of choice architecture raises moral and political questions. For example, evidence suggests that exposure to alcohol advertising and media coverage increases alcohol consumption among young people because it changes alcohol-related cognitions that determine motivation to drink, including expectancies about alcohol use and willingness to use alcohol (Anderson, de Bruijn, Angus, Gordon, & Hastings, 2009; Dal Cin et al., 2009). Yet when the UK charity "Alcohol Concern" investigated alcohol advertising and audience profiles for the Batman film, "Dark Knight," released in the United Kingdom in 2008, they found that almost half of the advertising loop for the film was made up of alcohol advertisements and that 810,000 7- to 14-year-olds were exposed to these alcohol adverts before watching the film, with up to a further 590,000 likely to have been exposed. Given the extent of alcohol advertising it is not surprising that children as young as 10 years old can readily identify alcohol brands, logos, and characters from alcohol adverts (Alcohol Concern, various). The effectiveness of such techniques raises questions about the need for national regulation of advertising, sports sponsorship, product placement, product labeling, other forms of choice architecture engineering (House of Lords, 2011; Marteau et al., 2011). Certainly a range of effective change techniques are available to those who control our environments. These can promote health-risk behavior patterns, including overeating and risky alcohol consumption. Regulation of these techniques and employment of alternative choice architecture engineering could promote health protective behavior patterns. Thus some behavior change problems are best tackled at organizational, institutional, and legislative levels.

Alcohol Concern (various)—see reports at:

1. http://www.alcoholconcern.org.uk/wp-content/uploads/ woocommerce_uploads/2014/12/stick_to_the_facts_report.pdf
2. http://www.alcoholconcern.org.uk/wp-content/uploads/ woocommerce_uploads/2015/02/Childrens-Recognition-of-Alcohol-Marketing_Briefing.compressed.pdf
3. http://www.alcohol-services.co.uk/pdfs/don-shenker-presentation. pdf

WHAT'S IN A BEHAVIOR CHANGE INTERVENTION?

Table 1.1 (taken from Abraham, Conner, Jones, & O'Conner, 2016) lists 12 broadly defined characteristics of any behavior change intervention. This list was adapted from a similar table presented by Davidson et al. (2003) and provides a useful checklist for intervention designers. The characteristics are listed in the order they are usually considered in the intervention planning process (see in subsequent sections). This list emphasizes, at a glance, why the planning stages in intervention design must be interlinked and iterative. For example, if those who need to deliver the intervention do not have the skills to do so or if the proposed delivery methods are unacceptable in the intended setting, then a rethink of the planning process is needed. Similarly, an evidence-based intervention that cannot be sustained in context over time due to a lack of resources will not have on-going real-world impact and so is unlikely to contribute to public health improvement (Glasgow, Bull, Gillette, Klesges, & Dzewaltowski, 2002). Thus, without anticipation of implementation in early planning, interventions may not be adopted or may be partially delivered and so be ineffective.

Planning Intervention Design: Intervention Mapping

Producing effective interventions depends on careful, systematic design, and a range of useful frameworks to guide planning are available (Craig et al., 2008; Centres for Disease Control and Prevention, 1999).

TABLE 1.1 Twelve Broad Characteristics of Behavior Change Interventions (Abraham et al., 2016)

1. Specific behavior change/s targeted
2. Modifiable processes (or mechanisms) operating at different levels that regulate relevant behavior patterns
3. Change techniques known to alter identified regulatory process/mechanisms
4. The delivery methods or formats used (e.g., face-to-face meetings, telephone calls, interactive online programs, leaflet distribution, and so on)
5. Intervention components, that is, the collection of materials and methods employed
6. The setting in which the intervention will be delivered (e.g., worksite, school, and so on)
7. The fit between intervention components and the cultural and practical context in which it will be used
8. Characteristics, qualifications, and training of the those delivering the intervention (e.g., relationship to recipients, skill bases, and so on)
9. Intensity (e.g., contact time in each session)
10. Duration (e.g., number sessions and overall period of intervention)
11. Fidelity of delivery (e.g., were lessons/meetings delivered as designed)
12. Evaluation, including outcome, process, and economic evaluations

TABLE 1.2   The IM Approach to Behavior Change Intervention Design (Bartholomew et al., 2011)

---

1. Needs assessment
2. Defining intervention objectives
3. Identifying regulatory processes and effective change techniques
4. Assembling the intervention
5. Planning delivery and implementation in context
6. Planning intervention evaluation

Here we focus on the IM approach (Bartholomew, Parcel, Kok, Gottlieb, & Fernandez, 2011; www.interventionmapping.com) because it provides a comprehensive and practical guide to optimal design and evaluation procedures (Abraham et al., 2016; Denford et al., 2015).

Table 1.2 summaries six design stages involved in IM and is based on a more detailed model presented by Bartholomew et al. First, a needs assessment determines what (if anything) needs to be changed for whom. Second, primary and secondary intervention objectives are defined. This involves specifying precisely the behavior changes participants will be expected to make (characteristic 1 in Table 1). Third, underlying regulatory processes or mechanisms that maintain current (unwanted) behavior patterns and/or are capable of generating new (wanted) behavior patterns are identified. This, in turn, facilitates selection of change techniques that have been found to alter those identified regulatory processes (characteristics 2–4 in Table 1). At this stage, for example, designers might decide that changing the environment by making a product or service more accessible or less expensive should be the focus of the intervention, rather than techniques capable of generating intrapersonal, individual change. Fourth, having identified evidence-based techniques relevant to the intervention's behavior change objectives, practical ways of delivering these techniques are developed and assembly of the intervention can begin (characteristics 4–7 in Table 1). Fifth implementation planning involves anticipating how the intervention will be used or delivered in everyday contexts (characteristics 7–11 in Table 9). For example, is the intervention engaging, acceptable, practical, and sustainable? The final stage is evaluation (characteristics 11 and 12). Does the intervention change the specified behaviors in context? Lloyd, Wyatt, and Creanor (2012) describe how IM approach can facilitate systematic intervention design and planning.

Needs assessment involves identifying the problem caused by specified behavior patterns. This usually involves reading or undertaking literature reviews and consulting with stakeholders. In some cases a needs assessment may reveal that intervention is not necessary or feasible, or that dissemination of best practice/usual care is the optimal response.

A thorough needs assessment can avoid wasting time and resources on unnecessary or ineffectual intervention development.

Defining intervention objectives, in stage 2, depends on a precise definition of the behavior changes required. These vary widely across interventions. For example, in a sexual health intervention, the design group might consider a series of behaviors that could facilitate successful condom use and so reduce transmission of sexually transmitted diseases (the identified need for intervention). For example, acquiring condoms (which may depend on price and accessibility), carrying condoms when out, discussing condom use with potential partners and correct use of condoms might all be targets depending on the findings of the needs assessment. This could generate a series of interventions targeting, for example, accessibility and price, knowledge of correct use, attitudes toward carrying condoms, normative beliefs concerning condom carrying and skills-training in sexual negotiation and condom handling. This stage is critical to future planning.

Stage 3 necessitates an understanding of how target behavior patterns are regulated. If designers make incorrect assumptions about the key drivers of behavior and behavior change, then they are likely to employ change techniques that are suboptimal or ineffective in relation to the intervention objectives. For example, public health campaigns frequently employ messages that highlight health risk or threat. Unfortunately, perceived threat does not always prompt behavior change so, in some circumstances, fear appeals may be the wrong choice of change technique (Albarracin et al., 2005). For example, among a motivated target audience different regulatory processes and change techniques are needed. The utility of fear appeals may also depend on psychological readiness among the target audience. Das, De Wit, and Stroebe (2003) found that fear appeals generated favorable cognitive responses and consequent attitude change *when* participants felt susceptible to the threat (Witte & Allen, 2000). So matching techniques to the target audience is critical. This may involve exploratory or "elicitation" research to identify the needs of the target group (Fisher & Fisher, 1992), subsequent to the initial needs assessment.

Poorly designed interventions may not only be ineffective, they may have negative effects. For example, if people are not persuaded by a fear appeal they interpret to mean the threat is not relevant to them (I'm not like those people), this may undermine attitudes and motivation toward change. Alternatively, if people acknowledge a threat but do not believe that they can protect themselves (i.e., they have low self-efficacy; Bandura, 1997) they may protect themselves psychologically through defensive cognitive responses such as dismissing the message as untrustworthy or rejecting its relevance to them (Ruiter, Abraham, & Kok, 2001). Thus careful selection of combinations of change techniques is often critical. For example, if a fear appeal is selected as an appropriate technique, strong threat and susceptibility messages combined with messages known to bolster self-efficacy are likely to optimize effectiveness.

Many categories of change techniques have been identified and many lists of such categories are available. See, for example, Abraham and Michie (2008) for a succinct list of frequently used individual-level change techniques, Kok et al. (2015) for an extended list linked to the Intervention Mapping Framework, including environmental change techniques and van Beurden, Greaves, Smith, and Abraham (2016) for a list of technique categories relevant to regulating weight-loss relevant impulsive processes. However, designers need to consider carefully whether these categories of techniques are relevant to their particular mapping of their behavior change challenge and also to pay attention to the detail of how any type of technique is implemented in practice.

Once the relevant regulatory processes are understood and appropriate change techniques selected, questions of delivery must be addressed. Effectiveness depends on exactly *how* change techniques are applied (Table 1.1). For example, a metaanalysis by Noar et al. (2015) found that 12 of 17 experimental tests showed that fear appeals using pictures on cigarette packets generated greater psychological change than warnings without pictures. Pictorial warnings held attention for longer, led to stronger cognitive and emotional responses and elicited more negative attitudes toward smoking and stronger intentions to avoid or quit smoking. So delivery mode design is critical to the construction of effective behavior change interventions. This, of course, necessitates careful consideration of the implementation context.

The fifth stage involves anticipating how the intervention will be used or delivered in everyday contexts. For example, what are the motivations, skills, and resources of those who will deliver the intervention? Will the recipients like the intervention and be able to engage with it? Will those meant to deliver the intervention be able to do so? Once developed, interventions should be piloted to ensure that the intervention is acceptable to the target population. Cocreation with recipients and those who will deliver the intervention not only facilitates ownership of the intervention but can highlight practical challenges which need to be overcome during the design phases. Table 1.1 highlights the importance of facilitators in face-to-face intervention delivery. Competent delivery may require additional training. For example, a review of competence in motivational interviewing found that of the 11 studies that had assessed clinician competence, only 2 studies reported that 75% of trained clinicians were proficient (Hall, Staiger, Simpson, Best, & Lubman, 2015). Thus, when developing face-to-face interventions it is important to develop and evaluate quality training programs for those delivering the program. Imprecise decision making at this stage is likely to mean that the intervention is not delivered as designed, that is there is poor delivery fidelity, or that the intervention is not maintained over time.

The final stage is evaluation planning. Although listed last, it is critical to anticipate evaluation from the outset. For example, when the desired behavior changes are defined in stage 2, designers can address the challenge of measuring those changes (assessing whether or not condom use has increased or alcohol consumption reduced) to determine whether or not the intervention has been effective. Similarly once regulatory mechanisms are identified, designers can select appropriate measures to assess the change processes by which the intervention is assumed to work. For example, how should we measure normative beliefs about condom carrying and use or self-efficacy in relation to smoking cessation?

CHOICE OR HABIT

Often behavior change is conceptualized as helping people make the right choices. This perspective may, however, sometimes be misleading. "Choice" implies deliberation or rational consideration of the pros and cons of alternate courses of action. Yet many problematic behavior patterns may be enacted without thought or deliberation; they may be automatic or habitual in particular contexts. So changing the context may be crucial to changing the behavior. So, for some behavior patterns, changing "choice architecture" may be better conceptualized as changing architecture of habit.

A series of "dual-process" models have been developed to explain the difference between choices and habits. These models characterize two distinct systems that regulate everyday behavior patterns (Borland, 2014; Kahneman, 2011; Strack & Deutsch, 2004). One system regulates conscious, deliberative control of action (choice) while the other operates automatic action involving low levels of conscious awareness and monitoring (habit). The same behavioral sequence may involve one or both systems in different contexts. Consider, for example, leaving your home and locking the outer door. If you have lived in the same place for a while you may do this while thinking of other things. The behavioral sequence can be been initiated and completed automatically with little conscious monitoring and, consequently may be difficult or impossible to remember later. Of course, you are conscious while locking the door and so can engage in conscious control. For example, if, while you are leaving, a friend says, "Don't forget to lock the door and take your key," then you may more carefully monitor your actions, and make changes to your usual routine such as checking the door a second time. Such activation of conscious control facilitates change in routine or automatic behavior patterns (or habits) and enhances action recall.

Many of the behavior patterns we may wish to change can be enacted in an automatic manner. These include "addictions," such as smoking, as well as many "habitual" behavior patterns, including eating, physical activity, and computer use. For example, we may eat and drink many times during a day. Each one of these action sequences is unlikely to be carefully consciously monitored. Having another spoonful or another drink can be initiated by internal impulses or external cues with little conscious deliberation or monitoring. Many well-practiced behavioral sequences are controlled automatically with low levels of conscious monitoring. The problem with such "mindless" behavior patterns (see Wansink's 2007 discussion of "mindless eating") is they can become increasingly independent of conscious control, being prompted by well-learnt environmental cues. This can result in us doing things repeatedly that, on reflection, we do not want to do. When this happens we experience a lack of control over our behavior patterns and our motivation no longer predicts our actions. For example, a person may be highly motivated to consume less calories but, nonetheless, find themselves eating and drinking more calories than they inteded to.

An important advance in conceptualizing these two regulatory systems was made by Strack and Deutsch (2004) when they developed the Reflective Impulsive Model (RIM) which has been elaborated by Borland (2014) as the Context, Executive and Operational Systems (CEOS) model. The two regulatory systems (referred to in the RIM as reflective and impulsive systems) operate in parallel on a moment-to-moment basis with the reflective system responding to aspects of impulsive functioning. For example, when people talk about "urges," and cravings" they are referring to the reflective system's conscious awareness of the impulsive system regulating perceptions and action initiation processes. This is important because awareness of such "urges" is critical to regaining control of impulsive behavior patterns by deploying the reflective system to realign intentions and action sequences.

Understanding interactions between these two systems is foundational to the development of effective behavior change interventions in stage 3 of the IM process. For example, just as a friend's reminder can prompt monitoring of locking a door, so a food diary that is completed each time a person eats or drinks can change the regulation of eating and drinking. Deliberately monitoring and recording a particular set of actions reduces mindless or impulsive initiation and regulation. Using self-monitoring in this way illustrates how a change technique can be selected through our understanding of underpinning regulatory processes (Abraham & Michie, 2008; Michie, Abraham, Whittington, McAteer, & Gupta, 2009). The use of conscious control to self-monitor is, however, taxing. By exerting conscious control over one set of actions we may reduce the reflective system's capacity to consciously regulate other action sequences

(Baumeister, Bratslavsky, Muraven, & Tice, 1998). So while activation of the reflective system is critical to behavior change, reliance on its capacity to override the impulsive system may be unsustainable. Sustainable behavior change involves practice in context so that new behavioral routines become automatic and can be initiated and completed with little reflective control. Thus behavior change involves both breaking unwanted habits and making new ones (Dean, 2013).

Information, Motivation, and Behavioral Skills: A Reflective Perspective

The IMB skills model (Fisher & Fisher, 1992; Fig. 1.1) provides a useful and well-tested model for designing individual-level behavior change interventions targeting reflective regulatory processes. The model proposes that changes in the operation of the reflective system occur when individuals are well informed, highly motivated and have the skills necessary to perform a desired behavior. Consequently, intervention designers should assess which informational, motivational, or skill antecedents are lacking in a target population and address these in interventions designed to change behavior patterns within that population. This framework can be applied as designers work through the IM process.

Provision of information may be critical when motivated, skilled people lack an understanding of their behavior or its consequences. For example, to lose weight, individuals may benefit from information about the number of calories in everyday foods and drinks, and the amount and type of exercise needed to burn off the calories consumed so that they can develop everyday skills to create energy deficits. Similarly, if people are not aware that their behavior patterns may lead to long-term illness, then providing such information allows people to choose to change their behavior. For example, if a group of parents are not aware that children playing in the sun without sun protection may cause long-term skin cancer, providing this information is the first step in enabling change. An extensive literature review on effective information provision is

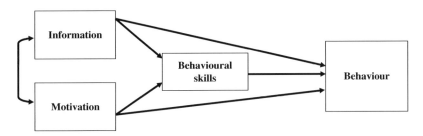

FIGURE 1.1   The IMB Skills model (Fisher & Fisher, 1992).

available (Abraham & Kools, 2011; and see http://www.gov.scot/Publications/2003/10/18378/28162 for a useful website on quality information provision in health care).

Some target audiences are well informed but not motivated to change. In such cases, techniques known to change determinants of motivation may be effective. There are many models of motivation available (see Abraham et al., forthcoming for a review). However, a simple model generated by Fishbein et al. (2001) provides a useful starting point for identifying which processes may be most important in designing motivational interventions. These researchers highlighted five key determinants of motivation as follows:

1. an individual's beliefs about the advantages of changing their behavior outweighing the disadvantages,
2. the anticipation that changing behavior will lead to a positive emotional reaction,
3. the belief that others will approve of the proposed change,
4. the belief that the behavior change is consistent with the person's self-image or identity,
5. and, finally, that the person feels capable of changing their behavior, that is, they have high self-efficacy.

Assessing each of these five determinants of motivation in elicitation research can identify which broadly defined change targets could be used to increase motivation in an unmotivated audience, as part of stage 3 planning. Once such motivational processes are specified, change techniques known to boost particular determinants of motivation can be selected. Self-efficacy is a key element of motivation but also a foundation for the development of behavioral skills. We do not usually continue to exert effort on unattainable goals. People who believe they can succeed (i.e., have high self-efficacy) set themselves more challenging goals, exert more effort, use more flexible problem-solving strategies and are more persistent (Bandura, 1997).

Well-informed, motivated individuals with high self-efficacy can fail to change their behavior patterns because they lack the skills to undertake action sequences or to reestablish reflective control over impulsively regulated behavior patterns. In such cases, information provision and motivation-building techniques are unlikely to lead to behavior change. Sustained weight management, for example, may necessitate learning new cooking or exercising skills and skills to manage social situations that involve food (e.g., refusing a slice of cake a friend has baked or avoiding Saturday night takeaways with friends). The development of behavioral skills involves instruction, and sometimes modeling, practice, receiving feedback on performance, and where necessary further instruction and practice. This skill-development process ensures proficiency of execution, enhances self-efficacy, and builds habits.

Three broad classes of skills can be defined. First self-regulatory skills; Control Theory provides a useful way of thinking about self-regulation (Carver & Scheier, 1982). At its simplest, the theory proposes that individuals' behavior is goal directed: we set goals, assess how close (or far away) we are to attaining the goal, take action to get closer to the goal, monitor progress, and again take action to bring reality closer to our goal. This feedback loop continues until monitoring shows that goal has been attained. Control Theory provides a useful way of thinking about goal striving and the process by which we attain new skills, including self-regulatory skills.

A series of cognitive skills can be assessed and, where needed, taught to enhance self-regulation. For example, we can help people to (1) consider longer term consequences of current action patterns, (2) set attainable goals, (3) self-monitor their behavior, (4) evaluate their current behavior against their goals, (5) set new goals in light of the feedback from self-monitoring, (6) prioritize goals in the face of other demands, (7) plan action before and during goal-relevant experiences, and (8) prompt exertion of appropriate effort when opportunities present themselves.

We can teach people to set SMART goals (Doran, 1981). The acronym stands for Specific (that is, specifying particular actions in particular contexts), Measurable (that is, we can test whether the goal has been attained), Assignable (that is, we know who will take action, although the "A" also sometimes used stands for "attainable" when it is already clear who needs to take action), Realistic (that is, the goal is attainable within the person's developing skill set and their environment), and Time-specified (that is, we know when or by what date action will be taken). A key part of realistic goal setting is beginning with easier tasks and only moving to more challenging goals as these are attained.

New motor skills constitute a second class of skills which may be involved in adopting health-related behaviors. For example, before using a gym, people need to be taught to use exercise machines. Similarly, certain medication regimes necessitating using devices such as inhalers or needles which patients may need to be taught how to use (see Abraham & Kools, 2011 for a discussion of how to provide such instruction in text). Even apparently simple skills such as handwashing to avoid infection, may need special instruction to ensure competence (Pittet, 2001). Thus analysis of any health behavior targeted in an intervention should involve an assessment of the motor skills required and the extent to which the targeted recipients are proficient or lacking in these skills. Of course, technological advances can make the skills involved in health behaviors easier to learn. Extra-fine needles make it easier for diabetics to inject themselves, alcohol wipes make handwashing easier and the development of a once-a-day single pill for HIV control makes adherence much easier than if patients have to take 36 pills a day! Sometimes skill deficits reveal an important role for organizational or technological, rather than individual, change.

Finally, we also require social skills to negotiate change in behavior patterns with others and seek their support. For example, the skills to negotiate condom use with a reluctant partner or the skills to explain why we will not take part in alcohol drinking games or round buying or eat traditional (but unhealthy) foods. These social skills required are likely to be determined largely by the target behavior and the social resources available to individuals planning change. However, assertiveness training (that is, being able to express one's own wants and needs in an honest and nonaggressive manner) and negotiation skills are often prerequisite to managing interactions which arise when individuals begin to change their behavior patterns. Other useful techniques include role play, especially with modeling and video feedback, and live filming followed by video feedback and praise for interactions that demonstrate desired skills. This approach to skills development is exemplified in the practice of Video Interaction Guidance (Kennedy, Landor, & Todd, 2011).

A number of successful behavior change interventions have been based on the IMB, particularly in relation to HIV-preventive behavior (Fisher, Fisher, Williams, & Malloy, 1994) and some of these have been evaluated using longer term follow up (e.g., at 12 months in the case of Fisher, Fisher, Bryan, & Misovich, 2002). Table 1.2 provides an illustration of an IMB-based intervention. The IMB model is useful because it highlights the need to assess behavior-relevant deficits among the target group prior to intervention design (IM stage 1) and provides a framework for defining the intervention objectives (IM stage 2), identifying key regulatory processes and, thereby, candidate change techniques that may be crucial to intervention effectiveness (IM stage 3). The model proposes that behavior change intervention designers need to discover whether the (precisely defined) target group lack any behavior-relevant information, whether the key determinants of motivation are in place among this target group and whether the target group lack any skills required to translate motivation into behavior.

CHANGING IMPULSIVE PROCESSES

Research into how environmental change shapes behavior patterns provides an important background for interventions designed to change habits regulated by impulsive, rather than reflective, regulatory processes. For example, Skinner's (1938) *Behavior of Organisms* systematically explained how the environment shapes behavior. For example, we perceive aspects of the environment that, in the past, have been associated with rewarding experiences and we respond to repeat those experiences. Over time this process of operant conditioning establishes automatic responses to particular environmental stimuli, or cues, which, through sequencing, can be built up into complex impulsively regulated behavior patterns. Such analyses models can be applied to identify potentially effective change techniques capable of modifying impulsive processes (in stage 3 of IM). For example, research into pairing a desired object that is usually approached with a stop signal can help recipients ignore or reject the approach stimuli. If this is done repeatedly then the established (conditioned) impulse to approach may be inhibited because the object becomes associated with nonresponse or rejection. For example, in the "go-no-go" paradigm pictures of food may be paired with cues that the recipient is asked to respond to, for example, by touching a screen, or refrain from responding to, for example, by not touching a screen. Two different tones can be used to signal whether the recipient should touch, or not touch, the image. If recipients are conditioned not to touch desirable food images over many pairings this may strengthen inhibitory control and, thereby, help people inhibit automatic approach responses in the real world (Lawrence, Verbruggen, Morrison, Adams, & Chambers, 2015; Veling, Aarts, & Stroebe, 2013). For example, if one is trained not to respond to pictures of doughnuts or chocolate this may make it easier to ignore or refuse these foods subsequently. A metaanalysis of 19 experimental studies, conducted mainly with undergraduates, suggested that inhibition training of this kind may be effective in changing health behavior patterns (Allom, Mullen, & Hagger, 2015).

Inhibition training is one of many change techniques that can be used to alter impulsive processes. In a systematic review of 92 experimental studies van Beurden et al. (2016) sought to identify and categorize techniques used to modify or manage impulsive processes involved in unhealthy eating. These authors defined 17 distinct categories of impulse management techniques and described the regulatory processes they target; summarizing the findings of 92 experimental studies. This review illustrates that, in just one behavioral domain, a large number of techniques based on a variety of theoretical explanations have been tested. The work also emphasizes the importance of detailed analyses in stage 3 of the IM approach.

When elicitation research shows that the target audience is already motivated then targeting the determinants of motivation is unlikely to be effective. Implementation intention formation, or if-then planning, has proved promising as a technique type that can help motivated people to translate their intentions into action (Gollwitzer & Sheeran, 2006). Luszczynska, Sobczyk, and Abraham (2007) added a single training session focusing on if-then action planning to an existing group-based weight loss intervention. Recipients who were randomly assigned to receive this additional training session lost twice as much weight over a 2-month follow up and 54% lost 5% of body weight compared to only 8% in the unenhanced intervention. Moreover, increased self-reported planning was found to statistically mediate the effect of the enhanced intervention on weight loss, that is, the change in self-reported planning accounted for the difference in weight loss between the intervention and control group. This mediation analyses was consistent with the hypothesized mechanism of action, or logic model (developed in IM stage 3).

If-then planning is an interesting category of change technique in that these techniques involve *both* the reflective and impulsive systems. The plan is formulated by activating the reflective system, but the pairing of a cue (the "if") with an imagined response (the "then") has the capacity to change impulsively regulated processes when the cue is encountered following training that is to prompt a new response to the cue.

Breaking unwanted habits by changing the operation of the impulsive system may require use of multiple change techniques targeting various regulatory mechanisms delivered using various methods tailored to the target population (IM stages 3 and 4). Dean (2013) discusses the stages involved in "habit reversal therapy" for people with Tourette's syndrome. The objective of this intervention is to reduce the incidence of unwanted, unconsciously elicited behavioral tics. The therapy focuses on becoming aware of the tics and the situations in which they occur and then practicing a competing behavior. The therapy is effective but is also intensive, involving more than 10 h of therapeutic contact (McGuire et al., 2014).

The process Kessler (2009) calls "food rehabilitation" has interesting parallels with "habit reversal therapy." The former also begins with building awareness, both of cues in our everyday environment that prompt overeating and of our own "premonitionary urges" or feelings that we are about to revert to a habitual response. By training the reflective system to identify urges generated by the impulsive system just before we respond to cues, we can create space for reflective initiation of competing behaviors, just as a friend's reminder can change how we lock our front door. The next stage of food rehabilitation is the specification and learning of relevant competing behaviors, such as deliberately walking by the doughnut shop or taking another route to work. Kessler emphasizes cognitive and emotional reconstruction, that is, learning to reflectively nurture new thoughts and emotions in relation to conditioned cues. Over time this results in attitude change that further bolsters motivation to change. For example, one person having undergone food rehabilitation noted that, "Once I thought a big plate of food was what I wanted and needed to feel better … now I see it for what it is … fat on fat on sugar on fat that will never provide lasting satisfaction and only keeps me coming back for more." This is a radical cognitive and emotional reconstruction of food cues that might previously have prompted excitement and positive thoughts. Such reconstruction serves to sustain motivation to avoid unhealthy foods and reduce impulsive prompting of unhealthy eating. Reconditioning the impulsive system requires multiple learning opportunities because the associations that regulate the system have themselves developed through repeated pairings. Thus "food rehabilitation" and other habit breaking interventions require practice and yet more practice. Moreover, since such interventions can be very challenging to complete requiring considerable time, effort, and social support.

DETAILED TAILORING IS CRITICAL TO EFFECTIVE PLANNING

The examples considered above clarify the detail needed to identify critical change processes and effective techniques in stage 3 of IM and the potential complexity of intervention assembly in IM stage 4.

Consider problems of encouraging people to turn up for medical/ therapy appointments. Let us assume that our target audiences are motivated to attend, and further, that we have decided that if-then planning could be effective in increasing appointment uptake. In this case some of the IM stage 3 planning is complete; a broad understanding of the change mechanisms and a category of potentially useful techniques have been established. Is it then obvious how to proceed to stage 4? Not yet. Let us further assume that elicitation research has suggested that recipients will complete questionnaires and that, consequently, this is the chosen delivery mechanism for the intervention. Even now, using this relatively simple intervention design process, careful analyses and planning is critical to designing an intervention appropriate to the target audience.

Consider two if-then planning intervention evaluations. Sheeran and Orbell (2000) found that inclusion of a planning prompt in a questionnaire increased attendance for cervical cancer screening. The prompt advised questionnaire recipients that they would be more likely to go for a cervical smear if they decided when and where to go. They were then given space to write "when, where and how you will make an appointment." In this intervention, motivated respondents who had not yet made an appointment were prompted to make specific action plans (e.g., specifying a time) to prompt a response that they had the skills to enact (making an appointment). This technique was effective in changing attendance behavior; 92% of those offered this planning opportunity attended for screening compared to 67% in the control group, despite equivalent levels of reported motivation across the two groups.

Now consider a different behavior change challenge. Sheeran, Aubrey, and Kellett (2007) aimed to increase attendance at psychotherapy appointments among those who had already made appointments. These researchers undertook a needs assessment and identified that being worried about the appointment was a common precursor to missing an appointment. Consequently, recipients were advised to use a self-talk technique to terminate such worrying, "As soon as I feel concerned about attending my appointment I will ignore that feeling and tell myself this is perfectly understandable." Unlike the technique employed by Sheeran and Orbell (2000), this is does not prompt "action" planning, no behavioral response is specified. This is a thought-regulation technique designed to reduce cognitive elaboration of appointment-related worries. Note too that it is *not* an example of thought suppression (Wenzlaff & Wegner, 2000) which has been found to be ineffective (Erskine, Georgiou, & Kvavilashvili, 2010). Recipients were not advised *not to think* about appointment concerns but rather to avoid elaborating appointment-related concerns when they became aware of them. Those who received a questionnaire containing this advice were more likely to attend their psychotherapy appointment with 75% attending compared to 63% in the control group.

These two experimental evaluations demonstrate the potential effectiveness and versatility of if-then change techniques as well as the variability in implementation needed to precisely tailor such techniques to audience-relevant barriers to action. If-then planning is not a "behavior change technique" but a category of change techniques that work because they engage both the reflective and impulsive regulatory systems and can be adapted to a wide range of behavior change problems involving quite different problems, for example, not scheduling and prioritizing appointment-making versus elaboration of concerns about a booked appointment. Without such detailed analyses at stages 3 and 4 of Intervention Planning bland, off-the-peg interventions may fail to incorporate the detailed tailoring on which effectiveness depends; so highlighting the importance of needs assessment, elicitation research and a detailed analyses of the regulatory process that need to change in order to facilitate behavior change.

EVALUATION OF BEHAVIOR CHANGE INTERVENTIONS

The last stage of the IM is evaluation. We can distinguish between three broad types, (1) outcome evaluations (that answer the question, did the intervention change the behavior it targeted?), (2) process evaluations (that answer the question, how did the intervention work and did it change the regulatory mechanisms targeted?), and (3) economic evaluations (that answer the question, how much does the intervention cost for a given degree of effectiveness).

Once the intervention objectives are defined in stage 2 of IM, it is important to identify measures to be used in the evaluation. Outcome measures may include assessments of health or behavior patterns or both, depending on the intervention objectives. Assessing health outcomes (such as weight loss or sexually transmitted disease prevalence) allows tests of hypothesized links between behavior change and health enhancement or disease incidence.

Process evaluations focus on understanding how mechanisms of change, intervention delivery, and contextual factors determine effectiveness/ineffectiveness (Moore et al., 2014). Stage 2 of IM involves defining a logic model that specifies the change mechanisms that the intervention targets, so measuring these is critical to understanding whether an effective intervention worked as hypothesized or whether an ineffective intervention failed because (1) it failed to change the targeted process or (2) while successfully changing targeted processes it, nonetheless, failed to change behavior patterns. Process measures may include measures of attitude, self-efficacy (see Fishbein et al., 2001; model of key determinants of motivation) or planning (Luszczynska et al., 2007). Such measurement allows mediation analyses to be conducted, testing whether the hypothesized change mechanisms account for the success or failure of the intervention.

Process evaluations also investigate intervention delivery as specified in stage 5 of the IM process, for example, do different delivery formats change effectiveness. An important element of process evaluation is the assessment of fidelity of delivery, that is, was the intervention designed as planned. This includes "dose," that is, did recipient receive enough of the intervention? Glasgow et al. (2002) and Green and Glasgow (2006) provide a useful framework model for evaluating intervention delivery and implementation: the RE-AIM (Reach, Effectiveness, Adoption, Implementation, and Maintenance) framework. Reach refers to how many of the target population were involved in an evaluation and how representative they were. For example, if an intervention was evaluated using economically advantaged participants then questions would arise as to whether it would also be effective for economically less advantaged people, or, for example, with those with more severe health problems then the intervention participants. Effectiveness relates to the range of effects an intervention might have. For example, even if it changed behavior, did it enhance overall quality of life or have any unintended consequences (e.g., did participants find it onerous or upsetting)? Adoption refers to whether the users (e.g., nurses, teachers, managers, members of the public) are persuaded of the utility of the intervention and use it. Adoption depends on how easy the intervention is to implement, whether those who will deliver it and/or their clients like and value it and whether it is compatible with their other main goals (Paulussen, Kok, & Schaalma, 1994). Since cost is important to most people, interventions are unlikely to be used if adopters cannot afford them. Understanding this adoption and diffusion process is critical to the overall impact of any intervention (Rogers, 2003). Even effective interventions have no impact on public health if they are not adopted and translated into everyday practice. Implementation refers to the ease and feasibility of faithful delivery. If an intervention is complex, expensive, or requires specialist training or teams of people to deliver it then it is less likely to be sustainable in real-world settings so it may not be adopted or, if adopted, may be delivered with poor fidelity. Maintenance refers to the longer term sustainability of the intervention in real-world settings. For example, if an organization or community does not have the resources to deliver an intervention then, no matter how effective, it will be dropped over time. Similarly, if implementation problems are encountered then even if the intervention is retained it may be changed and adapted to the setting which may mean altering or dropping change techniques critical to its initial effectiveness, so rendering it ineffective. These practical, real-world considerations are critical to translating potentially efficacious interventions into sustainable enhancement of routine health preventive and health care services. They need to be carefully considered in stages 1 and 5 of the IM process.

When an intervention is found to be effective an economic evaluation can clarify how much it will cost to implement the intervention. This is important because health care funds are limited and implementing expensive interventions may require cuts in other services. It is worth noting, however, that when preventive health behavior interventions are effective they are likely to be cost effective because of high treatment costs. For example, the lifetime cost of treating an HIV positive person in the United States has been estimated at more than £240,000 so even expensive HIV-preventive interventions are likely to be cost saving if they are effective in reducing HIV incidences. Similarly, an intervention that prevents obesity, heart attacks, or falls among the elderly is very likely to be cost saving and, therefore, cost effective.

CONCLUSIONS

We know a lot about behavior change intervention design. By carefully following tried and tested intervention planning procedures we can optimize intervention effectiveness. This involves understanding the detail of the regulatory processes that shape our behavior and the detail of tailored design and implementation. Simplified categorizations and formulaic approaches to interventions design may sometimes generate good results but also lack the versatility to match change techniques to specific behavior change problems and, so, fail to progress a science of behavior change. Design of effective interventions also necessitates an understanding of the developing experimental literature relevant to the targeted behavior pattern. Scientific mapping of the processes, techniques, delivery formats, and implementation challenges that determine the effectiveness or ineffectiveness of behavior change interventions is in its infancy. Behavior change science has long way to go before establishing an engineering paradigm equivalent to that used by rocket scientists but careful planning and rigorous evaluation, including process evaluation, advances our science project by project.

References

Abraham, C., Conner, M., Jones, F., & O'Conner, D. (2016). Health Psychology. Routledge.

Abraham, C., & Kools, M. (Eds.). (2011). *Writing health communication: An evidence-based guide.* London: SAGE Publications Ltd.

Abraham, C., & Michie, S. (2008). A taxonomy of behavior change techniques used in interventions. *Health Psychology, 27*(3), 379–387.

Albarracin, D., Gillette, C. J., Earl, A. N., Glasman, L. R., Durantini, M. R., & Ho, M. (2005). A test of major assumptions about behavior change: a comprehensive look at the effects of passive and active HIV prevention interventions since the beginning of the epidemic. *Psychological Bulletin, 131,* 856–897.

Allom, V., Mullen, B., & Hagger, M. (2015). Does inhibitory control training improve health behaviour? A meta-analysis. *Health Psychology Review, 10,* 168–186.

Anderson, P., de Bruijn, K., Angus, K., Gordon, R., & Hastings, G. (2009). Impact of alcohol advertising and media exposure on adolescent alcohol use: a systematic review of longitudinal studies. *Alcohol and Alcoholism, 44,* 229–243.

Bandura, A. (1997). *Self-efficacy: The exercise of control.* New York: Freeman.

Bartholomew, L. K., Parcel, G. S., Kok, G., Gottlieb, N. H., & Fernandez, M. E. (2011). *Planning health promotion programs: An intervention mapping approach.* London: Willey Press.

Baumeister, R. F., Bratslavsky, E., Muraven, M., & Tice, D. M. (1998). Ego depletion: is the active self a limited resource? *Journal of Personality and Social Psychology, 74,* 1252–1265.

Behavioural Insights. (2014). *EAST: Four simple ways to apply behavioural insights.* London: Behavioural Insights.

Belloc, N. B., & Breslow, L. (1972). Relationship of physical health status and health practices. *Preventive Medicine, 1,* 409–421.

Borland, R. (2014). *Understanding hard to maintain behaviour change: A dual process approach.* West Sussex, UK: Wiley and Sons.

Butland, B., Jebb, S., Kopelman, P., McPherson, K., Thomas, S., Mardell, J., & Parry, V. (2007). Foresight. Tackling obesities: future choices. Project report. *Foresight. Tackling obesities: future choices. Project report.*

Carver, C. S., & Scheier, M. F. (1982). Control theory: a useful conceptual framework for personality–social, clinical and health psychology. *Psychological Bulletin, 92,* 111–135.

Centres for Disease Control and Prevention (CDC). (1999). Framework for program evaluation in public health. *Morbidity and Mortality Weekly Report, 48,* RR-11.

Craig, P., Dieppe, P., Macintyre, S., Michie, S., Nazareth, I., & Petticrew, M. (2008). Developing and evaluating complex interventions: the new Medical Research Council guidance. *British Medical Journal, 337,* a1655.

Dal Cin, S., Worth, K. A., Gerrard, M., Gibbons, F. X., Stoolmiller, M., Wills, T. A., & Sargent, J. D. (2009). Watching and drinking: expectancies, prototypes, and friends' alcohol use mediate effect of exposure to alcohol use in movies on adolescent drinking. *Health Psychology, 28,* 473–483.

Das, E. H., De Wit, J. B., & Stroebe, W. (2003). Fear appeals motivate acceptance of action recommendations: evidence for a positive bias in the processing of persuasive messages. *Personality and Social Psychology Bulletin, 29*(5), 650–664.

Davidson, K. W., Goldstein, M., Kaplan, R. M., et al. (2003). Evidence-based behavioral medicine: what is it and how do we achieve it? *Annals of Behavioral Medicine, 26,* 161–171.

Dean, J. (2013). *Making habits, breaking habits.* Boston, MA: De Capo Press.

Deci, E. L., Koestner, R., & Ryan, R. M. (1999). A meta-analytic review of experiments examining the effects of extrinsic rewards on intrinsic motivation. *Psychological Bulletin, 125,* 627–668.

Denford, S., Abraham, C., Smith, J., Lloyd, J. J., White, M., Tarrant, M., Wyatt, K., Greaves, C., & Dean, S. (2015). Designing and evaluating behavior change interventions to promote health. In K. J. Reynolds, & N. R. Branscombe (Eds.), *The psychology of change: Life contexts, experiences, and identities* (pp. 151–169). New York, NY: Psychology Press.

Denford, S., Taylor, R. S., Campbell, J. L., & Greaves, C. J. (2013). Effective behavior change techniques in asthma self-care interventions: systematic review and meta-regression. *Health Psychology, 33,* 577–587.

Department of Health. (2013). Reducing obesity and improving diet. Available from https://www.gov.uk/government/policies/reducing-obesity-and-improving-diet

Doran, G. T. (1981). There's a SMART way to write management's goals and objectives. *Management Review, 70*(11), 35–36.

Erskine, J. A. K., Georgiou, G. J., & Kvavilashvili, L. (2010). I suppress therefore I smoke. *Psychological Science, 21,* 1225–1230.

Fishbein, M., Triandis, H. C., Kanfer, F. H., Becker, M., Middlestadt, S. E., & Eichler, A. (2001). Factors influencing behavior and behavior change. In A. Baum, T. A. Revenson, & J. E. Singer (Eds.), *Handbook of health psychology* (pp. 3–17). Mahwah, NJ: Lawerence Erlbaum.

Fisher, J. D., & Fisher, W. A. (1992). Changing AIDS-risk behavior. *Psychological Bulletin, 111,* 455–471.

Fisher, J. D., Fisher, W. A., Bryan, A. D., & Misovich, S. J. (2002). Information-motivation-behavioral skills model-based HIV risk behavior change intervention for inner-city high school youth. *Health Psychology, 21,* 177–186.

Fisher, J. D., Fisher, W. A., Williams, S. S., & Malloy, T. E. (1994). Empirical tests of an Information-Motivation-Behavioral Skills model of AIDS preventive behavior. *Health Psychology, 13,* 238–250.

Flegal, K., Kit, B., Orpana, H., & Graubard, B. (2013). Association of all-cause mortality with overweight and obesity using standard body mass index categories: a systematic review and meta-analysis. *JAMA, 309*(1), 71–82.

Glasgow, R. E., Bull, S. S., Gillette, C., Klesges, L. M., & Dzewaltowski, D. M. (2002). Behavior change intervention research in healthcare settings: a review of recent reports with emphasis on external validity. *American Journal of Preventive Medicine, 23,* 62–69.

Gollwitzer, P. M., & Sheeran, P. (2006). Implementation intentions and goal achievement: a meta analysis of effects and processes. *Advances in Experimental Social Psychology, 38,* 69–121.

Greaves, C., Sheppard, K., Abraham, C., Hardeman, W., Roden, M., Evans, P., & Schwarz, P. The IMAGE Study Group. (2011). Systematic review of reviews of intervention components associated with increased effectiveness in dietary and physical activity interventions. *BMC Public Health, 11*(1), 119Available from http://www.biomedcentral.com/1471-2458/11/119.

Green, L. W., & Glasgow, R. E. (2006). Evaluating the relevance, generalization, and applicability of research: issues in external validation and translation methodology. *Evaluation and the Health Professions, 29,* 126–153.

Guh, D. P., Zhang, W., Bansback, N., Amarsi, Z., Birmingham, C. L., & Anis, A. H. (2009). The incidence of co-morbidities related to obesity and overweight: a systematic review and meta-analysis. *BMC Public Health, 9*(1), 88.

Hall, K., Staiger, P. K., Simpson, A., Best, D., & Lubman, D. I. (2015). After 30 years of dissemination, have we achieved sustained practice change in motivational interviewing? *Addiction, 111,* 1144–1150.

Haslam, C., Haslam, S. H., Knight, C., Gleibs, I., Ysseldyk, R., & McCloskey, L. (2014). We can work it out: group decision-making builds social identity and enhances the cognitive performance of care residents. *British Journal of Psychology, 105,* 17–34.

Herculano-Houzel, S. (2009). The human brain in numbers: a linearly scaled-up primate brain. *Frontiers in Human Neuroscience, 3,* 31.

Heil, S. H., Higgins, S. T., Bernstein, I. M., Solomon, L. J., Rogers, R. E., Thomas, C. S., et al. (2008). Effects of voucher-based incentives on abstinence from cigarette smoking and fetal growth among pregnant women. *Addiction, 103,* 1009–1018.

House of Lords. (2011). *Behaviour change (HL paper 179).* The Stationary Office, London: House of Lords, Science and Technology Committee.

Jepson, R. G., Harris, F. M., Platt, S., & Tannahill, C. (2010). The effectiveness of interventions to change six health behaviors: a review of reviews. *BMC Public Health, 10,* 538, Available from: WOS:000282239600005.

Johnson, E. J., & Goldstein, D. (2003). Do defaults save lives? *Science, 302,* 1338–1339.

Johnson, B. T., Scott-Sheldon, L. A., & Carey, M. P. (2010). Meta-synthesis of health behavior change meta-analyses. *American Journal of Public Health, 100,* 11.

Kahneman, D. (2011). *Thinking, fast and slow.* New York: Macmillan.

Kennedy, H., Landor, M., & Todd, L. (2011). *Video interaction guidance: A relationship-based intervention to promote attunement, empathy, and wellbeing.* London: Jessica Kingsley Publishers.

Kessler, D. A. (2009). *The end of overeating: Taking control of the insatiable American appetite.* Emmaus, PA: Rodale.

Kok, G., Gottlieb, N. H., Peters, G. -J. Y., Mullen, P. D., Parcel, G. S., Ruiter, R. A. C., Fernández, M. E., Markham, C., & Bartholomew, L. K. (2015). A taxonomy of behavior change methods; an intervention mapping approach. *Health Psychology Review, 10,* 297–312.

Kunz, A. H., & Pfaff, D. (2002). Agency theory, performance evaluation, and the hypothetical construct of intrinsic motivation. *Accounting Organizations and Society, 27,* 275–295.

Kvaavik, E., Batty, G. D., Ursin, G., Huxley, R., & Gale, C. R. (2010). Influence of individual and combined health behaviors on total and cause-specific mortality in men and women: the United Kingdom health and lifestyle survey. *Archives of Internal Medicine, 170,* 711–718.

Laatikainen, T., Dunbar, J., Chapman, A., Kilkkinen, A., Vartiainen, E., Heistaro, S., et al. (2007). Prevention of Type 2 Diabetes by lifestyle intervention in an Australian primary health care setting: Greater Green Triangle (GGT) Diabetes Prevention Project. *BMC Public Health, 7,* 249.

Lawrence, N. S., Verbruggen, F., Morrison, S., Adams, R. C., & Chambers, C. D. (2015). Stopping to food can reduce intake. Effects of stimulus-specificity and individual differences in dietary restraint. *Appetite, 85,* 91–103.

Lloyd, J. J., Wyatt, K. M., & Creanor, S. (2012). Behavioral and weight status outcomes from an exploratory trial of the Healthy Lifestyles Programme (HeLP): a novel school-based obesity prevention programme. *BMJ Open, 2,* e000390.

Luszczynska, A., Sobczyk, A., & Abraham, C. (2007). Planning to lose weight: RCT of an implementation intention prompt to enhance weight reduction among overweight and obese women. *Health Psychology, 26,* 507–512.

Marteau, T. M., Ogilvie, D., Martin, R., Suhrcke, M., & Kelly, M. P. (2011). Judging nudging: can nudging improve population health? *British Medical Journal, 342,* d228.

Maslin, M. A., & Christensen, B. (2007). Tectonics, orbital forcing, global climate change, and human evolution in Africa: introduction to the African paleoclimate special volume. *Journal of Human Evolution, 53,* 443–464.

McGuire, J. F., Piacentini, J., Brennan, E. A., Lewin, A. B., Murphy, T. K., Small, B. J., & Storch, E. A. (2014). A meta-analysis of behavior therapy for Tourette Syndrome. *Journal of Psychiatric Research, 50,* 106–112.

Michie, S., Abraham, C., Whittington, C., McAteer, J., & Gupta, S. (2009). Effective techniques in healthy eating and physical activity interventions: a meta-regression. *Health Psychology, 28*(6), 690.

Moore, G., Audrey, S., Barker, M., Bond, L., Bonell, C., Hardeman, W., Moore, L., O'Cathain, A., Tinati, T., Wight, D., & Baird, J. (2014). *Process evaluation of complex interventions: Medical Research Council guidance.* London: MRC Population Health Science Research Network.

Noar, S. M., Hall, M. G., Francis, D. B., Ribisl, K. M., Pepper, K. J., & Brewer, N. (2015). Pictorial cigarette pack warnings: a meta-analysis of experimental studies. *Tobacco Control, 25,* 341–354.

Paulussen, T., Kok, G., & Schaalma, H. (1994). Antecedents of adoption of classroom-based HIV-education in secondary schools. *Health Education Research, 9,* 485–496.

Pittet, D. (2001). Improving adherence to hand hygiene practice: a multidisciplinary approach. *Emerging Infectious Diseases, 7,* 234.

Reynolds, K., & Branscombe, N. R. (Eds.). (2015). *The psychology of change: Life contexts, experiences, and identities* (pp. 151–169). New York: Psychology Press.

Ruiter, R. A., Abraham, C., & Kok, G. (2001). Scary warnings and rational precautions: a review of the psychology of fear appeals. *Psychology and Health, 16,* 613–630.

Rogers, E. M. (2003). *Diffusion of innovations* (5th ed.). New York: Free Press.

Sargent, R. P., Shepard, R. M., & Glantz, S. A. (2004). Reduced incidence of admissions for myocardial infarction associated with public smoking ban: before and after study. *British Medical Journal, 328,* 977–980.

Sheeran, P., Aubrey, R., & Kellett, S. (2007). Increasing attendance for psychotherapy: implementation intentions and the self-regulation of attendance-related negative affect. *Journal of Consulting and Clinical Psychology, 75,* 853–863.

Sheeran, P., & Orbell, S. (2000). Using implementation intentions to increase attendance for cervical cancer screening. *Health Psychology, 19,* 283–289.

Shepherd, L., O'Carroll, R. E., & Ferguson, E. (2014). An international comparison of deceased and living organ donation/transplant rates in opt-in and opt-out systems: a panel study. *BMC medicine, 12*(1), 1.

Skinner, B. F. (1938). *The behavior of organisms: An experimental analysis.* Oxford, England: Appleton-Century.

Strack, F., & Deutsch, R. (2004). Reflective and impulsive determinants of social behavior. *Personality and Social Psychology Review, 8,* 220–247.

Tarrant, M., Hagger, M. S., & Farrow, C. V. (2011). Social categorization, social consensus and the promotion of health behaviour. In J. Jetten, S. A. Haslam, & C. Haslam (Eds.), *The social cure: Identity, health, and well-being.* New York: Psychology Press.

Thaler, R. H., & Sunstein, C. (2008). *Nudge: Improving decisions about health, wealth, and happiness.* New York: Yale University Press.

van Beurden, S. B., Greaves, C. J., Smith, J. R., & Abraham, C. (2016). Techniques for modifying impulsive processes associated with unhealthy eating: a systematic review. *Health Psychology, 35*(8), 793–806.

Veling, H., Aarts, H., & Stroebe, W. (2013). Using stop signals to reduce impulsive choices for palatable unhealthy foods. *British journal of health psychology, 18*(2), 354–368.

Volpp, K. G., John, L. K., Troxel, A. B., Norton, L., Fassbender, J., & Loewenstein, G. (2008). Financial incentive-based approaches for weight loss. a randomized trial. *Journal of the American Medical Association, 3000,* 2631–2637.

Wansink, B. (2007). *Mindless eating: Why we eat more than we think.* London: Random House Digital, Inc..

Wenzlaff, R. M., & Wegner, D. M. (2000). Thought suppression. *Annual Review of Psychology, 51*(1), 59–91.

Whitlock, G., Lewington, S., Sherliker, P., Clarke, R., Emberson, J., Halsey, J., … Peto, R. (2009). Body-mass index and cause-specific mortality in 900 000 adults: collaborative analyses of 57 prospective studies. *Lancet, 373*(9669), 1083–1096.

Witte, K., & Allen, M. (2000). A meta-analysis of fear appeals: implications for effective public health campaigns. *Health Education and Behavior, 27,* 591–615.

World Health Organization. (2015). Obesity and overweight. Fact sheet No. 311. Available from http://www.who.int/mediacentre/factsheets/fs311/en/

Designing and Delivering Interventions for Health Behavior Change in Adolescents Using Multitechnology Systems: From Identification of Target Behaviors to Implementation

L.A. Condon, N.S. Coulson

School of Medicine, Nottingham University, Nottingham, United Kingdom

OVERVIEW

The chapter details the importance of gaining an in-depth understanding of target behavior(s), and the issues surrounding implementation, adherence, and acceptance of an intervention for health behavior change among a target population. Discussion around how these issues affect the design of a behavior change intervention is presented, along with a case study from a multitechnology health behavior change intervention designed to optimize healthy dietary and exercise behaviors in European adolescents through promotion of health awareness, motivation, and engagement; the PEGASO project (EU FP7 Grant Ref: 610727). Attention is paid to the method of understanding the target behaviors within this target population and how behavior change frameworks can aid intervention content and design, and issues relating to the barriers and facilitators of the implementation pathway for health behavior change interventions.

Behavior Change Research and Theory. http://dx.doi.org/10.1016/B978-0-12-802690-8.00001-3

BACKGROUND

When designing health behavior change interventions (HBCIs) it is fundamental to gain insight into the factors that will shape and guide this process from the outset. Before embarking upon any element of the intervention design, researchers should always first gain an in-depth understanding of the following:

1. The target behavior of interest that will be the focus of the intervention.
2. The characteristics of the target population for which the HBCI is intended.
3. The factors surrounding implementation of the intervention which may be identified through investigating the behavioral patterns of the target population, their environment, social context, and the resources available to them.

Gathering the information stated earlier (particularly in point 3) has a twofold advantage of also helping to identify and anticipate potential problems that may arise with the implementation of the intervention and allow them to be considered and addressed during the planning stages of the intervention. For example, specific factors that may arise could include acceptance of the intervention by the target population; possible peer group/social/environmental/financial influences resulting in good levels of acceptance yet high levels of nonadherence to the intervention; effective and appropriate modes of intervention delivery that are both acceptable, accessible, and feasible, among the target population.

The chapter discusses the importance of understanding the target behavior in context of the order to inform the intervention design process, and presents a case study from a large EU FP7 funded project (Grant Ref: 610727) to develop a personalized multitechnology guidance service for optimizing healthy dietary and exercise lifestyle behaviors in European teenagers through increasing health awareness, motivation, and engagement (PEGASO).

THE IMPORTANCE OF UNDERSTANDING THE TARGET BEHAVIOR IN CONTEXT

To change behavior we need to understand it. The starting point of designing any HBCI is to gather evidence about the target behavior and investigate what type of intervention is needed. Starting at the point of synthesizing existing research evidence through comprehensive literature searches and (ideally) a systematic review will enable a more comprehensive understanding to be formed about the research that already exists in

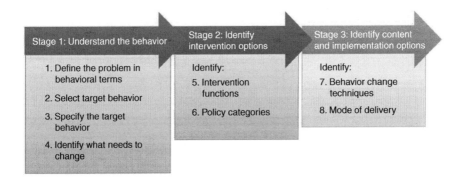

FIGURE 2.1 **Development stages in the design of behavior change interventions.**
Source: Taken from Michie, S., van Stralen, M. M., & West, R. (2011). The behaviour change wheel: A new method for characterising and designing behaviour change. Implementation Science, <u>6</u>, 42.

the area concerning the target behavior and the target population, in general. Most importantly, this will provide the first step in ensuring that the intervention is focused upon the *actual problem,* not what is *assumed to be the problem.* It also provides background information concerning what functions the intervention needs to perform, termed "intervention functions" (Michie, van Stralen, & West, 2011), and what suite of behavior change techniques (BCTs) will be the most appropriate to serve those intervention functions (Michie et al., 2011, 2013; see Fig. 2.1), along with information on the nature of the interventions that already exist in the area.

However, synthesizing secondary data sources alone is not sufficient to provide a well-rounded overview of the problem, or an in-depth understanding of the target behavior. Primary empirical data from the target population is needed in order to gain deeper insight into what needs to change, termed the "behavioral diagnosis" (Michie et al., 2011), and then move into designing the intervention. Such approaches are advocated by behavior change intervention design frameworks, such as "The Behaviour Change Wheel" (Michie et al., 2011; see Fig. 2.2), and the "Person Centred Approach" (Yardley, Morrison, Bradbury, & Muller, 2015).

Methodological Approaches to Empirical Data Collection

If a HBCI, or any behavior change intervention, is going to be useful and assist the people that it is being designed for it must be grounded in a thorough understanding of the perspectives and the psychosocial context of this target population. Particularly in the case of HBCIs, it is widely held among the eHealth research community that this is a vital criterion of good practice in the intervention design and development process (Pagliari, 2007; van Gemert-Pijnen et al., 2011; Baker, Gustafson, & Shah, 2014).

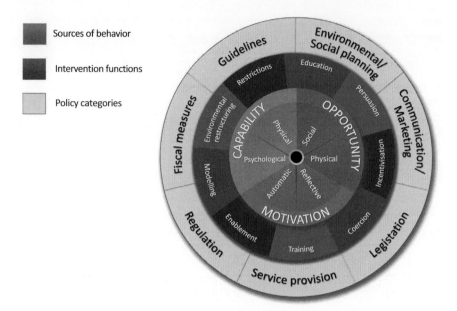

FIGURE 2.2   **The behavior change wheel framework.** *Source: Taken from Michie, S., van Stralen, M. M., & West, R. (2011). The behaviour change wheel: A new method for characterising and designing behaviour change.* Implementation Science, 6, 42.

Mixed-Methods Approach

Qualitative research methods can be useful in providing in-depth information to understand target behaviors. Temporally they can be used either at a single data time-point (i.e., interviews/focus groups conducted only once with the target population to understand the target behavior at the start of the intervention design process) or in an iterative data collection approach over multiple time-points during this phase to understand the behavioral patterns of target behaviors that are likely to fluctuate regularly, particularly when there is the risk of relapse (i.e., smokers during cessation, weight loss through dieting).

However, using a mixed-methods approach to combine both qualitative and quantitative empirical data from the target population have some advantages. Primarily, the combined strengths of both qualitative and quantitative approaches offers the most optimal methodology to build a fuller insight into the target behavior and the target population; quantitative approaches can reveal the attitudes, beliefs, and experiences; qualitative techniques allow enquiry into how and why people do or do not engage and adhere. As such a combined approach can provide an in-depth understanding of the target behavior that might be missed through using only a single data collection method. Mixed methodology also enables verification of the research findings through comparison across multiple sources, and can mutually dilute the biases or weaknesses of different data collection methods (Creswell, 2014). Researchers already familiar with conducting behavioral mapping studies will know the importance of triangulating the data in this way to ensure that all of the nuances that characterize the natural, (i.e., preintervention) behavioral patterns of the target population are captured, and ensure the data is valid and reliable in order to give a sufficiently detailed representation of the target behavior.

Behaviors Don't Occur in Isolation

The decision about which methods to include in mixed-methods data collection will depend upon the contextual variables of the target population and it's subpopulations, environment, geographical area, psychosocial context, and number of target behaviors of interest. For example, when there are multiple target behaviors of interest under investigation (e.g., physical activity and nutrition behaviors) data collection will be quite labor intensive in terms of both time and manpower required, particularly if an observational study is needed. In the case of multiple target behaviors it is also important to investigate how these behaviors interact with each other to give a thorough understanding of how this may affect the possible outcomes of the intervention and whether there will be any unexpected effects. For example, an intervention designed to encourage healthy eating *and* increase physical activity may reveal a positive correlation between increasing exercise levels and increasing caloric intake from energy dense foods. However, does this mean that the intervention has not been effective?

Understanding the interactions between multiple target behaviors in context will allow issues that are specific to these interactions to be addressed. Furthermore, it will raise the question of what data collection methods are the most appropriate. For example, using self-report techniques to assess sensitive topics may be open to social desirability response bias (Krumpal, 2013). Social desirability response biases may arise when a person wishes to make themselves stand out from their peer group, become appealing to their peer group, or conform to the group norm (Brechwald & Prinstein, 2011). The tendency to seek social approval of a peer group may vary according to specific peer group norms relating to the target behavior (Johnson & van de Vijver 2002), and are likely to vary across cultural orientations. For example, in individualist cultures societal norms are related to personal values, attitudes, and goals, whereas in collectivist cultures societal norms value good relationships with others and to work together for the goodness of the society (Lalwani, Shavitt, & Johnson, 2006) all of which may result in over- or underinflated responses on self-report response measures which will cause a negative impact upon the data.

Going back to the previous example, social desirability response biases have been found relating to multiple target behaviors, particularly physical activity and nutritional health behaviors, and particularly when the outcome measure is weight loss (Carels, Cacciapaglia, Rydin, Douglass, & Harper, 2006; Adams et al., 2005). So, when the likelihood of the data being affected by social desirability response bias is high, using a different data collection method other than a self-report technique would be the most appropriate way to ensure fidelity and validity of the data. Taking a mixed-methods approach to data collection would allow verification of the data gathered via a self-report response method (i.e., in the form of questionnaires, surveys, or interviews) with an observational study of the target behaviors to compare what the participants say they do and what they actually do. This will then identify where the problematic behaviors are, when and where they need to be addressed, and who are the primary agents of this behavior (e.g., the participants themselves, their significant others, their peers).

This highlights the importance of understanding the psychosocial influences over the target behaviors related to peer group norms and peer group conformity, and may merit thorough investigation particularly when designing interventions for childhood and adolescent target populations.

Resource Limitation

The choice of mixed-methodologies will also depend upon practical considerations that ensure you are working within the means of your research capacity and capabilities, such as the amount of time you have allocated to the background data collection phase, the allocated budget, and the logistics of collecting and analyzing large volumes of data (i.e., timescale, manpower, and capabilities of the research team). In the case where HBCIs are part of large-scale studies spanning different study sites, types of institutions/settings, and even different countries, care should be taken to maintain fidelity of study methods particularly when data will be gathered simultaneously or in parallel by different researchers. For example, if it is a large-scale multinational study then differences in language barriers need to be overcome, not least through accurate translation of study materials to be administered (i.e., questionnaires, surveys) and data quality checking for fidelity of raw data transfer during the process of translation → back-translation before analysis is attempted. As such careful planning and coordination of this phase is needed, not least to allow adequate allocation in the study timeline during this baseline data collection phase; it has been suggested that this phase should account for the first 6 months of the study (see Yardley et al., 2015, and Table 2.1). Nevertheless, whichever methods are decided upon they must answer all of the fundamental

TABLE 2.1   An Overview of how the Person-Based Approach can be Incorporated at thePlanning and Design Stage of the Development of Digital HBCIs

Intervention stage	Target output of the person-based approach	Specific person-based approach processes undertaken	Activities that may be undertaken as part of wider intervention development context
Step 1: Planning (months 0–6)	Identification of key behavioral issues, needs, and challenges the intervention must address	Synthesize previous qualitative studies of user experiences of similar interventions Carry out primary qualitative research using open-ended questions to elicit user views of the planned behavior changes (including relevant previous experience, barriers, and facilitators)	Consultation with experts, members of user groups, other stakeholders (e.g., purchasers of health care services) Examination of relevant theory and evidence from previous trials Observation of real-life context of intended health care product/ service (user-centerd design)
Step 2: Design (months 3–9)	Creation of guiding principles to help developers summarize and easily refer to features of the intervention identified as central for achieving the intervention objectives	Create guiding principles, comprising: key intervention design objectives (addressing key behavioral issues, needs, challenges identified in Step 1), and key (distinctive) features of the intervention needed to achieve objectives (drawing on intervention planning in Step 1	Theoretical modeling (complex intervention development), for example, creation of logic model describing hypothesized mechanisms of action of intervention, and/ or intervention mapping of behavioral determinants and behavior change techniques

Taken from Yardley, L., Morrison, L., Bradbury, K., & Muller, I. (2015). The person-based approach to intervention development: application to digital health-related behaviour change interventions. Journal of Medical Internet Research, 17(1), e30.

questions needed to accurately represent all of the nuances of the target behavior needed to determine the intervention functions: *who, what, when, where, how often, and with whom?*

BEHAVIOR CHANGE INTERVENTION DESIGN FRAMEWORKS

In recent years developments in the field of health psychology have seen the emergence of comprehensive frameworks intended to guide the design and development of behavior change interventions. Two of the most recent and comprehensive design frameworks are "The Behavior Change Wheel" (Michie et al., 2011), and the "Person Centred Approach" (Yardley et al., 2015).

The Behavior Change Wheel

This framework, referred to hereafter as BCW, operates upon the underlying assumption that effective behavior change interventions must be constructed using a systematic approach that is firmly grounded in the research evidence base for specific target behavior(s) in context (i.e., fruit & vegetable consumption; increased walking activity, etc.) or which is relevant to a specific target population (i.e., adolescents, the elderly, pregnant women, etc.).

The BCW (Fig. 2.2) is a comprehensive framework which integrates over 19 behavior change frameworks from the research evidence base (Michie et al., 2011). It is based upon three domains; sources of human behavior (center circle), functions of the behavior change intervention (middle circle), and the categories of official policies/guidelines concerning behavior change interventions (outer circle) (Fig. 2.2). This framework provides behavior change researchers with a way of conceptualizing the components that explain, or determine, an individual's behavior, which in turn allows researchers to design more successful behavior change interventions.

At the core of the BCW framework is a psychological model of human behavior (B) incorporating the psychological components associated with behavior change: Capability (C), Opportunity (O), and Motivation (M) (The COM-B Model, see Fig. 2.3). COM-B components are applicable to all human behaviors and are the starting point for developing and designing behavior change interventions. Each component in the COM-B model directly influences behavior, and interacts with the other components. In combination they can provide the explanation for the barriers that prevent the target behavior being performed by the target population, and this then identifies the appropriate barriers to be addressed to bring about a

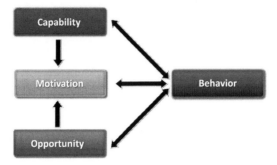

FIGURE 2.3   **The COM-B model of behavior.** *Source: Taken from Michie, S., van Stralen, M. M., & West, R. (2011). The behaviour change wheel: A new method for characterising and designing behaviour change.* Implementation Science, 6, 42

change in that specific target behavior. In this way all of the components of the COM-B model are interdependent, and work in unison to help change a target behavior, or support the long-term maintenance of a target behavior once an individual has adopted it into their regular pattern of behavior (i.e., habit formation). Each component of the COM-B model is divided into subcomponents which are used to capture the more refined details of the COM-B components that are specific to the target behavior.

Capability is defined as the individual's psychological and physical capacity to engage in the activity concerned. The subcomponents being "Psychological Capability"; the capacity to engage in the necessary thought processes, and "Physical Capability"; the capacity to engage in the necessary physical processes.

Opportunity is defined as the factors that lie outside the individual that make the behavior possible, or prompt the behavior. The subcomponents being "Physical Opportunity"; opportunities to engage in the desired behavior that are provided by the environment, and "Social Opportunity"; the cultural situation that dictates how we think about things.

Motivation is defined as the brain processes that energize and direct the individual's behavior. The subcomponents being "Reflective Motivation"; evaluating action and making plans, and "Automatic Motivation"; the emotions and impulses which arise from associative learning, and/or innate personality characteristics.

The COM-B model can be applied to target behaviors both at the individual level, or at the group level. When applied to a target population the components of the model should be used to determine what proportion/percentage of the target population is displaying which behavioral components and subcomponents of the COM-B model in relation to the target behavior. This is more beneficial to intervention design than taking a broad spectrum approach across the whole target population, as particular components of the COM-B model may not be displayed as frequently in relation to the target behavior among all of the members of the target population. Therefore caution must be taken not to apply the BCTs too generically across the target population as a whole because the individuals that make up each target population will all have a different set of factors influencing their patterns of behavior. Not least is the importance of mapping interactions between different behavioral subcomponents in the COM-B model which contribute to overall patterns of behavior. For example, when considering motivation, the drive to perform a behavior is influenced by both evaluating and planning (reflective motivation) and our desires, needs, and impulses (automatic motivation). In this way motivation at any one time goes beyond reason and choice, and is temporally fluid and dynamic depending upon the behavior in context. The structure of human motivation to action is represented in PRIME Theory (West, 2006) which provides a hierarchical view with higher levels of motivation generated in response to stimulation by both the internal and external environment, and so permitting greater response flexibility. These act as stimuli for lower levels of motivation that are well established within the individual, such as reflex responses and intrinsic needs. Our actions are therefore influenced by what we want (the anticipated pleasure or satisfaction of performing an action) or need (the anticipated relief from mental or physical discomfort) at any given moment in time, and so, there is a degree of competition between wants and needs for momentary control over our actions. However, having self-awareness introduces reflective processes in relation to our actions and our internal mental representations of self and exert a degree of self-control over our behavior to reinforce this mental representation, or identity; establishing identity is an important predeterminant of behavior change. Thus when responding to competing stimuli, whereas acting upon impulse may allow the stimulus with the strongest motivational force in relation to our wants and needs to control our behavior, conversely, reflective evaluation of our intention to act in relation to future desires may lead a deferral in our priorities at that moment in favor of future action planning (goal-directed behavior).

Defining the contributions of behavioral subcomponents of the model must be investigated thoroughly in the preliminary stages of understanding the target behavior in context. Ensuring an in-depth understanding of how the target behaviour is performed in context, and the facilitators and barrier for this within the intended target population has important implications for intervention design. When considering the motivational content of an intervention, for example, defining the contributions of automatic and reflective behavioral subcomponents, and the interactions between them, both within a target population and within context via COM-B analysis will inform the intervention design approach, leading to the utility of the appropriate suites of BCTs within an appropriately developed and tailored intervention. Failure to do so may risk nonadherence and/or nonengagement with an intervention if it is not designed to sufficiently meet the needs of its intended target population.

In addition, there is also the likelihood that there will be both interindividual variability among members of a target population, and also, intraindividual variability over the time-course of the intervention. In such cases tailored approaches to intervention design have the benefit of allowing for these differences (Noar, Benac, & Harris, 2007; Noar, Harrington, van Stee, & Aldrich, 2011). In order to detect behavioral fluctuations over time, regarding levels of motivation, for example, may also require interventions to be designed with additional outcome measures at salient time points to track behavioral trends and adapt the intervention accordingly; for example, by delivering ecological momentary interventions in both clinical and research settings using mobile technologies (Heron & Smyth, 2010). Also, using dynamic tailoring methods, such as a "just-in-time" approach (Intille, 2004; Maheshwari, Chatterjee, & Drew, 2008) allows instant data collection and analysis for interventions to be adapted in real-time to allow for behavioral trend fluctuations over time. This type of tailoring in intervention delivery is consequently becoming widely used in mHealth interventions, particularly when behavioral trend fluctuations are anticipated, for example, in motivation toward behavioral goal attainment or in seeking opportunities for engagement with a target behavior.

Therefore, understanding the contributions of behavioral subcomponents of the COM-B model will enable the design of behavior change interventions with both fixed elements (across all members of the target population) and flexible elements (applied on an individual basis); this can be addressed by building personalized, tailored, elements into the design of the intervention, and considering the most appropriate mode of delivery to fulfill the intervention functions.

The Person-Centered Approach

This development framework, referred to hereafter as PCA, was designed to inform the development of digital interventions to help people with the self-management of their health and/or illness. The framework focuses on the perspectives of the people who will use an intervention in order to improve uptake, encourage adherence, and improve outcomes. Its aim is essentially: "…to ground the development of behavior change interventions in a profound understanding of the perspective and psychosocial context of the people who will use them, gained through iterative in-depth qualitative research." (Yardley et al., 2015).

The PCA is intended to be used alongside theory-based and evidence-based approaches to intervention development which provide models of predicting and describing possible influences upon the target behavior which can then be mapped onto appropriate BCTs. The PCA enhances these approaches by incorporating user perspectives into the intervention development process by providing a systematic method for investigating the context specific behavioral patterns of a target population in relation to the target behavior of interest. Table 2.1 shows an overview of the PCA in relation to understanding the target behavior, and incorporating the user perspective, during the planning stages of intervention development.

IDENTIFYING IMPLEMENTATION FACTORS

Understanding the target behavior(s) in context will also provide important information about the barriers and facilitators for the successful implementation of the HBCI.

Addressing Acceptance, Accessibility, Adherence: to Tailor, or not to Tailor Interventions

Developing an in-depth understanding of the target behavior will enable the intervention design to include elements intended to establish positive acceptance of the intervention, provide ease of accessibility, and good levels of adherence within the intended target population. However, using solely rigid intervention designs to fulfill the intervention functions may result in wide disparities in levels of acceptance and adherence among the target population. This is due, in part, to the fact that when trying to change behavior, individual differences exist between drivers of motivation and self-efficacy. One solution to overcome this is to tailor the intervention to the individual needs of each user within the study sample.

Providing tailored feedback is arguably seen as one of the most personalized approaches to encourage health behavior change (Kreuter & Strecher, 1996; Noar et al., 2007; Krebs, Prochaska, & Rossi, 2010) and has been shown to be effective in a variety of target populations over a variety of different behaviors particularly when addressing chronic disease and health promotion, such as smoking cessation, physical activity, eating a healthy diet, and receiving regular breast cancer screening (Krebs et al., 2010). The process of tailoring interventions can be seen as the strategies and information which are applied to a specific person, related to the outcome of interest, and based upon their personal characteristics (Kreuter, Farrell, Olevitch, & Brennan, 1999b; Kreuter, Bull, Clark, & Oswald, 1999a; Kreuter & Skinner, 2000).

Incorporating mobile (mHealth) and Internet (eHealth) technologies into the delivery of behavior change interventions, HBCIs particularly have some advantages when delivering a tailored intervention. Providing tailored feedback via text messages, for instance, is thought to foster behavior change by providing personally relevant feedback for the individual. Personalization of text message content can be selected using a process of "computer-tailoring," which assesses individuals on parameters that are relevant to the target behavior (e.g., the components of a behavior change model, such as the COM-B model), and then selects communication content using embedded data-driven decision rules (algorithms) that automatically trigger feedback from a repository of message content. For example, making an assessment of an individual's capability, opportunity, motivation, and self-efficacy to increase their fruit and vegetable consumption, and then providing feedback tailored to address the different needs of the individual on each of the COM-B components (e.g., to increase motivation for dealing with periods of low willpower, or a tailored reminder of their health goal at mealtimes). Although effective, tailoring an intervention requires a significant time and manpower allocation, and if delivering a digital or Internet based intervention then input into the intervention design process by software developers and mobile App developers may be needed. Above all, an in-depth understanding of the target behavior is fundamental to decide whether tailoring is appropriate to fulfill the intervention functions, or not.

Addressing Acceptance, Accessibility, Adherence: Solutions From mHealth and eHealth

Computer-tailored interventions have become increasingly prevalent in designing and developing behavior change interventions, particularly HBCIs with the adoption of mHealth as a novel approach to intervention delivery and measurement strategies (O'Reilly & Spruijt-Metz, 2013). As mentioned in the previous section, delivering personalized feedback via text messages has great potential for HBCIs, not least because mobile phones are ubiquitous across age groups and populations. This affords them great potential as both a cost-effective and acceptable implementation tool for health behavior change and maintenance by providing a delivery method that is easily accessible to its intended users. The widespread nature of mobile technologies, particularly smartphones, means that mHealth tools, applications, and interventions are able to fit seamlessly into people's everyday lives. This provides opportunities for novel ways to assess behavior in a real-time ecologically valid context across a range of settings. Similarly, it also affords the opportunity to collect data using real-time, objective, data lifestyle tracking methods, such as on-body sensor devices, and to transmit this real-time behavioral and bio-feedback data instantly (Patrick, Griswold, Raab, & Intille, 2008; Atienza & Patrick, 2011) increasing acceptability by minimizing the level of burden needed for significant time-investment by the user (i.e., through manual data input). mHealth also opens a direct communication channel with the user, giving rise to the potential to provide salient and timely reminders and instantaneous feedback in an adaptive "just-in-time" manner (Bickmore, Gruber, & Intille, 2008; Intille, 2004; Intille, Kukla, Farzanfar, & Bakr, 2003; Intille, Larson, & Kukla, 2002; Nahum-Shani et al., 2014).

Although mHealth has the potential to foster good levels of acceptance resulting from convenience, accessibility, and minimal user burden, one of the major challenges for HBCIs is maintaining adherence and long-term behavior change. A major advantage of mHealth is that during the design process it can fulfill the needs of the users identified from the data collected to understand the target behavior relating to what motivates and engages the target population with mobile technologies. Interventions can then implement design features that are not only acceptable but also enjoyable for individuals to use, including mobile applications and mobile games (Gotsis, Hua Wang, Spruijit-Metz, Jordan-Marsh, & Valente, 2013; O'Reilly & Spruijt-Metz, 2013) to encourage and preserve good levels of engagement.

eHealth & mHealth also includes online social networks, available both as web-based and mobile-based platforms. Social support has been proposed as a central concept for health and well-being (Cohen & Hoberman, 1983) with positive effects of social support being seen in relation to a variety of health outcomes in long-term health conditions, such as epilepsy (Amir, Roziner, Knoll, & Neufeld, 1999), mental health (Lakey et al., 2002; Solberg & Viliarreal, 1997) and diabetes (Williams & Bond, 2002), and also in adhering to HCBIs (Richardson et al., 2010).

DESIGNING AND DELIVERING HBCIS FOR ADOLESCENTS

Case study: PEGASO – A personalized ICT guidance service for optimizing healthy dietary and exercise lifestyle behaviours in European teenagers through increasing health awareness, motivation and engagement.

Obesity in childhood and adolescence is a global public health crisis, accounting for up to 7% of healthcare costs in the European Union (WHO, 2000; Sun Guo, Wu, Chumlea, & Roche, 2002) and significantly predicts obesity in adulthood (WHO, 2009). However knowledge alone is not enough to motivate teenagers to adopt healthy lifestyles. Over 50% of all mobile phones owned in the EU5 countries (Spain, Germany, Italy, France, and the United Kingdom) are smartphones with ownership at around 29% among children and teenagers aged 5–15 years (Ofcom, 2013a, 2013b) with initiatives delivered through mobile technologies and the Internet proving an effective approach to encourage healthy lifestyles in this target population.

The EU FP7 funded PEGASO project (Grant Ref: 610727) aims to develop a multitechnology system to motivate teenagers to learn and adopt healthy lifestyle habits in order to prevent obesity, and the development of obesity-related diseases in adulthood. The system is designed with minimal time investment burden to the user so that it can fit effortlessly into their lifestyle. As such, the PEGASO system has been designed to use the smartphone as the main mode of delivery of the intervention to the users. The smartphone has been chosen as the mode of delivery because the current generation of teenagers already perceives it as a personal companion and this relationship is predicted to become stronger in the future (Siewiorek, 2012). In the PEGASO project, the smartphone will provide a set of applications that will enable teenagers to access multiple "in-App" services and games that aim to promote healthy lifestyles, motivate them to take part in physical activity, and adopt healthy eating habits. The applications and services will each be specialized toward a particular function (i.e., the food record application allows the teenagers to monitor and self-manage their dietary patterns) but will all be interrelated within the system.

To understand the target behaviors and inform the design of the PEGASO system a mixed-methodology approach was used. First, the target health behaviors that compose a healthy lifestyle within this age group were determined in an exercise of expert consensus for physical activity behaviors, and dietary behaviors (10 in total). Next, an extended series of systematic literature reviews were completed for each target health behavior to examine the psychosocial influences upon teenagers in relation to performing and adopting each healthy behavior into their daily life, in addition to a systematic review on the use of technology systems (including multiple technologies) in delivering interventions to encourage the adoption of healthy lifestyle behaviors.

In order to understand the views and perspectives of European teenagers toward using technology to support their health, and to explore what they, as users, desire and need from a multitechnology system to support a healthy lifestyle, we conducted several focus groups in three countries: Italy, Spain, and the United Kingdom. During these focus groups, teenagers expressed views that informed the subsequent design of the PEGASO system, namely that: the use of the smartphone is perceived as a means to acquire information about healthy lifestyles for personal motivation; the display of information on the smartphone should not be tiring; the use of multimedia content, especially images, is attractive and engaging; the applications and "in-App" services and games should be interesting; the idea of serious aspects of healthy lifestyle through interactive games "gamification" is an interesting and appealing system component that would ensure engagement with the PEGASO system.

Consequently, gaining these valuable insights has enabled the PEGASO smartphone applications system prototype to be designed to incorporate interactive visual feedback displays to the user on their performance toward achieving their health goals, and interconnectivity between the applications and a health game where points can be earned by engaging in healthy behaviors. The focus group results also showed that the teenagers felt that feedback and goal setting were a highly desirable function, and consequently a potentially very effective motivational BCT in this target population. Therefore, the PEGASO system takes a user-led goal setting approach with interactive data collection through an on-body sensor component of the system. Instant feedback is then provided to the user via direct data communication to the smartphone applications which enables the PEGASO system to evolve with the user and interactively track their performance toward their user-defined, personal, health behavior goals to encourage and motivate behavior change.

CONCLUSIONS

In conclusion, understanding target behaviors in context with the intended target population should be the foundation of the design process for behavior change interventions. This is important to ensure that behavior change interventions meet the needs of the target population and that potential facilitators and barriers to implementation are controlled for in the design and delivery process to make every effort to ensure that there is the maximum opportunity for intervention, engagement, and adherence. A mixed-methodological approach has many benefits in building a thorough understanding of target behaviors in context, as well as the interaction between them. Intervention design framework, such as the Person-Based Approach and the BCW can help to identify and understand the interactions between behavioral components and subcomponents that contribute to the performing target behaviors, particularly COM-B. These, in turn, can be translated into an appropriate suite of BCTs for behavior change intervention content. Pathways to implementation of behavior change interventions should also try to address issues relating to intervention acceptance, accessibility, and adherence. Of particular importance is the mode of intervention delivery, which should fit discretely and seamlessly into the lifestyle of the intended target population. Mobile technologies have the potential to deliver mHealth and eHealth interventions on a large scale due to their wide reaching, pervasive, and ubiquitous use among the majority of the population as a whole. These offer opportunities to develop bespoke and tailored interventions for target populations who are pervasive users of mobile technologies, such as adolescents.

References

Adams, S. A., Matthews, C. E., Ebbeling, C. B., Moore, C. G., Cunningham, J. E., Fulton, J., & Hebert, J. R. (2005). The effect of social desirability and social approval on self-reports of physical activity. *American Journal of Epidemiology, 161*(4), 389–398.

Amir, M., Roziner, I., Knoll, A., & Neufeld, M. Y. (1999). Self-efficacy and social support as mediators in the relation between disease severity and quality of life in patients with epilepsy. *Epilepsia, 40*, 216–224.

Atienza, A. A., & Patrick, K. (2011). Mobile health: the killer app for cyber infrastructure and consumer health. *American Journal of Preventative Medicine, 40*(S2), S151–S153.

Baker, T. B., Gustafson, D. H., & Shah, D. (2014). How can research keep up with eHealth? Ten strategies for increasing the timeliness and usefulness of eHealth research. *Journal of Medical Internet Research, 16*(2), e36.

Bickmore, T., Gruber, A., & Intille, S. (2008). Just-in-time automated counseling for physical activity promotion. *AMIA Annual Symposium Proceedings, Nov. 6*, 880.

Brechwald, W. A., & Prinstein, M. J. (2011). Beyond homophily: a decade of advances in understanding peer influence processes. *Journal of Research on Adolescence, 21*(1), 166–179.

Carels, R. A., Cacciapaglia, H. M., Rydin, S., Douglass, O. M., & Harper, J. (2006). Can social desirability interfere with success in a behavioural weight loss program? *Psychology & Health, 21*(1), 65–78.

Cohen, S., & Hoberman, H. M. (1983). Positive events and social supports as buffers of life change stress. *Journal of Applied Social Psychology, 13*, 99–125.

Creswell, J. W. (2014). *Research design: Qualitative, quantitative, and mixed method approaches* (4th ed.). California: Sage Publications.

Gotsis, M., Hua Wang, H., Spruijit-Metz, D., Jordan-Marsh, M., & Valente, T. (2013). Wellness partners: the design and evaluation of a web-based physical activity diary with social gaming features for adults. *Journal of Medical Internet Research Protocols, 2*(1), e10.

Heron, K. E., & Smyth, J. M. (2010). Ecological momentary interventions: incorporating mobile technology into psychosocial and health behaviour treatments. *British Journal of Health Psychology, 15*, 1–39.

Intille, S. S. (2004). Ubiquitous computing technology for just-in-time motivation of behaviour change. *Studies in Health Technology & Informatics, 107*, 1434–1437.

Intille, S. S., Larson, K., & Kukla, C. (2002). Just-in-time context-sensitive questioning for preventative health care. In: *Proceedings of the AAAI workshop on automation as caregiver: the role of intelligent technology in elder care*. Edmonton, Canada.

Intille, S. S., Kukla, C., Farzanfar, R., & Bakr, W. (2003). Just-in-time technology to encourage incremental, dietary behaviour change. In: AMIA *annual symposium proceedings;American medical informatics association* (p. 874).

Johnson, T., & van de Vijver, F. J. (2002). Social desirability in cross-cultural research. In J. Harness, F. J. van de Vijver, & P. Mohler (Eds.), *Cross-cultural survey methods* (pp. 193–202). New York: Wiley.

Krebs, P., Prochaska, J. O., & Rossi, J. S. (2010). Defining what works in tailoring: a meta-analysis of computer tailored interventions for health behaviour change. *Preventative Medicine, 51*(3–4), 214–221.

Kreuter, M. W., & Skinner, C. S. (2000). Tailoring: what's in a name? *Health Education Research, 15*, 1–4.

Kreuter, M. W., & Strecher, V. J. (1996). Do tailored behaviour change messages enhance the effectiveness of health risk appraisal? Results from a randomized trial. *Health Education Research, 11*, 97–105.

Kreuter, M. W., Bull, F. C., Clark, E. M., & Oswald, D. L. (1999a). Understanding how people process health information: a comparison of tailored and untailored weight loss materials. *Health Psychology, 18*(5), 1–8.

Kreuter, M. W., Farrell, D., Olevitch, L., & Brennan, L. (1999b). *Tailored health messages: Customizing communication with computer technology*. Mahwah, NJ: Lawrence Erlbaum Associates.

Krumpal, I. (2013). Determinants of social desirability bias in sensitive surveys: a literature review. *Quality & Quantity, 47*(4), 2025–2047.

Lakey, B., Adams, K., Neely, L., Rhodes, G., Lutz, C. J., & Sielky, K. (2002). Perceived support and low emotional distress: the role of enacted support, dyad similarity, and provider personality. *Personality and Social Psychology Bulletin, 28*, 1546–1555.

Lalwani, A. K., Shavitt, S., & Johnson, T. (2006). What is the relation between cultural orientation and socially desirable responding? *Journal of Personality and Social Psychology, 90*, 165–178.

Maheshwari, M., Chatterjee, S., & Drew, D. (2008). Exploring the persuasiveness of "just-in-time" motivational messages for obesity management. In *Persuasive Technology* (pp. 258–261). Berlin, Heidelberg: Springer.

Michie, S., van Stralen, M. M., & West, R. (2011). The behaviour change wheel: a new method for characterising and designing behaviour change. *Implementation Science, 6*, 42.

Michie, S., Richardson, M., Johnston, M., Abraham, C., Francis, J., Hardeman, W., Eccles, M. P., Cane, J., & Wood, C. E. (2013). The behaviour change technique taxonomy(v1) of 93 hierarchically clustered techniques: building an international consensus for the reporting of behaviour change interventions. *Annals of Behavioural Medicine, 46*, 81–95.

Nahum-Shani, S., Smith, S. N., Tewari, A., Witkiewitz, K., Collins, L. M., Spring, B., & Murphy, S. A. (2014). Just-in-Time Adaptive Interventions (JITAIs): An organizing framework for ongoing health behaviour support. (Technical Report No. 14-126). University Park, PA: The Methodology Center, Penn State.

Noar, S. M., Benac, C. N., & Harris, M. S. (2007). Does tailoring matter? Meta-analytic review of tailored print health behaviour change interventions. *Psychological Bulletin, 133*(4), 673–693.

Noar, S. M., Harrington, N. G., van Stee, S., & Aldrich, R. S. (2011). Tailored health communication to change lifestyle behaviours. *American Journal of Lifestyle Medicine*(5), 112–122.

O'Reilly, G. A., & Spruijt-Metz, D. (2013). Current mHealth technologies for physical activity assessment and promotion. *American Journal of Preventative Medicine, 45*(4), 501–507.

Ofcom (2013a). *Communications market report, 2013.* Retrieved from: http://stakeholders.ofcom.org.uk/binaries/research/cmr/cmr13/2013 UK CMR.pdf

Ofcom (2013b). *Children and parents: media use and attitudes report.* Retrieved from: http://stakeholders.ofcom.org.uk/binaries/research/media-literacy/october-2013/research07Oct2013.pdf

Pagliari, C. (2007). Design and evaluation in eHealth: challenges and implications for an interdisciplinary field. *Journal of Medical Internet Research, 9*(2), e15.

Patrick, K., Griswold, W., Raab, F., & Intille, S. (2008). Health and the mobile phone. *American Journal of Preventative Medicine, 35*(2), 177–181.

Richardson, C. R., Buis, L. R., Janney, A. W., Goodrich, D. E., Sen, A., Hess, M. L., Mehari, K. S., Fortlage, L. A., Resnick, P. J., Zikmund-Fisher, B. J., Strecher, V. J., & Piette, J. D. (2010). An online community improves adherence in an Internet-mediated walking program. Part 1: results of a randomized controlled trial. *Journal of Medical Internet Research, 12*(4), e71.

Siewiorek, D. (2012). Generation smartphone. *IEEE Spectrum, 49*(9), 54–58.

Solberg, V. S., & Viliarreal, P. (1997). Examination of self-efficacy, social support, and stress as predictors of psychological and physical distress among Hispanic college students. *Hispanic Journal of Behavioural Sciences, 19*, 182–201.

Sun Guo, S., Wu, W., Chumlea, W. C., & Roche, A. F. (2002). Predicting overweight and obesity in adulthood from body mass index values in childhood and adolescence. *American Journal of Clinical Nutrition, 76*, 653–658.

van Gemert-Pijnen, J. E., Nijland, N., van Limburg, M., Ossebaard, H. C., Kelders, S. M., Eysenbach, G., et al. (2011). A holistic framework to improve the uptake and impact of eHealth technologies. *Journal of Medical Internet Research, 13*(4), e111.

West, R. (2006). *Theory of addiction.* Oxford: Blackwell.

World Health Organization (2000). Obesity: preventing and managing the global epidemic. *WHO Technical Report Series 894*. Geneva.

World Health Organization (2009). Population-based prevention strategies for childhood obesity: report of a WHO forum and technical meeting. Geneva.

Williams, K., & Bond, M. (2002). The roles of self-efficacy, outcome expectancies and social support in the self-care behaviours of diabetics. *Psychology, Health & Medicine, 7*, 127–141.

Yardley, L., Morrison, L., Bradbury, K., & Muller, I. (2015). The person-based approach to intervention development: application to digital health-related behaviour change interventions. *Journal of Medical Internet Research, 17*(1), e30.

Software Design Patterns for Persuasive Computer–Human Dialogue: Reminder, Reward, and Instant Feedback

M. Oduor*, T. Alahäivälä*, H. Oinas-Kukkonen**

*Department of Information Processing Science, University of Oulu, Oulu, Finland; **Oulu Advanced Research on Software and Information Systems, Oulu, Finland

OVERVIEW

Digital interventions are transforming health care and the well-being sector and can be seen as prime candidates for the application of key behavioral science theories and principles to promote healthier behaviors and also generate new elements to health care and healthier living (Langrial, Lehto, Oinas-Kukkonen, Harjumaa, & Karppinen, 2012; Lehto & Oinas-Kukkonen, 2011). There is an extensive research showing that computer-based health interventions can be efficacious and as computing has migrated to the Web, so have the plethora of behavior change support systems (BCSSs) (Oinas-Kukkonen, 2013; Lenert, Munoz, Perez, & Bansod, 2004). The Web has ability to provide efficient, interactive, and tailored content to the user and computer-tailored interventions have induced significant changes in smoking, diet, and physical activity (Langrial & Oinas-Kukkonen, 2012; Lehto & Oinas-Kukkonen, 2011; Spittaels, De Bourdeaudhuij, Brug, & Vandelanotte, 2007; Womble et al., 2004), and have the potential to provide individualized behavior change information to many individuals (Ritterband, Thorndike, Cox, Kovatchev, & Gonder-Frederick, 2009).

Behavior Change Research and Theory. http://dx.doi.org/10.1016/B978-0-12-802690-8.00003-7

BCSSs are socio-technical systems that emphasize users' goals and are concerned with both psychological and behavioral outcomes (Ploderer, Reitberger, Oinas-Kukkonen, & van Gemert-Pijnen, 2014). BCSSs have been defined as information systems that form, alter, or reinforce attitudes, behaviors, or acts of complying without using deception or coercion (Oinas-Kukkonen, 2013). They have proven successful in problem areas, such as health and sustainability; research into BCSSs focuses on the approaches, methodologies, processes, and tools for their design, as well as their potential effects (Oinas-Kukkonen, 2013). There are many features that add to the persuasiveness of a system, such as those contributing to support users' goals, interaction with the system, systems' credibility, or social influence (Oinas-Kukkonen & Harjumaa, 2009). In this chapter we focus on conceptualizing software design patterns for specifically providing *persuasive computer–human dialogue* in BCSSs. That is, facilitating interaction between the user and the system. The conceptualization is based on the dialogue support design principles in the persuasive systems design (PSD) model (Oinas-Kukkonen & Harjumaa, 2009).

Although a prominent research area, BCSSs have in prior studies been described at a generally undetailed technical level (cf. Bennett & Glasgow, 2009; Lehto & Oinas-Kukkonen, 2011). This has partly been due to a lack of understanding of how to apply the knowledge from the relevant theories and a lack of guidance for software developers of persuasive systems on the principles to apply (Oduor, Alahäivälä, & Oinas-Kukkonen, 2014). For understanding persuasion in a system, its use, user, and technology contexts should be recognized. The use context covers the characteristics of the problem domain in question, the user context considers the differences between individuals, and the technology context contains the technical specifications of a system (Oinas-Kukkonen & Harjumaa, 2009).

A lack of precision in describing the technological context has been common in prior studies on BCSSs, making it difficult to understand the persuasiveness of these systems as a whole (Oinas-Kukkonen, 2013). Describing systems without knowledge of their internals, or so-called "blackbox approach," makes it difficult to argue generalizable results related to systems design (Oinas-Kukkonen, 2013; Oduor et al., 2014). By utilizing more software engineering-oriented approaches and tools, such as software architectures (Alahäivälä, Oinas-Kukkonen, & Jokelainen,2013), and software design patterns (Oduor et al., 2014), BCSS research can be enhanced from proof-of-concepts to concrete software development guidelines.

There has been prior research on Web design patterns (Díaz, Aedo, & Rosson, 2008; Taleb, Seffah, & Abran, 2007) and design patterns for persuasive systems. For example, discovering persuasive patterns in social networks, introducing a set of general patterns for influencing user behavior through design and more recently, conceptualization of design patterns for social influence (Weiksner, Fogg, & Liu, 2008; Lockton, Harrison, & Stanton, 2010; Oduor et al., 2014). While covering many aspects of persuasive design, these patterns have mostly been presented at a high conceptual level and are mainly graphical user interface (GUI) based. Although Oduor et al. (2014) provide practical examples of how software design patterns can enhance PSD and development.

We propose and aim to reach a more detailed technical view into PSD by inspecting patterns also from the object-oriented modeling and code implementation levels. Our view is that use of design patterns will emphasize the importance of the features, help to distinguish between different persuasive strategies, and how they have been applied in various systems. This in turn makes our results applicable to both researchers studying PSD and practitioners implementing future BCSSs.

The rest of the chapter is organized as follows: in Section 2 we present issues related to computer–human dialogue in PSD and overall pattern thinking. Based on this, Section 3 introduces three design patterns for computer–human dialogue. Section 4 describes an example implementation of the patterns in a prototype to evaluate their applicability. In Section 5, the discussion is presented and then conclusions are given.

THEORETICAL BACKGROUND

Dialogue Support in Persuasive Systems Design

Behavioral treatments were first introduced in the 1970s and researchers advocating these approaches argue that the most effective way to change behaviors is by changing environmental factors. These factors could either precede behavior–restricting or forbidding certain foods, prompting regular intake of water by placing a bottle of water on one's desk—or be the result of behavior—receiving points for healthy behaviors, criticism for unhealthy behaviors, and a growing interdisciplinary body of literature explores sociological and psychological aspects of computer-mediated communication (CMC) (Chiu et al., 2009; Purpura, Schwanda, Williams, Stubler, & Sengers, 2011). According to Lehto and Oinas-Kukkonen (2011), at the heart of health promotion or any treatment program is changing people's behavior; behavior that significantly affects, for example, cancer and heart disease that are among the major causes of premature mortality.

Computer-based interventions are most effective when they are interactive and when persuaders adjust their influence tactics as the situation evolves. Computers can be more effective than humans in persuasion because of their persistence, anonymity, ability to manage huge volumes of data, modality, scalability, and ubiquity (Fogg, 2002, pp. 7–11). Technology does not in itself seek to influence, rather, because it provides a platform where services can be built on; it facilitates and simplifies the behavior change process (Lockton, 2012). The multimodality and high interactivity of Web technologies enables creation of self-regulatory skills and also provide various options for engaging, educating, and equipping individuals; in addition to constant access, the Internet also offers anonymity that could possibly encourage individuals who would prefer privacy (Lustria, Cortese, Noar, & Glueckauf, 2009; Womble et al., 2004).

The various persuasive roles—tool to increase capability, medium for interactive experiences, and social actor that creates relationships—computers can imply different kinds of implementations and design for persuasive systems, and their overall influence (Fogg, 2002). Building on from Fogg's (2002) study on computer-based persuasion is Oinas-Kukkonen and Harjumaa's (2009) PSD model for designing and evaluating persuasive systems and mapping persuasive design principles to system requirements. The model states that the development of persuasive systems requires three steps: understanding the key design issues related to persuasive systems, analyzing the persuasion context, and then designing the systems' features (Oinas-Kukkonen & Harjumaa, 2009).

Concerning the design of the actual *software features* of persuasive systems, Oinas-Kukkonen and Harjumaa (2009) have proposed four categories of design principles: primary task, dialogue, system credibility, and social support. These design principles function as guidelines for determining software requirements, as well as an evaluation method for persuasive systems (Oinas-Kukkonen & Harjumaa, 2009). Kelders, Kok, Ossebaard, and Van Gemert-Pijnen (2012) in their review on persuasive systems and their efficacy found—although not conclusively—that extensive employment of dialogue support features, such as reminders can significantly predict better adherence in subjects and the effectiveness of Web-based interventions.

The dialogue support category contains design principles concerning the dialogue between a system and its users. These features improve communication between users and the system, especially in terms of system's feedback to better guide the user through the intended behavior change process. The features should be incorporated to keep users involved and motivated in continued interaction with the system toward achieving their behavioral goal(s) (Langrial & Oinas-Kukkonen, 2012; Lehto & Oinas-Kukkonen, 2011; Oinas-Kukkonen & Harjumaa, 2009). The dialogue support features include praise, rewards, reminders, suggestion, similarity, liking, and social role.

By offering *praise* for the target behavior, users can be made more prone to persuasion. Praise can be via words, images, symbols, and act as a means of providing feedback based on the user's behavior. System should *reward* target behaviors to help motivate the user to learn and progress through a behavior change program and in order to produce long-term engagement and playful interaction. For example, a child user can be rewarded for completing a module or unit within a pediatric intervention by making an online game available (Ritterband et al., 2009). A *reward* system can make the process more enjoyable and help users get pleasure from their tasks (Ritterband et al., 2009; Sohn & Lee, 2007). *Reminders* for target behaviors will more likely lead to achievement of goals and research (Chiu et al., 2009; Langrial, Oinas-Kukkonen, Lappalainen, & Lappalainen, 2013) has shown that reminders help in task completion. They could be in the form of automated emails sent to all users, personalized emails sent based on predetermined algorithms, or from an individual and phone calls triggered by the program or clinician (Ritterband et al., 2009). The effectiveness of behavior change interventions is also enhanced if reminders are frequent and there is also personal contact with a counselor where applicable (Fry & Neff, 2009). Offering *suggestions* matching the desired target behavior will have greater persuasive power in ensuring that the users' decisions are in line with their desired outcome (Purpura et al., 2011). *Similarity* between users and the systems makes the user more persuadable; *liking* means making the systems look and feel pleasurable to use; and the system may also adopt a *social role* for users more likely to use it (Oinas-Kukkonen & Harjumaa, 2009).

The dialogue support features are usually not well covered in the literature and a majority of those reviewed, such as Lehto and Oinas-Kukkonen (2011); Ritterband et al. (2009); Sohn and Lee (2007); Fry and Neff (2009); Langrial and Oinas-Kukkonen (2012); Langrial et al. (2013) focus mostly on rewards, reminders, and/or suggestions. Although with the continued development in studies related to the use of game design elements in nongame contexts (gamification), (e.g., Hamari, Koivisto, & Sarsa, 2014; Rapp, 2015; Deterding, 2015), the dialogue support features are becoming more prevalent.

Software Design Patterns

Patterns reflect factual and experience knowledge that can be applied in different situations to solve tangible engineering problems (Wentzlaff & Specker, 2006). Especially, as idea generation and problem solving is based on the premise that there are truly no new inventions and that the process of recognizing problem situations is similar to those faced previously (Lockton et al., 2010). Patterns have mainly been used to preserve common problem-solving knowledge as they describe recurring problems together with their solutions; they have been tailored to suit the needs of various disciplines and over time have evolved to dealing with specific problems (Kruschitz & Hitz, 2010a; Wentzlaff & Specker, 2006). Patterns are reusable solutions that can be applied to commonly occurring problems in software design and enable building of systems with good object-oriented design qualities. Patterns are not the source of programmable code, but rather provide solutions to general design problems, to be applied to specific applications. They serve as templates that can be used in different ways for solving problems (Gamma, Helm, Johnson, & Vlissides, 1994).

Patterns guide and are also enhanced as development progresses and they primarily address issues concerning changes in software. Most patterns allow some part of a system to vary independently of all other parts and these varying parts are often encapsulated (Gamma et al., 1994). Furthermore, they aid in avoiding design alternatives that compromise reusability and can also help improve documentation and maintenance of existing systems by providing explicit specifications of class and object interactions and their underlying intent (Gamma et al., 1994; Zemin, 2009).

Patterns depict the static and dynamic structures and collaborations of successful solutions to problems that arise when developing applications within a particular context and have four essential characteristics:

1. The *pattern name* is a common term that eases the communication among stakeholders and enables design at a higher abstraction level while simplifying thoughts on designs and communicating these and their trade-off to others.
2. The *problem* describes when a pattern should be applied and its context.
3. The *solution* provides an abstract description of a design problem and how a general arrangement of elements (classes and objects) solves it.
4. The *consequences* are the results and tradeoffs of applying the pattern (Gamma et al., 1994).

Patterns can further be classified according to what they do (purpose) and whether they apply primarily to classes or objects (scope) (Gamma et al., 1994). Gamma et al. (1994) further elaborate on the classification of patterns and their functions, which includes: initializing of classes and objects, their relationships, and distribution of responsibility.

Most of the studies on software design patterns have focused on different phases and aspects of systems development, such as reuse and the challenges involved in evaluation of architectures. For example, Zemin (2009) and Peña-Mora and Vadhavkar (1997) detail application of patterns in software reuse, where an effective method of software development based on pattern reuse is proposed. Both papers provide a framework with valuable insights on the use of patterns for development and analysis of reusable software systems. Gestwicki and Sun (2008) using game development as an example, show how design patterns could be taught with emphasis on object-orientation and patterns integration. The study provides relevant examples of how patterns could be used to implement various features of a system's architecture (Gestwicki & Sun, 2008).

Others have focused on the challenges involved in software architecture evaluation; formalization and unification of human–computer interaction (HCI) patterns to aid different groups including software engineers in their work with patterns; and visualization of software systems as a set of design patterns and possible solutions through use of UML class diagrams to document a system's static structure (Kruschitz & Hitz, 2010b; Trese & Tilley, 2007; Zhu, Babar, & Jeffery, 2004).

Another stream of research (Ning, Liming, Yanzhang, Yi-bing, & Jing, 2008; Thung, Ng, Thung, & Sulaiman, 2010) mainly concentrates on architectural features which detail the use of the Model-View-Controller (MVC) in Web information system development. In Leff and Rayfield (2001), a model of flexible Web application partitioning that can be implemented using the constructs of MVC is proposed.

Taleb et al. (2007) and Díaz et al. (2008) provide a classification of different Web design patterns and discuss how they can be combined in the development process, and show how the patterns have been used in the redesign of a website. Díaz et al. (2008), for example, visually represent Web design patterns by integrating them with goal-oriented design to assist both end users and casual developers in selecting the right patterns needed for specific design projects, determining the complexity of the project, and the relationships and trade-offs of each (Díaz et al., 2008).

Others (Franch, 2013; Aversano, Canfora, Cerulo, Del Grosso, & Di Penta, 2007; Kobayashi & Saeki, 1999; Peña-Mora & Vadhavkar, 1997) have focused on the changes of patterns in the software development process where each of the stages has their own styles that could be reused in other development processes. Franch (2013), for example, has particularly concentrated on patterns in the requirements phase of systems development. Initially, a suitable pattern has to be chosen then instantiated to make it adaptable to the problem in order to be able to get an artifact Franch (2013) adds. According to Aversano et al. (2007), pattern change frequency and amount of cochange does not depend on the pattern type, but rather on the role played by the pattern to support the application features. Use of patterns provides a shared language that maximizes the value of communication among developers, thus reducing the time spent on making design decisions related to feature changes (Gamma et al., 1994).

Even though there is a certain set of well-known patterns, choosing the one to use especially for inexperienced developers can be a problem (Kruschitz & Hitz, 2010a, 2010b; Wentzlaff & Specker, 2006). Therefore, when thinking of future developments, patterns could be more domain-specific and tailored to particular focus areas, such as software-oriented architecture (SOA), mobile systems, and Web 2.0, that are yet to be properly covered by the pattern languages (Buschmann, Henney, & Schmidt, 2007). Moreover, as software design patterns do not also cover all aspects of interactivity in online systems (Buschmann et al., 2007), there are opportunities for development of persuasive patterns for enhanced *computer–human dialogue* in BCSSs. Thus the following sections based on the discussions earlier seek to develop persuasive patterns intended for dialogue support.

SOFTWARE DESIGN PATTERNS FOR COMPUTER– HUMAN DIALOGUE SUPPORT IN BCSSs

To conceptualize software design patterns for *computer–human dialogue* in BCSSs, we adapted the design principles from the PSD model (Oinas-Kukkonen & Harjumaa, 2009). In the dialogue support features similarity, liking, and social role mainly relate to systems design at the user-experience level, and they may not be easily operationalized as software design patterns. For this reason, we will focus on praise, suggestion, reminders, and rewards. *Reminder* and *reward* patterns are implemented as such, but because both *praise* and *suggestion* are means of providing feedback based on users' (targeted) behavior, they are combined into the *Instant Feedback* pattern (Fig. 3.1).

The system and the patterns are designed for BCSS and implemented using modern de-facto Web technologies and architectures, such as the model/view/controller (MVC) and representational state transfer (REST) approaches (Fielding & Taylor, 2002; Krasner & Pope, 1988; Leff & Rayfield, 2001). MVC is a common design pattern to distribute the software functionalities into distinct components for the sake of maintainability: models, views, and controllers (Krasner & Pope, 1988). Although this is not exactly the case in modern-day Web applications, many Web development frameworks still roughly retrace the MVC pattern in their separation

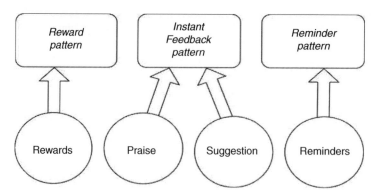

FIGURE 3.1   Computer–human dialogue support features recognized in the PSD model and the corresponding software design patterns.

of application concerns (Leff & Rayfield, 2001). REST again implies that an application's resources are identified and resolved by a particular uniform resource locator (URL). The application's data is then accessed by performing hypertext transfer protocol (HTTP) requests on the resource specified in the URL. A REST application usually provides an interface for performing Create, Read, Update, and Delete (CRUD) actions on its resources (Fielding & Taylor, 2002).

Building on MVC and REST approaches, we presume that the application's resources are implemented as their corresponding Models, Views, and Controllers with CRUD actions. There are at least two generalizable resource entities that are necessary for a BCSS: the User resource and the Entry resource. The User resource depicts the users of the systems, containing their account information and possible behavioral profiles. The Entry resource is an abstraction of the data that the user submits to the system to monitor their behavioral habits; for example, weight measures in a weight-monitoring application, or individual exercise activities in exercise-tracking application. Next we describe the patterns, stating the needed components and their relations to implement the dialogue support features adapted from the PSD model.

Instant Feedback Pattern

A BCSS or any persuasive system should provide its users with immediate feedback upon completion of a task to enable them to know how they are doing in adapting their target behavior. This feedback can be in the form of praise and/or suggestions. Users can be made more open to persuasion by offering praise on expected behaviors (Toscos, Faber, An, & Gandhi, 2006). Also, offering suggestions during the use of a system will ensure that the users' decisions are in line with their desired outcome (Purpura et al., 2011). A simple way to implement this sort of instant feedback is to include logic for analyzing every entry upon submission to the system. Following the MVC and REST approaches, this would be placed on the *Create* action of the *Controller* of an *Entry*. Based on the analysis, a praising or suggesting message is selected. The appropriate feedback message is then passed on to the corresponding View that is shown to the user instantly. See Fig. 3.2 for a flow chart of the pattern and Table 3.1 for a structured presentation in natural language explaining the problem and solution.

Reminder Pattern

Research has shown that reminders help in task completion (Chiu et al., 2009; Langrial et al., 2013). Possible forms of reminders are automated emails sent to all users or personalized emails sent based on

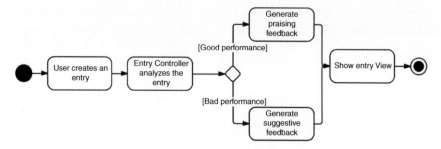

FIGURE 3.2   **Activity diagram of the instant feedback pattern.**

TABLE 3.1   Instant Feedback Pattern

Pattern name	Instant feedback
Problem	The system should give real-time comments on the user's performance, so they can get immediate feedback on their progress. Good performance should be praised and relapses should be met with appropriate suggestions for the next action taken
Components	User, Entry (Controller)
Solution	Upon creation of an Entry to a BCSS system, it should be analyzed in the Create action of its Controller, and an appropriate feedback message should be passed on the View that is shown to the user, containing (1) a praising message for good performance or (2) a suggestion how to correct one's behavior
Consequences	The user always receives appropriate feedback when submitting an entry of a behavioral action. Based on the feedback the users can reexamine the progress made and possibly make adjusting moves to their habits

predetermined algorithms (Ritterband et al., 2009). In order for a Web-based BCSS to include the functionality for sending persuasive reminders, the *User, Mailer,* and *Scheduler* components could be implemented (Fig. 3.3).

The User component contains the user profiles, most prominently their email address and any possible preferences for providing tailored content. Mailer component should contain methods and logic for different cases of reminder delivery. These could include, for example, a weekly newsletter, a reminder after not logging in for the past week, or additional reminders for users submitted for tailored content according to their behavioral profiles. The Scheduler component should then include the functionality to implement the delivery of the reminders according to the set schedule.

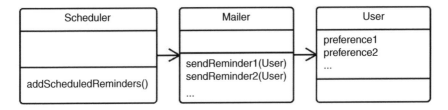

FIGURE 3.3 **Reminder pattern.**

TABLE 3.2 Reminder Pattern

Pattern name	Reminder
Problem	The system should continuously reach out to users to strengthen their habit to regularly visit the system
Components	User, Mailer, Scheduler
Solution	The system should contain the User, Mailer, and Scheduler components for handling the reminder functionality. The scheduler component contains the preferences on when to call the Mailer component to send the appropriate reminders to the users
Consequences	The user is sent a regular reminder email or SMS to encourage visiting the system. If the user has not logged in during a certain time frame, an additional reminder can be sent. This keeps the users more engaged. Too frequent use of reminder may irritate the users though, so the interval of the reminders should be carefully evaluated

Instead of email, for example, short message service (SMS) could be used to reach the users. In this, case, the Mailer component should be implemented as a corresponding SMS sending component. See Table 3.2 for summary.

Reward Pattern

Rewards and virtual achievements are powerful motivational tools. A reward system can make the process more enjoyable and help users get pleasure from their tasks (Ritterband et al., 2009; Sohn & Lee, 2007). For issuing virtual rewards in a Web-based BCSS, the performance of its users must be monitored. This can be efficiently done utilizing the well-known object-oriented *Observer* design pattern, which defines and maintains a one-to-many dependency between objects such that a change in

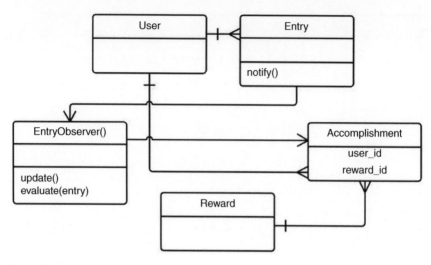

FIGURE 3.4   **Reward pattern.**

one object leads to all its dependents being notified and being updated automatically. Hence, for providing rewards functionality in BCSS, *User*, *Entry*, *EntryObserver*, *Reward*, and *Accomplishment* components are needed (Fig. 3.4).

The *User* object is an instantiation of the User model, which contains the profile information of a certain user. *Entry* depicts an action that the user submits to the system, being an actualization of a pursued behavioral habit. *Reward* contains the description of the reward in question. *Accomplishment* depicts the relationship between the User and the Reward and is used for maintaining the record of the rewards users have gained. *EntryObserver* then contains the logic that observes upon creation of Entries, if they account for a reward and if so, creates the corresponding *Accomplishment*, depicting the relationship between the user and the entry (Table 3.3).

EXAMPLE IMPLEMENTATION

In order to demonstrate and verify our suggested software design patterns, we used them to develop a nonfunctional software prototype for a conceptual BCSS based on the "Don't Break the Chain" method (http://lifehacker.com/281626/jerry-seinfelds-productivity-secret). This motivational approach is based on the idea that for adapting behaviors, one should choose a habit and start performing it on a daily basis. Each day the habit is successfully kept up should be marked down to keep track of

TABLE 3.3 Reward Pattern

Pattern name	Reward
Problem	The system should give virtual rewards to users to further motivate them to stay involved
Components	User, Entry, EntryObserver, Reward, Accomplishment
Solution	The resources in the system should be modeled to implement the User, Entry, EntryObserver, Reward, and Accomplishment components. When the User submits an Entry to the system, the EntryObserver component observers whether the action is eligible for issuing a reward to the user
Consequences	Rewarding users for performing after their target behavior motivates them and assists their goal setting. But it should be minded that all users might not find rewards as desirable

the amount of consecutive days the target behavior has been followed. Thus, the longer the "chain," the more resilient the user is in maintaining the behavior. The basic functionality of the system conceptualized here would be for the user, to choose the habits to follow and then keep marking down their performance every day.

We now inspect how the persuasiveness of the system could be presumably incremented using our presented software design patterns. As a fundamental system the components we implemented, the User and Entry resources to handle managing the users of the system and their daily submissions of completed activities that consecutively form a chain. We now apply the features suggested in our patterns to the system. The example implementation uses the Ruby programming language with Ruby on Rails web framework (see the Appendix for the pseudocode). For presentation purposes, we have omitted all but the features specifically implied by the design patterns in our demonstration. Ellipses in the code indicate intentionally omitted implementation details.

Instant Feedback Pattern

In our example application, we want to praise the user whenever they add an entry that maintains a chain. If a chain is broken, we give a remark suggesting corrective behavior. We apply the Instant Feedback pattern by adding the logic for giving praise or suggestions into the create action of the controller class for the Entry resource.

The example is very basic and does not analyze the content in anyway other than if it is part of a chain or not. More intricate logic could be added for more personalized feedback. But it should be noted that when following the MVC approach, adding logic to display information should be rather separated into view components rather than the controller. This suggests revision of the pattern when applied to more complex occasions.

Reminder Pattern

To implement the Reminder pattern (see Appendix for the pseudo-code), we set up the system to send its users a regular email every Monday morning to nudge them to sign in and maintaining their chains. The UserMailer component is created to contain the method definitions of the intended persuasive reminders.

The User model is then complemented with a method call for sending out the reminders to every user. We acknowledge, that this may not be the best possible approach though, since it makes the User model somewhat complicated to understand if there will be a multitude of different reminder methods.

As the Scheduler component, we use the open-source *Whenever* software package. In its configuration file we add a call to the reminder method in the User model to be added to the *crontab* file of the server, which handles running scheduled processes:

The user now receives the reminder every week. More reminders can easily be added, and they could also easily be personalized or tailored according to user profiling, based on the data that is stored in the User model.

Reward Pattern

In our example application we give people virtual rewards for getting and maintaining long chains. To implement this using the Reward pattern (see the Appendix for pseudocode), we first setup the many-to-many relationships between User and Reward through the Accomplishment model to allow keeping track of the gained rewards.

An observer is then created to observe if new Entries are submitted. Upon the creation of an entry, the observer checks if it is entitled to a reward and if so, creates the corresponding accomplishment record between the user and the reward.

The system will now automatically deliver rewards to users when their entries entitle for it, and each user's rewards can be easily retrieved.

DISCUSSION

The current practice in developing persuasive systems, while based on well-developed and researched cognitive and social psychological principles, lacks the support of clear, well-defined, flexible, and generalizable software design patterns that could inform and aid in automating the development process (Oduor et al., 2014). The presented work delves into aspects of improving the design and development of persuasive systems by defining appropriate patterns based on Oinas-Kukkonen and Harjumaa's (2009) PSD model. This is because patterns are based on the premise that there rarely are new problems and almost all problems have been faced and solved earlier and the solutions for these can be applied using the same basis in a different setting or context (Lockton et al., 2010).

Design patterns are an important tool for knowledge sharing and they help to identify and document best practice solutions as it is important not to reinvent the wheel each time a system is to be created so as to save time and avoid making erroneous implementation interpretations (Kruschitz & Hitz, 2010b; Wentzlaff & Specker, 2006). Thus patterns can be useful for enhancing the development of persuasive systems by providing reusable frameworks that enhance standardization of the development process and one not overly affected by factors that cause changes in software. Three persuasive software design patterns for computer–human dialogue support features that could be implemented in BCSSs have been suggested. We evaluated the applicability of the patterns by implementing them in a figurative prototype BCSS. The implementation of the patterns in the prototype seems to provide support for our argument that the patterns as we suggest could be useful in developing persuasive systems. However, as the patterns at this stage are only a conceptualization of the dialogue support features in the PSD model, there is still need for further research and additional testing on a more elaborate persuasive system.

The suggested patterns are therefore limited as they were developed only for describing the development of a demonstrative system prototype. For further proof, more complex applications applying the patterns should be developed; rather than just focusing on the PSD principles, the patterns could be applied in systems for making recommendations based on information generated from sensors or other connected applications. The application of the patterns in different programming environments, languages, and frameworks should also be studied. For example, whether the patterns apply in the development of a native mobile application, as well as of a Web-based BCSS could be studied.

The presented patterns solely concern the computer–human dialogue features in a system, and there still remain many other persuasive system features that could be covered when studying persuasive software design patterns. Thus, future work will involve definition and verification of the presented patterns and development and integration with others focusing on different aspects of PSD, such as social influence as described in Oduor et al. (2014). Additionally, evaluation of the patterns flexibility, their ability to inform system design and improve communication among developers, or their capability to improve design quality and/or reduce development time should be evaluated. Moreover, more concrete examples of the code and graphical user interface (GUI) features that serve as a source for the patterns, how they could be connected with other patterns (to form a pattern language), and accessible from a repository where patterns can be stored as noted in Kruschitz and Hitz (2010a, 2010b) for easy access should also be looked at.

This chapter's implications for research are in providing an intricate implementation level view of the software development aspects of BCSSs. The object-oriented design and code level findings presented are meant to break out from black-box thinking in PSD, allowing researchers to inspect the internals of software components needed to produce persuasive applications. This therefore serves as a first step in providing evidence of why patterns could be an important component in enhancing the persuasive intent of BCSSs' development. Especially because in BCSSs unlike in general persuasive systems, the focus is more on the users' needs and goals rather on specific features and/or system developers' goals (Ploderer et al., 2014). Enhancement of systems' persuasiveness will depend on implementation of features that align both a system's and users' intent. Practitioner-wise, the use of persuasive design patterns will assist in creating conventions to bootstrap future BCSSs development.

CONCLUSIONS

In this chapter, persuasive software design patterns for computer–human dialogue have been presented. The patterns are the first step in standardization of the development of persuasive systems and could facilitate the development of robust and easily modifiable system specifications. These systems will also provide better linkage between users' interaction with the systems and the intent of the systems designers. First, the patterns are instantiations of well-known features from the PSD model that are implemented in various persuasive systems to facilitate user engagement and interaction with and through the respective systems. Second, through use of patterns starting from natural language requirements and problem definition and then moving on to context diagrams and example implementation, we illustrate how a design requirement can be instantiated into actual system features applying the MVC architectural framework. This has also served to demonstrate how patterns can provide standardized methods for implementing persuasive features, how they can be modeled differently when developing BCSSs and other persuasive systems that cater for different behaviors. Therefore, we have paved the way for a research track in persuasive software patterns with implications for further investigation on the use of patterns for future design of persuasive systems. A natural next step would be to implement the patterns in fully functional software systems in order to get a more detailed conception of their software implementations and present these to other developers and see how they are used to support a variety of other needs as discussed in the previous section.

References

Alahäivälä, T., Oinas-Kukkonen, H., & Jokelainen, T. (2013). Software architecture design for health BCSS: Case Onnikka. In *Proceedings of the 8th international conference on persuasive technology* (pp. 3–14). Berlin, Heidelberg: Springer-Verlag.

Aversano, L., Canfora, G., Cerulo, L., Del Grosso, C., & Di Penta, M. (2007). An empirical study on the evolution of design patterns. In *Proceedings of the the 6th joint meeting of the European software engineering conference and the ACM SIGSOFT symposium on the foundations of software engineering* (pp. 385–394). New York, NY: ACM.

Bennett, G. G., & Glasgow, R. E. (2009). The delivery of public health interventions via the internet: actualizing their potential. *Annual Review of Public Health, 30*(1), 273–292.

Buschmann, F., Henney, K., & Schmidt, D. C. (2007). Past, present, and future trends in software patterns. *IEEE, Software*, 31–37.

Chiu, M. -C., Chang, S. -P., Chang, Y. -C., Chu, H. -H., Chen, C. C. -H., Hsiao, F. -H., & Ko, J. -C. (2009). Playful bottle: a mobile social persuasion system to motivate healthy water intake. In *Proceedings of the 11th international conference on ubiquitous computing* (pp. 185–194). New York, NY: ACM.

Deterding, S. (2015). The lens of intrinsic skill atoms: a method for gameful design. *Human–Computer Interaction, 30*(3–4), 294–335.

Díaz, P., Aedo, I., & Rosson, M. B. (2008). Visual representation of web design patterns for end-users. In *Proceedings of the working conference on advanced visual interfaces* (pp. 408–411). New York, NY: ACM.

Fielding, R. T., & Taylor, R. N. (2002). Principled Design of the Modern Web Architecture. *ACM Transactions on Internet Technology, 2*(2), 115–150.

Fogg, B. J. (2002). *Persuasive technology: using computers to change what we think and do (interactive technologies)*. San Francisco: Morgan Kauffman.

Franch, X. (2013). Software requirement patterns. In *Proceedings of the 2013 international conference on software engineering* (pp. 1499–1501). Piscataway, NJ: IEEE Press.

Fry, J. P., & Neff, R. A. (2009). Periodic prompts and reminders in health promotion and health behavior interventions: systematic review. *Journal of Medical Internet Research, 11*(2), e16.

Gamma, E., Helm, R., Johnson, R., & Vlissides, J. (1994). *Design patterns: elements of reusable object-oriented software*. Reading: Addison-Wesley.

Gestwicki, P., & Sun, F. -S. (2008). Teaching design patterns through computer game development. *Journal of Educational Resources in Computing, 8*(1), 2:1–12.

Hamari, J., Koivisto, J., & Sarsa, H. (2014). Does gamification work?—a literature review of empirical studies on gamification. *47th Hawaii International Conference on System Sciences* (HICSS).

Kelders, S. M., Kok, R. N., Ossebaard, H. C., & Van Gemert-Pijnen, J. E. W. C. (2012). Persuasive system design does matter: a systematic review of adherence to web-based interventions. *Journal of Medical Internet Research, 14*(6), e152.

Kobayashi, T., & Saeki, M. (1999). Software development based on software pattern evolution. *Proceedings. Sixth Asia Pacific. Software Engineering Conference*. (APSEC '99).

Krasner, G., & Pope, S. (1988). A description of the {model-view-controller} user interface paradigm in the smalltalk-80 system. *Journal of Object Oriented Programming, 1*(3), 26–49.

Kruschitz, C., & Hitz, M. (2010a). Are human-computer interaction design patterns really used? In *Proceedings of the 6th Nordic conference on human-computer interaction: extending boundaries* (pp. 711–714). New York, NY: ACM.

Kruschitz, C., & Hitz, M. (2010b). Bringing formalism and unification to human-computer interaction design patterns. In *Proceedings of the 1st international workshop on pattern-driven engineering of interactive computing systems* (pp. 20–23). New York, NY: ACM.

Langrial, S., Lehto, T., Oinas-Kukkonen, H., Harjumaa, M., & Karppinen, P. (2012). Native mobile applications for personal well-being: A persuasive systems design evaluation. *Proceedings PACIS*.

Langrial, S., & Oinas-Kukkonen, H. (2012). Less fizzy drinks: A multi-method study of persuasive reminders. In M. Bang, & E. Ragnemalm (Eds.), *Persuasive technology. Design for health and safety SE—23* (pp. 256–261). (Vol. 7284). Berlin, Heidelberg: Springer.

Langrial, S., Oinas-Kukkonen, H., Lappalainen, P., & Lappalainen, R. (2013). Rehearsing to control depressive symptoms through a behavior change support system. In *CHI'13 extended abstracts on human factors in computing systems*, April (pp. 385–390). ACM.

Leff, A., & Rayfield, J. T. (2001). Web-application development using the model/view/controller design pattern. In *Proceedings of the 5th IEEE international conference on enterprise distributed object computing* (pp. 118–127). Washington, DC: IEEE Computer Society.

Lehto, T., & Oinas-Kukkonen, H. (2011). Persuasive features in web-based alcohol and smoking interventions: a systematic review of the literature. *Journal of Medical Internet Research*, *13*(3), e46.

Lenert, L., Munoz, R. F., Perez, J. E., & Bansod, A. (2004). Automated e-mail messaging as a tool for improving quit rates in an internet smoking cessation intervention. *Journal of the American Medical Informatics Association*, *11*(4), 235–240.

Lockton, D. (2012). Persuasive technology and digital design for behaviour change. *Available from: SSRN 2125957*.

Lockton, D., Harrison, D., & Stanton, N. A. (2010). The Design with intent method: a design tool for influencing user behaviour. *Applied Ergonomics*, *41*(3), 382–392.

Lustria, M. L. A., Cortese, J., Noar, S. M., & Glueckauf, R. L. (2009). Computer-tailored health interventions delivered over the Web: review and analysis of key components. *Patient Education and Counseling*, *74*(2), 156–173.

Ning, W., Liming, L., Yanzhang, W., Yi-bing, W., & Jing, W. (2008). Research on the web information system development platform based on MVC design pattern. *International conference on Web Intelligence and Intelligent Agent Technology*. WI-IAT IEEE/WIC/ACM.

Oduor, M., Alahäivälä, T., & Oinas-Kukkonen, H. (2014). Persuasive software design patterns for social influence. *Personal and Ubiquitous Computing*, *18*(7), 1689–1704.

Oinas-Kukkonen, H. (2013). A foundation for the study of behavior change support systems. *Personal and Ubiquitous Computing*, *17*(6), 1223–1235.

Oinas-Kukkonen, H., & Harjumaa, M. (2009). Persuasive systems design: key issues, process model, and system features. *Communications of the Association for Information Systems*, *24*(1), 28.

Peña-Mora, F., & Vadhavkar, S. (1997). Augmenting design patterns with design rationale. *AI EDAM*, *11*(02), 93–108.

Ploderer, B., Reitberger, W., Oinas-Kukkonen, H., & van Gemert-Pijnen, J. (2014). Social interaction and reflection for behaviour change. *Personal and Ubiquitous Computing*, *18*(7), 1667–1676.

Purpura, S., Schwanda, V., Williams, K., Stubler, W., & Sengers, P. (2011). Fit4Life: The design of a persuasive technology promoting healthy behavior and ideal weight. In *Proceedings of the SIGCHI conference on human factors in computing systems* (pp. 423–432). New York, NY: ACM.

Rapp, A. (2015). Designing interactive systems through a game lens: An ethnographic approach. *Computers in Human Behavior*.

Ritterband, L. M., Thorndike, F. P., Cox, D. J., Kovatchev, B. P., & Gonder-Frederick, L. A. (2009). A behavior change model for internet interventions. *Annals of Behavioral Medicine*, *38*(1), 18–27.

Sohn, M., & Lee, J. (2007). UP health: ubiquitously persuasive health promotion with an instant messaging system. In *CHI'07 extended abstracts on human factors in computing systems*, April (pp. 2663–2668). ACM.

Spittaels, H., De Bourdeaudhuij, I., Brug, J., & Vandelanotte, C. (2007). Effectiveness of an online computer-tailored physical activity intervention in a real-life setting. *Health Education Research, 22*(3), 385–396.

Taleb, M., Seffah, A., & Abran, A. (2007). Patterns-oriented design applied to cross-platform web-based interactive systems. *IEEE international conference on Information Reuse and Integration*, IRI.

Thung, P.L., Ng, C.J., Thung, S.J., & Sulaiman, S. (2010). Improving a web application using design patterns: a case study. *International symposium in Information Technology* (ITSim).

Toscos, T., Faber, A., An, S., & Gandhi, M. P. (2006). Chick clique: persuasive technology to motivate teenage girls to exercise. In *CHI'06 extended abstracts on human factors in computing systems*, April (pp. 1873–1878). ACM.

Trese, T., & Tilley, S. (2007). Documenting software systems with views V: Towards visual documentation of design patterns as an aid to program understanding. In *Proceedings of the 25th annual ACM international conference on design of communication* (pp. 103–112). New York, NY: ACM.

Weiksner, G. M., Fogg, B. J., & Liu, X. (2008). Six patterns for persuasion in online social networks. In *Persuasive Technology* (pp. 151–163). Berlin, Heidelberg: Springer.

Wentzlaff, I., & Specker, M. (2006). Pattern-based development of user-friendly web applications. In *Workshop proceedings of the sixth international conference on web engineering*. New York, NY: ACM.

Womble, L. G., Wadden, T. A., McGuckin, B. G., Sargent, S. L., Rothman, R. A., & Krauthamer-Ewing, E. S. (2004). A randomized controlled trial of a commercial internet weight loss program. *Obesity Research, 12*(6), 1011–1018.

Zemin, Z. (2009). Study and application of patterns in software reuse. *IITA international conference on Control, Automation, and Systems Engineering*. CASE.

Zhu, L., Babar, M.A., & Jeffery, R. (2004). Mining patterns to support software architecture evaluation. In *Proceedings Fourth Working IEEE/IFIP Conference on Software Architecture*. WICSA.

APPENDIX. PSEUDOCODE, FOR EXAMPLE, IMPLEMENTATION

Instant Feedback Pattern

```
class EntriesController < ApplicationController
  def create
    @entry = Entry.new(params[:entry])
    if @entry.save
      if is_good_performance(@entry)
        redirect_to @entry, notice: 'Good! You're doing great.'
      else
        redirect_to @entry, notice: 'You should keep going
                                     every day to get results.'
      end
    end
  end
  ...
  # Logic for evaluating performance
  private
    def is_good_performance(entry)
      entry.is_in_chain ? true : (return false)
    end
end
```

Reminder Pattern

UserMailer Component

```
class UserMailer < ActionMailer::Base
  ...
  def weekly_email(user)
    ...
  end
end
```

Reminders

```
class User < ActiveRecord::Base
  ...
    def self.send_weekly_emails
      @users = User.all
      @users.each do |u|
        UserMailer.weekly_email(u).deliver
      end
    end
  ...
end
```

Scheduler

```
every :monday, at: "10:00 AM" do
  runner "User.send_weekly_emails"
end
```

Reward Pattern

Many-to-Many Relationships

```ruby
class User < ActiveRecord::Base
  has_many :entries
  has_many :accomplishments
  has_many :rewards, :through => :accomplishments
end
 class Reward < ActiveRecord::Base
  has_many :accomplishments
  has_many :users, :through => :accomplishments
end
class Accomplishment < ActiveRecord::Base
  belongs_to :user
  belongs_to :reward
end
```

Observer

```ruby
class Auditor < ActiveRecord::Observer
  observe :entry
  def after_create(entry)
    if gives_reward(entry)
      Accomplishment.create(:user_id => entry.user_id,
                            :reward_id => gives_reward(entry))
    end
  end
  private
    # Returns either the id of the gained reward or false
    def gives_reward(entry)
    ...
    end
end
```

4

Evaluating Mobile-Based Behavior Change Support Systems for Health and Well-Being

S. Langrial*,†, P. Karppinen*, T. Lehto*,
M. Harjumaa**, H. Oinas-Kukkonen*

*Oulu Advanced Research on Software and Information Systems,
Department of Information Processing Science, University of Oulu, Oulu,
Finland; **VTT Technical Research Center of Finland, Oulu, Finland;
†Sur University College, Sur, Sultanate of Oman

BACKGROUND

Mobile computing devices have brought a new dimension in the field of behavior change technologies (Oinas-Kukkonen, 2010). Pervasive information systems are being developed and improved for several purposes including learning, preventive health, and social networking. Technological advances are facilitating system designers to better plan and develop such systems especially in terms of data storage and processing of information in real time. It was Fogg (2002) who envisioned the scope of persuasion through computing. He devised the term Persuasive Technology (PT) that received extensive attention resulting in a new research discipline encompassing psychology, persuasion, and computing technologies. Building upon the formative work of Fogg (2002), Oinas-Kukkonen (2013) presented the inference of BCSSs. He defines BCSSs as *"a socio-technical IS with psychological and behavioral outcomes designed to form, alter or reinforce attitudes, behaviors or an act of compliance without using coercion or deception"* (cf., Oinas-Kukkonen, 2013). He further adds that BCSSs are an object of

Behavior Change Research and Theory. http://dx.doi.org/10.1016/B978-0-12-802690-8.00007-4

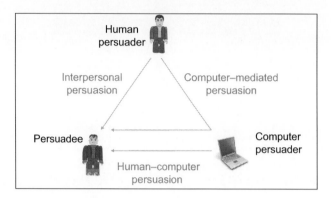

FIGURE 4.1   Channels of persuasion.

study within the field of PT, that is, a given BCSS is essentially persuasive in nature.

This chapter recommends that BCSSs differ from conventional persuasive information systems because they are expected to be augmented with software features that facilitate continuous accessibility, enhanced human–computer interaction, ease of use, and social support without being obtrusive (Oinas-Kukkonen, 2013). A large number of BCSSs can be found that target behavior change in different areas, for instance, physical activity, preventive medicine, and healthy diet. As mentioned earlier, all BCSSs are persuasive in nature and employ superior computer–human and computer-mediated persuasion (Fig. 4.1). In other words, computer-mediated persuasion implies that people use technological means (e.g., emails, IM, SNS) to influence others.

Mobile-Based Behavior Change Support Systems

Mobile-based BCSSs have shown great potential in assisting people to improve their lifestyles (Connelly, Faber, Rogers, Siek, & Toscos, 2006; Patrick, Griswold, Raab, & Intille, 2008) However, it is proposed that system designers need to appreciate that stable behavior change involves great deal of effort that infuses everyday life and the social world. A large number of mobile-based BCSSs (in this case, mobile apps) are designed to support people in achieving their goals, for instance, to have an active lifestyle. While such BCSSs have been subject to evaluations, nevertheless the focus of most evaluations has mainly been on Usability. It is argued that there are obvious limitations relating with Usability testing. For example, generally they are performed in laboratory settings and lack pragmatism as reviewed by Beck, Christiansen, Kjeldskov, Kolbe, and Stage (2003). However, such limitations do not undermine the value of Usability evaluations. Researchers from the field of persuasive information systems have been conducting studies to discover the extraordinary acceptance and usage of mobile-based BCSSs. To the best of our knowledge, only a few persuasive design features have been reported unequivocally to date.

Identifying the said research gap, a study was performed to identify and evaluate persuasive software features in a set of preselected iPhone applications for health and general well-being. For the purpose of evaluation, the PSDM (Oinas-Kukkonen & Harjumaa, 2009) and the O/C Design Matrix (Oinas-Kukkonen, 2010) were utilized. These were the existing frameworks that are used for both planning, developing, and evaluating BCSSs. The frameworks highlight the importance of intended behavioral outcomes, technological features, and persuasive strategies that are incorporated in mobile-based BCSSs. The next section provides a brief overview of the PSD Model.

The PSD Model

The model promotes itemized and systematic analyses of the persuasion context (i.e., what are the designers' purposes in terms of changing users' behaviors, or attitudes), the event (i.e., whether the designers have a clear idea about the context of use and users while their interaction) and the persuasion strategy (i.e., cautiously crafting the persuasive message and selecting the route for delivering the message). The PSD Model features seven key postulates that are key for the planning and design. They include: (1) Information Technology is never neutral. On the contrary, it is designed in such a way that it almost always influences users; (2) people have an intrinsic drive to stay unswerving in terms of their attitudes and actions; (3) persuasion is an incremental process; (4) persuasive messages can be delivered through direct or indirect routes; (5) BCCSs should be easy to interact with; (6) BCSSs should not be obtrusive; and (7) the designers' intentions should be devoid of manipulation or deception.

The PSD model offers sociotechnological propositions for the HCI discipline too. In line with the user models that suggest that user experience is an outcome of users' internal state of mind (Hassenzahl and Tractinsky, 2006), the PSD model promotes comprehensive analyses of the use and user context when planning, designing, and implementing mobile-based BCSSs. In addition to the seven postulates, the model specifies categorical persuasive design principles underlining software features. The four categories are: (1) primary task support; (2) human–computer dialogue support; (3) system credibility support, and (4) social support. A brief description of each category is provided:

1. Primary Task Support: BCSSs should be incorporated with software features that help users in reaching their goals.
2. Human–Computer Dialogue Support: BCSSs should be enhanced with software features that inspire users for an extended interaction.

3. System Credibility: A BCSS should be trustworthy.
4. Social Support: BCSSs should be incorporated with software features that facilitate social interaction between users.

The O/C Design Matrix is briefly explained in the next section.

The Outcome/Change Design Matrix

The fundamental objective of a BCSS is not to prompt a temporary change in users' behaviors or attitudes. Quite the reverse, BCSSs can provide opportunities to facilitate potential changes in users' behaviors or attitudes in accord with the system designers' intents. Manifestly emerging technologies are facilitating design and implementation of mobile-based BCSSs for well-being. However, from the existing literature, limitations are also evident. Although it might be too early to expect IS researchers to agree upon a unified framework for planning, developing, and evaluating BCSSs, nevertheless, there is huge potential when it comes to methodologies for evaluating information systems (Consolvo, Landay, & McDonald, 2009; Fogg, 2009). We propose the O/C Design Matrix (Oinas-Kukkonen, 2010) for gaining better understanding of the design process. The O/C Design Matrix complements the PSD model by categorizing different design intents and persuasive strategies that are much needed for developing effective mobile-based BCSSs. The O/C Design Matrix lays a specific focus on how to support A-change, B-change, and/ or C-change (attitude-, behavior-, or compliance-change).

Mobile-based BCSSs for health are rather complex interventions. Some researchers have outlined challenges for designers of e-Health interventions. According to Campbell, Fitzpatrick, Haines, and Kinmonth (2000) defining, implementing, and evaluating e-Health interventions are the basic challenges. It is argued that evaluators face difficulties because system designers do not fully explain and promote the interventions. Similarly, Craig et al. (2008) have highlighted the importance of identifying challenges while planning, developing, and evaluating e-Health interventions. They underscore several issues including pinpointing the target audience, variations in the expected outcomes, and scalability. It is worth noting that there is limited research that focuses on the anticipated outcome from the use of mobile-based BCSSs. Available literature provides little if any descriptions of the intentions of system designers, that is, whether the designer develop the systems with an intention to change users' behaviors, attitudes or both.

Among the challenges that mobile-based BCSSs developers face, identification and rationalization of the anticipated outcomes in users' behaviors or attitudes change is one. Further, current trend in research on behavior change is particularly focused on C-change (Compliance) and B-change (Behavior). Oddly, system designers and researchers have somehow overlooked the influence of A-change (Attitude change). In line with Oinas-Kukkonen (2013), it is proposed that attitudes direct how people act in real life. Therefore, attention must be paid to A-change while developing mobile-based BCSSs. Based on this argument, it is recommend to the PSD model and O/C Design Matrix for evaluating effective mobile-based BCSSs.

An approach that would exploit both the PSD model and O/C Design Matrix could enrich the design and evaluation process. While the PSD model provides a realistic framework with categorical persuasive software features, the O/C Design Matrix enables the designers to focus on the planned change type: whether the users comply with the newly acquired behavior (C-change), whether the change takes place in users' behavior (B-change) or the users receive support from the BCSS in order to change their attitudes rather than behavior only (A-change).

OBJECTIVES AND METHODOLOGY

A study was carried out to identify and categorize persuasive design strategies incorporated in mobile-based BCSSs. Expert evaluation approach (Jaspers, 2009) was applied where one or more specialists evaluate a given system against a list of design principles (in this case, the PSD model and O/C Design Matrix). The adopted methodology was similar to heuristic evaluation that is frequently applied in usability engineering, to feature usability problems, and test interactive technologies (Jaspers, 2009). Four computer scientists specializing in persuasive systems carried out the heuristic evaluations simulating real users walking through the mobile-based BCSSs (apps) step-by-step and performed regular tasks (i.e., cognitive walkthrough). According to Holzinger (2005), among other usability evaluation methods, heuristic and cognitive walkthroughs are a few. In heuristic evaluation (Holzinger, 2005) evaluators review the system independent of each other. Upon completion of the individual evaluations, each evaluator communicates with others and goes through the findings several times before final synthesis are created. Following the same pattern, four evaluators with diverse research interests and expertise performed the heuristics and cognitive walkthroughs. The lead researcher has a strong background in evidence-based psychology and digital interventions. The coresearchers are specialists in user experience (UX), knowledge-intensive services for health behavior change, and consumer health informatics. With their expertise from different scientific backgrounds, the coauthors added significant value to the research work.

Evaluated applications (BCSSs) were installed in iPhones and were methodically used to perform daily tasks. The evaluators worked independent of each other and autonomous appraisals were performed (including feature-by-feature analyses). All the four evaluators made notes based on their individual experiences and recorded their individual reflections using Excel spreadsheets. Each evaluator analyzed persuasive features by reading the descriptions of the applications predominantly from developers' websites. Once the evaluation process was finalized, the findings were merged. There were minor differences in the findings however they were resolved through in-depth discussions and reiterations. Additionally, it was mutually agreed that only those persuasive features would be narrated that were acknowledged by at least three out of the four evaluators.

The evaluations were aimed to identify and store a brief yet demonstrative pool of the preselected mobile-based BCSSs for health and well-being. All the applications were in English and designed to support users in changing health and wellness behaviors, according to the descriptions. It must be noted that the evaluated applications do not represent all the available mobile-based BCSSs (apps). However, a realistic effort was made to have an idea of the persuasive features and functionalities. The selected apps were: *AngerCoach* (ANG), *Awareness Lite* (AWA), *Healthy Habits* (HEA), *Live Happy* (LIV), *MiMood* (MIM), *MoodKit* (MOK), *Mood Meter Lite* (MOM), *Mood Runner* (MOR), *MyBalance* (MYB), *MyCalmBeat* (MYC), *SeeMyCity* (SEE), and *T2 Mood Tracker* (T2M).

Analyzing the Persuasion Context

The intent, event, and persuasion strategies for each BCSS (app) were evaluated because these are the parameters that frame the persuasion context (Oinas-Kukkonen & Harjumaa, 2009). Context is the information that can be used to describe the situation of a user (Dey, 2001). Based on the work by Langrial, Lehto, Oinas-Kukkonen, Harjumaa, and Karppinen (2012), selected mobile-based BCSSs were mapped to the O/C Design Matrix. The findings indicated that a majority of the evaluated apps were designed with an intent to bring a change in users' behaviors with only a few (that too elusively) targeted compliance to newly adopted behaviors, that is, supporting users to conform to new behaviors and/or attitudes. Table 4.1 illustrates the practical implications of the O/C Design Matrix in understanding the design intentions for BCSS designers and developers.

It is proposed that the ultimate goal of stimulating behavior change is to support them through the entire behavior change process with a specific focus on A-Change (Attitude change). This could lead to a state of improved self-confidence. Bandura (1977) outlines this as self-efficacy. Self-efficacy establishes whether people are actually driven to make an effort towards behavior change, and self-confidence is the key for people to overcome challenges in that process. Bandura (1977) approach further strengthens the proposition that A-Change needs a great deal of attention while designing BCSSs for health and well-being.

TABLE 4.1 The Intended Outcome/Change When Analyzed Using the O/C Design Matrix

Outcome/ change	C-change	B-change	A-change
F-Outcome	Forming a compliance (F/C) *QuitPal* not only helps users stop smoking but also supports people conform to new routine, that is, not smoking. It provides reminders, health milestone alerts, tips to overcome cravings, and personalized videos from loved-ones.	Forming a behavior (F/B) *HeathyHabits* supports people to form desirable habits, for example, eating healthy food	Forming an attitude (F/A) *LiveHappy* encourages people to form positive attitudes, keep a record of emotional patterns, and try to improve mood through virtual coaching
A-Outcome	Altering compliance (A/C) *AngerCoach* supports people over-come angry behaviors. Users are guided through the change process through expert videos as software feature	Altering a behavior (A/B) *NHS quit smoking* app supports users to alter smoking habits. The aim of the app is to support smokers through the process of gradually becoming a nonsmoker	Altering an attitude (A/A) *T2 Mood Tracker* helps users to monitor emotional experiences, such as stress and anxiety
R-Outcome	Reinforcing compliance (R/C) *Waterworks* supports people conform to consume desirable amount of water by providing visual graphics for motivation and goal achievement	Reinforcing a behavior (R/B) *MoodKit* helps people sustain positive moods through learning how to be in control of their lives. It allows people to set their goals, provides personalized content, and access to expert publications	Reinforcing an attitude (R/A) *AwarenessLite* supports users feel positive through inspirational quotes based on how the users are feeling

QuitPal and Waterworks were not included in the evaluated BCSSs. They were used to demonstrate practicality of the O/C Design Matrix.

Next, an attempt to explain the O/C Design Matrix is displayed using relevant examples. Several of the described examples can possibly be placed under multiple cells. However, the examples were assigned to the cells keeping in mind the apparent target change and outcome among the users: (1) *QuitPal was* allocated to F/C because the apparent intention was to help users conform to a new behavior; (2) *AngerCoach was* placed under A/C because its objective was to guide people through a change process and equip them with skills to sustain the change; (3) *WaterWorks* was categorized under R/C because it targeted people who already had a desirable behavior however they needed support in continuing to perform accordingly; (4) *HealthyHabits* was placed under the F/B category because it aimed to assist people in forming new habits; (5) *NHS Quit Smoking* was categorized as A/B because it was designed to help users break undesirable habits; (6) *MoodKit* belonged to the R/B category because it targeted reinforcement of desirable behaviors; (7) *LiveHappy* was placed under F/A because it aimed to support people to form new attitudes; (8) *T2 Mood Tracker* was categorized under A/A because it aimed to help people alter existing attitudes, and (9) *Awareness Lite* was placed under the R/A category because it intended to help users with positive attitudes conform to their attitudes.

The Intent

In the studied BCSSs, the intentions of the developers were vaguely described. Though, some of the applications were noticeably developed for business purposes (e.g., a book's publisher). Based on the findings, it is cautiously argued that applications, such as ANG, LIV, and MYC were developed for commercial purposes. For illustration, MYC encouraged paid membership for getting full access to the application. The remaining nine (9) applications were apparently developed to support users in everyday life. The evaluations were primarily based on the available descriptions provided by the developers. Therefore, it was exceptionally difficult to grasp definite intentions of the developers. Having said that, it is stated that other factors could play a critical part when it comes to designing BCSSs from the developer's perspective. For example, it could be argued that the developer was simply following the requirements of the client or that she/he was cautious in terms of privacy and ethical issues, etc. Notably, it was difficult to conclude whether any of the evaluated BCSSs were aimed at inducing behaviors or attitudes (i.e., change type).

The Event

The event pertains to understanding the target audience, the technology, and the use context. Based on the descriptions provided, the findings indicated that MIM, MOR, MOK, MOM, T2M, LIV, and SEE were developed for people who wished to track their moods. HEA was designed for people who either aimed to adopt new behaviors or get rid of old ones. MYB was designed for individuals who desired to improve well-being by monitoring their diet, fitness, and lifestyle. ANG was intended for people who needed help with anger, and AWA was designed for individuals who wished for a more peaceful lifestyle. MYC was developed for people who wanted to reduce stress by performing breathing exercises.

The Strategy

The PSD model highlights two conceivable strategies for persuading users (i.e., the message and the route). The message means the content of the persuasive communication in the form of rational arguments and the route relates to how the message is delivered. The route can be direct (using logical arguments), indirect (by using cues), or a mix of both. The results from the evaluations suggest that there were moderately compact presentations of persuasive messages.

Identified Persuasive Strategies and Software Features

Primary Task Support. The findings indicate that almost all the evaluated mobile-based BCSSs were incorporated with a reasonable level of primary task support software features. The only unexpected finding was that tailoring and simulation were not identified in any of the evaluated BCSSs. Table 4.2 represents identified features from the primary task support.

Dialogue Support. Augmented human–system interaction can inspire users toward continuous usage thus increasing the chance of behavior change. It was noted from the evaluations that dialogue support features were underutilized. For example, only two BCSSs were incorporated with praise (feedback) and virtual rewards. Reminders were most commonly used feature. It was a surprising finding. The findings related to dialogue support are described in Table 4.3.

Credibility Support. According to the Oinas-Kukkonen and Harjumaa (2009), credibility and trust are highly desirable features for an effective BCSS. We do admit that credibility could be a biased issue and it is also argued that people develop initial assessment of a system's credibility based on their first interaction. Conversely, it can also be maintained that at times, initial assessments could be made even before a user has interacted with the system. For example, while reading the description of a BCSS or going through peer reviews. We propose that third party endorsements from renowned sources can increase the credibility. The findings indicated that most of the applications were modestly credible. Nevertheless, it was again a subjective argument. The findings related to credibility support are described in Table 4.4.

TABLE 4.2   Noticeable Primary Task Support Features

Software feature	Description	Example implementation
Self-monitoring (12 out of 12 BCSSs)	Delivering means for users to track their behavior, performance, or status	Past behaviors measurements presented via graphs (MOM); pie charts, timelines (MYC)
Reduction (11 out of 12 BCSSs)	Reducing users' effort in performing target behavior/s	Predefined habit library (HEA); effortless goal-setting (MOK)
Personalization (4 out of 12 BCSSs)	Recommending personalized content and services	Personalized based on user-inputs and other known variables (e.g., Demographics) (HEA, MOK)
Rehearsal (3 out of 12 BCSSs)	Providing means for practicing target behavior/s	Breathing exercise supported by the application (MYC)
Tunneling (3 out of 12 BCSSs)	Guiding users by providing means for action that bring them closer to the target behavior/s	After filling out a questionnaire, the user is presented with an appropriate set of tools and means for action (ANG)

TABLE 4.3   Noticeable Dialogue Support Features

Software Feature	Description	Example
Reminders (5 out of 12 BCSSs)	Prompting users of their target behavior/s	Automatized reminders; customizable reminders via email/SMS /screen prompt
Praise (2 out of 12 BCSSs)	Praising users in the form of text, images, symbols, and/or sounds	Automated prompt praises the user for reaching a goal
Suggestion (2 out of 12 BCSSs)	Signifying that users carry out behaviors during use of the system	An application for healthier eating habits provides an option for coaching messages
Rewards (1 out of 12 BCSSs)	Rewarding for performing the desired action	Trophies, badges, icons, pictures, and other content provided to the user for successfully finishing a certain task

Social Support. Social learning can potentially boost users' inspiration to perform target behaviors. For example, users can compare their performance with fellow users. In the evaluated mobile-based BCSSs, users had an option of sharing their progress via email and/or Facebook. In our estimation, it is not social connectivity in the strongest form. Therefore, it is highlighted that the evaluated apps

TABLE 4.4 Noticeable Credibility Support Features

Software feature	Description	Example
Trustworthiness (8 out of 12 BCSSs)	Providing information that is true, unbiased, and equitable. The application must not exploit private user data	The system clearly states the privacy policy. The user has control over security settings (e.g., setting a pin/lock code; disabling/enabling location tracking; disabling/enabling data sharing)
Real-world feel (7 out of 12 BCSSs)	Providing information related to the organization and/or actual people behind its content and services.	The application specifies developers' contact details. Email address; physical address, etc. (HEA, T2M, AWA)
Expertise (4 out of 12 BCSSs)	Providing information that demonstrates knowledge, experience, and expertise	Expert videos (ANG). Users can ask questions from an expert (T2M)
Verifiability (3 out of 12 BCSSs)	Providing ways to verify the accuracy of site's content	Links to external resources and references to scientific publications (ANG, LIV, MOK)
Authority (2 out of 12 BCSSs)	Referring to people in positions of authority	Quoting an authority, such as a statement by the government health authority/office (ANG, T2M)

did not fully utilize social support features, for example, allowing users to compete with other users or public recognition for users who performed their target behavior (e.g., via personal stories of people who have succeeded in their target behaviors). The findings related to social support are described in Table 4.5.

The distinctive persuasive software features incorporated in the evaluated BCSSs are presented collectively in Table 4.6.

RESULTS

The findings suggest that there were limitations with regard to the persuasive design in the evaluated mobile-based BCSSs. In summary, primary task support features were fairly well utilized including self-monitoring; reduction and personalization were evidently used. In our view, it was a surprise that none of the evaluated mobile-based BCSSs used tailoring. This was identified as a serious limitation.

TABLE 4.5   Noticeable Social Influence Features

Software feature	Description	Example
Social comparison/ sharing (7 out of 12 BCSSs)	Providing techniques for comparing one's performance with other users	Users can share and compare information related to their health behavior via a social networking application (HEA, MOK)
Cooperation (1 out of 12 BCSSs)	Providing means for cooperation	Users can tag and share locations with other users (SEE)
Normative influence (1 out of 12 BCSSs)	Providing means for bringing together people who have the same goals	Users can share their information with similar users and view information from similar users (SEE)
Social facilitation (1 out of 12 BCSSs)	Providing means for identifying other users who are performing similar behavior	Users can recognize how many others are at the same location (SEE)

   Feedback in the form of praise and reward are essential for enhancing user-system interaction. According to Al-Natour and Benbasat (2009) IT entities are more like social actors. Likewise, it is reported that people consider their interactions with IT artifacts interpersonal in nature. In simple terms, people tend to engage with computing devices as though they are interacting with real life social situations (Lee, 2009; Fogg 2002). Therefore, augmented human-computer dialogue features can enhance users' interactivity with the system leading to persistent engagement with the intervention. It is hence proposed that for developing an effective mobile-based BCSS, enhanced user-system interaction could lead to greater task adherence and task completion. This is important because task-adherence has been an ongoing problem in the behavior change interventions (Kelders, Kok, Ossebaard, & Van Gemert-Pijnen, 2012).

   System credibility plays a critical role when users decide whether to use it and for how long they will be interested to use it. Research provides evidence (King & He, 2006) that users engage with systems that are trustworthy. Therefore, it is proposed that while designing mobile-based BCSSs, developers should keep the significance of credibility in mind. Finally, social relationships are increasingly maintained through technology-mediated communications. As outlined by Oinas-Kukkonen and Oinas-Kukkonen (2013), social web has already proven its potential to influence and change human lifestyle. Social networking platforms have pervaded daily lives (both leisure and work) for millions of individuals. Technology-mediated communications can support in forming and maintaining online relationships, which, in turn, can facilitate social support. Hence, it is advocated to carefully select social support features while developing mobile-based BCSSs.

TABLE 4.6 Persuasive System Features Observed in the Evaluated Mobile-BCSSs

Primary Task Support	ANG	AWA	HEA	LIV	MIM	MOM	MOK	MOR	MYB	MYC	SEE	T2M
Self-monitoring	✓	✓	✓	✓	✓	✓	✓	✓	✓	✓	✓	✓
Reduction	✓	✓	✓	✓	✓		✓	✓	✓	✓	✓	✓
Personalization			✓	✓			✓				✓	
Rehearsal		✓								✓		
Tunneling	✓			✓			✓					
Simulation							✓					
Tailoring												

Dialogue Support	ANG	AWA	HEA	LIV	MIM	MOM	MOK	MOR	MYB	MYC	SEE	T2M
Reminders		✓	✓				✓	✓				✓
Praise												
Suggestion												✓
Rewards												
Similarity												
Social role												

(Continued)

TABLE 4.6 Persuasive System Features Observed in the Evaluated Mobile-BCSSs (*cont.*)

Liking	Not evaluated											
	ANG	AWA	HEA	LIV	MIM	MOM	MOK	MOR	MYB	MYC	SEE	T2M
Credibility Support												
Trustworthiness	✓	✓	✓	✓				✓		✓		✓
Real-world feel	✓	✓	✓	✓			✓			✓		✓
Expertise	✓			✓			✓					✓
Verifiability	✓			✓			✓					
Authority	✓						✓					
Third-party endorsements												✓
Surface credibility	Not evaluated											
	ANG	AWA	HEA	LIV	MIM	MOM	MOK	MOR	MYB	MYC	SEE	T2M
Social Influence												
Social comparison			✓	✓	✓	✓	✓				✓	✓
Cooperation											✓	
Social facilitation						✓					✓	
Normative influence												
Competition												
Social learning												
Recognition												

Note: ✓, feature was found in the app; clear cell, feature was not found in the app.

DISCUSSION

Based on the findings, it is proposed that there is an apparent lack of systematic methodologies for planning, developing, and evaluating mobile-based BCSSs. This chapter demonstrates the practical use of the PSD model and O/C Design Matrix to gain a richer understanding of persuasive design strategies that are commonly incorporated by system designers. Presented work does not claim that the reviewed frameworks are the definitive tools for design and evaluation of mobile-based BCSSs; however, it can be suggested that they can be used as valuable tools for research purposes especially in terms of mobile-based BCSSs.

The PSD model and O/C Design Matrix do not explicitly provide guidelines for planning and development. On the contrary, they can be useful in developing strategies and procedures that web- and mobile-based BCSSs are incorporated with. To date several researchers have utilized the PSD model. For example, Harjumaa and coworkers (2009) performed a 3-month qualitative study addressing exercise and activity and reported the successful impact of dialogue support features on the participants. Kelders et al. (2012) performed a systematic review of the persuasive features on web-based interventions and reported that designers of such websites generally overlooked the importance of dialogue support features. Yetim (2011) evaluated the PSD model in terms of ethical and moral lessons for designing persuasive systems. The aforementioned examples provide evidence of the significance of the PSD model in the process of planning and developing systems that address behavior change.

Like most of research studies, presented work has its limitations. While the PSD model and O/C Design Matrix were used as tools for expert evaluation, it is also well-known that expert evaluations are subject to potential bias. To overcome these limitations, four evaluators were involved in the study. It is also acknowledged that the number of selected applications was not a representative pool. There are thousands of applications available that are apparently designed to help people change their habits or attitudes. Nevertheless, it is proposed that the weakness and strengths identified by the evaluators provide a fair idea of the importance of incorporating selected software features in the design process. Finally, it is acknowledged that ethics can have a significant impact on a designer's approach while developing mobile-based BCSSs. Software designers and healthcare researchers are recommended to pay close attention to sensitive issues including ethics, privacy, credibility, and moral values. Incremental innovation will bring significant benefits to the intriguing research field of mobile-based BCSSs.

Despite the ever-increasing development of mobile-based BCSSs for health and general well-being, there is a fairly narrow understanding of the persuasive design in terms of software features. The findings suggest that there is a lack of understanding when it comes to the designers' views about the persuasion context. In addition, it seems as though the system designers do not have a precise idea in terms of the anticipated outcome, that is, whether their system is targeting behavior change, attitude change, or compliance support. It is therefore proposed that the PSD model and O/C Design Matrix could help designers and researchers to overcome the identified design weaknesses.

Acknowledgments

The presented work was supported by SalWe Research Program for Mind and Body (Tekes–the Finnish Funding Agency for Technology and Innovation grant 1104/10). The first author would like to thank Sur University College, Sultanate of Oman for the support in continuing with his research efforts.

References

Al-Natour, S., & Benbasat, I. (2009). The adoption and use of IT artifacts: a new interaction-centric model for the study of user-artifact relationships. *Journal of the Association for Information Systems*, *10*(9), 661.

Bandura, A. (1977). Self-efficacy: toward a unifying theory of behavioral change. *Psychological Review*, *84*(2), 191.

Beck, E., Christiansen, M., Kjeldskov, J., Kolbe, N., & Stage, J. (2003). Experimental evaluation of techniques for usability testing of mobile systems in a laboratory setting. In *Proceedings of Ozchi 2003*, Brisbane, Australia.

Campbell, M., Fitzpatrick, R., Haines, A., & Kinmonth, A. L. (2000). Framework for design and evaluation of complex interventions to improve health. *British Medical Journal*, *321*(7262), 694.

Connelly, K. H., Faber, A. M., Rogers, Y., Siek, K. A., & Toscos, T. (2006). Mobile applications that empower people to monitor their personal health. *Elektrotechnik und Informationstechnik*, *123*(4), 124–128.

Consolvo, S., Landay, J. A., & McDonald, D. W. (2009). Designing for behavior change in everyday life. *IEEE Computer*, *42*(6), 414.

Craig, P., Dieppe, P., Macintyre, S., Michie, S., Nazareth, I., & Petticrew, M. (2008). Developing and evaluating complex interventions: the new Medical Research Council guidance. *British Medical Journal*, *337*, a1655.

Dey, A. K. (2001). Understanding and using context. *Personal and Ubiquitous Computing*, *5*(1), 4–7.

Fogg, B. J. (2002). Persuasive technology: using computers to change what we think and do. *Ubiquity*. December 5.

Fogg, B. J. (2009, April). A behavior model for persuasive design. In *Proceedings of the 4th international conference on persuasive technology* (p. 40). ACM.

Hassenzahl, M., & Tractinsky, N. (2006). User experience-a research agenda. *Behaviour & Information Technology*, *25*(2), 91–97.

Holzinger, A. (2005). Usability engineering methods for software developers. *Communications of the ACM*, *48*(1), 71–74.

Jaspers, M. W. (2009). A comparison of usability methods for testing interactive health technologies: methodological aspects and empirical evidence. *International Journal of Medical Informatics*, *78*(5), 340–353.

Kelders, S. M., Kok, R. N., Ossebaard, H. C., & Van Gemert-Pijnen, J. E. (2012). Persuasive system design does matter: a systematic review of adherence to web-based interventions. *Journal of Medical Internet Research*, *14*(6), e152.

King, W. R., & He, J. (2006). A meta-analysis of the technology acceptance model. *Information & Management*, 43(6), 740–755.

Langrial, S., Lehto, T., Oinas-Kukkonen, H., Harjumaa, M., & Karppinen, P. (2012, July). Native mobile applications for personal well-being: A persuasive systems design evaluation. In *PACIS* (p. 93).

Lee, E. J. (2009). I like you, but I won't listen to you: effects of rationality on affective and behavioral responses to computers that flatter. *International Journal of Human-Computer Studies*, 67(8), 628–638.

Oinas-Kukkonen, H. (2010). Behavior change support systems: The next frontier for web science. In *PERSUASIVE'10 Proceedings of the 5th international conference on Persuasive Technology*. ACM.

Oinas-Kukkonen, H. (2013). A foundation for the study of behavior change support systems. *Personal and Ubiquitous Computing*, 17(6), 1223–1235.

Oinas-Kukkonen, H., & Harjumaa, M. (2009). Persuasive systems design: key issues, process model, and system features. *Communications of the Association for Information Systems*, 24(1), 28.

Oinas-Kukkonen, H., & Oinas-Kukkonen, H. (2013). *Humanizing the web: Change and social innovation*. Chicago: Palgrave Macmillan.

Patrick, K., Griswold, W. G., Raab, F., & Intille, S. S. (2008). Health and the mobile phone. *American journal of Preventive Medicine*, 35(2), 177.

Yetim, F. (2011). Bringing discourse ethics to value sensitive design: pathways toward a deliberative future. *AIS Transactions on Human-Computer Interaction*, 3(2), 133–155.

Self-Affirmation Interventions to Change Health Behaviors

B. Schüz*, R. Cooke**, N. Schüz*, G.M. van Koningsbruggen[†]

*University of Tasmania, Hobart, TAS, Australia;
**Aston University, Birmingham, United Kingdom;
[†]Vrije Universiteit Amsterdam, Amsterdam, The Netherlands

WHEN HEALTH COMMUNICATION IS INEFFECTIVE…

In 2012, Australia became the first country in the world to adopt plain packaging legislation for tobacco products, with the United Kingdom adopting this legislation in 2016 and other countries set to follow. Since then, all tobacco products are sold in uniform packages in a visually unappealing color, using a standard font for the brand name and feature a large graphic health warning that covers most of the package.

These graphic health warnings range from abstract depictions (e.g., someone blowing smoke and a caption suggesting that smoking harms other people in one's vicinity) to very graphic and disgusting images (e.g., gangrenous feet). The stated aims of the introduction of plain packaging are "to reduce the attractiveness and appeal of tobacco products to consumers, particularly young people; to increase the noticeability and effectiveness of mandated health warnings; to reduce the ability of the retail packaging of tobacco products to mislead consumers about the harms of smoking" [Department of Health (Australia), 2014].

These goals are somewhat prototypical of health promotion attempts. Most of these attempts include a component of health education, that is, these interventions try to convey some aspect of health-related knowledge that the intended recipient either does not yet know, or try to expand existing knowledge with the underlying assumption that a sufficient amount of

Behavior Change Research and Theory. http://dx.doi.org/10.1016/B978-0-12-802690-8.00006-2

knowledge will eventually result in behavior change (in our plain packaging example: '…increase […] effectiveness of mandated health warnings' or 'reduce the ability […] to mislead […] about the harms of smoking'). This implies a knowledge-deficit model of health education—people who smoke don't know enough about this highly relevant health issue, and if they knew enough, that is, if we could increase the effectiveness of the mandated health warnings and reduce the ability of packaging to mislead them, they would adjust their behavior accordingly.

So far, so good; however, while there is some evidence that plain packages have reduced the visual appeal of cigarettes (Dunlop, Dobbins, Young, Perez, & Currow, 2014), other recent research shows that the health warnings are not as effective as intended in the people that encounter them most often—smokers (Schüz, Eid, Schüz, & Ferguson, 2016). In this study, daily smokers were asked to log every encounter they had with a plain packaging health warning together with some questions about their thoughts and feelings at the time. According to a deficit-driven model, the information provided on the packages (i.e., health warnings) should lead to increased risk perceptions in the smokers who encounter them and subsequently lead to reduced smoking rates. However, what this study showed instead is that neither individual risk perceptions nor intentions to reduce smoking changed as a result of repeated daily encounters with the health messages on plain packaging.

Sometimes, such health messages can even backfire—for example, smokers reported more positive cognitions toward smoking (Süssenbach, Niemeier, & Glock, 2013) and higher levels of craving and anxiety after being exposed to fear arousing graphic health warnings (Loeber et al., 2011). Similarly, in a study examining the effects of personalized feedback about risk for skin aging and skin cancer, participants who received such personalized risk feedback in the form of a UV photograph of their face actually *increased* the time they spent in the sun without sun protection (Schüz, Schüz, & Eid, 2013). We will revisit this study later to illustrate how such backfiring effects of health messages can be prevented.

Taken together, these studies pose the question—why are messages educating people about their health risks not more effective in changing health behaviors? This question can be answered in more than one way. What we aim at in this chapter is to use self-affirmation theory (Cohen & Sherman, 2014; Sherman & Cohen, 2006; Steele, 1988) to describe and examine conditions under which health education is more likely to lead to the desired outcomes and outline how these conditions could be used in health behavior change interventions.

Even though aspects of this theory have been labeled "esoteric" (McQueen & Klein, 2006), and we do agree with some of the notions that the basic tenets of the theory are formulated in less-than-precise and less-than-optimal ways, there are interesting if not intriguing applications of this theory in the health domain that warrant closer inspection (for reviews, see Epton, Harris, Kane, van Koningsbruggen, & Sheeran, 2015; Sweeney & Moyer, 2015).

First, we will describe self-affirmation theory and highlight which aspects of the theory apply to health behavior in particular. Next, we will review the effects of self-affirmation on health behavior change, highlighting some of the major challenges. Then, we will discuss mechanisms and conditions via which and under which self-affirmation is assumed to work and discuss how these could be important considerations in health behavior change as well. Finally, we will discuss how self-affirmation could be practically implemented in health behavior change interventions, a particular challenge, since most research in this area has been conducted in laboratory environments.

PROTECTING THE SELF—WHY HEALTH EDUCATION SOMETIMES JUST DOESN'T WORK

From the perspective of self-affirmation theory, the counter-intuitive reactions of people who encounter the health messages discussed earlier make perfect sense. In self-affirmation terms, these reactions can be understood as attempts of the individual to protect their view of themselves as generally good and adequate persons. This implies that we (in this case the collective "we" as sentient human beings) are motivated to feel good about ourselves, or to "maintain a global sense of self-integrity" (Sherman & Cohen, 2006). According to self-affirmation theory, this overall, global sense of self-integrity is based on the sum of all domains that are important to the individual, the self-system. Any external information that challenges any aspect of this global sense of self-integrity is accordingly a potential threat to our overall sense of being a generally good and adequate person.

Going back to health messages: a message which suggests that behaviors we engage in are damaging to our health is such a potential threat because it suggests that we have been doing something that is demonstrably unwise—and this notion is definitely not in accordance with being a good and adequate person. This notion is very similar to cognitive dissonance (Steele & Liu, 1983) that arises from engaging in behaviors while holding dissonant cognitions, such as continuing to smoke cigarettes despite knowing that it has disastrous consequences for one's health. Fig. 5.1 shows the steps an individual might engage in during this process, and the above corresponds to steps 1 (encountering a health warning that challenges one's perceptions of being a healthy person) and 2 (these challenges in turn threaten the integrity of the self-system, as they suggest one has been engaging in unwise behavior).

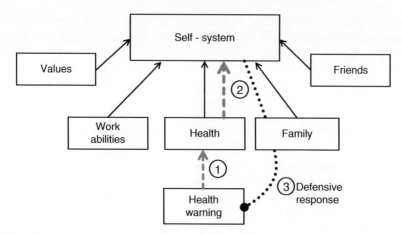

FIGURE 5.1   **Defensive responses to health messages serve the purpose of protecting the global integrity of the self-system.**

When faced with such threats, people turn to strategies to render these threats less consequential for their sense of self-integrity (Sherman & Cohen, 2006). Often, this involves reconstructing or reinterpreting a situation in a way that makes it less threatening (defensive responses). Cohen and Sherman (2014) have coined the metaphor of the self as a storyteller—one that is motivated to create an overarching coherent narrative of the self as being adequate and thus reinterprets information and recreates events so that they are coherent with this sense of global self-integrity. In the context of health messages, these attempts at retaining a coherent narrative of the self as being adequate would prompt defensive responses to health messages (step 3 in Fig. 5.1—the defensive responses aimed at reducing the threat arising from the health warning). Indeed, there is solid evidence that people often respond defensively to health information (van't Riet & Ruiter, 2013). For instance, people rationalize a potential health threat as being more common or less serious (Jemmott, Croyle, & Ditto, 1988), question the quality or the source of health information (Kunda, 1990), or plainly deny the implications of a health message (van Koningsbruggen & Das, 2009). These responses immediately make the content of the health message less threatening and thus contribute to maintaining a global sense of self-integrity.

From an interventionist's perspective, these defensive responses are detrimental, as they render many health communication measures less effective than they should be. Worse, there is research to suggest that defensive responses increase in intensity with the levels of risky behavior engaged in—for example, Kessels, Ruiter, and Jansma (2010) showed that defensive responses (in this case attentional avoidance) to tobacco-related health warnings were strongest in those who smoked most. Schüz et al.

(2013) in their study on sun protection similarly showed that those people who cherished a tanned appearance most, that is, those most at risk for engaging in risky tanning behavior, also were most likely to show reactance when provided with a UV photograph of their face—they increased their time in the sun without sun protection! Thus, people most in need of health behavior change are often the ones least likely to adaptively respond to health education efforts.

AFFIRMING THE SELF—REDUCING THE NEED FOR DEFENSIVE RESPONSES

What if there was a way to change people's appraisal of a health message as a threat to their self-integrity? A central tenet of self-affirmation theory is that the self-system, that is, all the aspects and concepts that we use to create the narrative of a coherent and adequate self, is in itself flexible. This means that the self can draw on a variety of roles and attributes to create and maintain this sense of self-integrity. Importantly, this does not imply that people strive to be superior, but good enough to feel adequate and a good person in general (Cohen & Sherman, 2014).

Consequently, this means that if there was a way to buffer the threat that, for example, a health message poses to one's overall sense of self-integrity to an acceptable degree at which the self-system would still retain adequate or good enough self-integrity, then the need for the self-system to respond defensively to challenging external information would decrease, and people could respond to this challenge in more adaptive ways.

This is what self-affirmations are assumed to do. Self-affirmations are any activity that demonstrate or reinforce one's sense of adequacy— basically anything that supports the global sense of integrity in the self-system. Going back to Fig. 5.1, this would mean that self-affirmation in another domain prevents step 1 (encountering the health warning) to be followed by step 2 (the threat to the overall integrity of the self-system), and thus reduces the need for step 3 (the defensive response to the health warning).

A review on experimental manipulations of self-affirmation (McQueen & Klein, 2006) suggests that the affirmations used most often in experimental research involve some sort of affirming personal values, either by having participants complete a values questionnaire (Reed & Aspinwall, 1998) or have them write about an important personal value and why this value might be of importance to them (Cohen, Aronson, & Steele, 2000).

Theoretically, as the self-system is assumed to be flexible in terms of which domains it draws self-integrity from, these affirmations should reinforce or reinstate one's overall sense of being adequate. When these affirmations are timed with a potentially threatening message (and it seems that these affirmations need to be completed before someone encounters a potentially threatening external message; Critcher, Dunning, & Armor, 2010), they then might enable the person to respond to these external messages in a less defensive, more adaptive way.

The fact that self-affirmations encompass a reflection on personally relevant aspects make these affirmations highly idiosyncratic, yet all the more relevant for the individual self-system. Further, and we will discuss this aspect later, this focus on personally relevant aspects, supports the idea to use self-affirmation components in individualized interventions. In the next section, we will first discuss research showing that manipulations of self-affirmation indeed have been found to reduce defensive responses to health information and to facilitate health behavior change.

SELF-AFFIRMATION AND HEALTH BEHAVIORS

Looking at the literature on self-affirmation in the health behavior domain, it becomes apparent that this topic has received increasing attention particularly in the years after 2010. Previously mainly examined in Social Psychology, the potential for application in health has become increasingly recognized, and a rough estimate would be that there are around 70 studies examining the effects of self-affirmation on health behavior or its determinants.

Two recent reviews (Epton et al., 2015; Sweeney & Moyer, 2015) have examined the effects of self-affirmation on health-related cognitions and health-related behaviors. Both reviews report small to medium effects of self-affirmation on health behaviors, and small effects on behavioral intentions. In addition, Epton et al. (2015) also report small effects of self-affirmation on message acceptance. Rather than reiterating these reviews, in this chapter, we review the effects of self-affirmation on predictors of health behavior change and, more specifically, on change in specific health behaviors (Table 5.1). We will first focus on the effects of self-affirmation on predictors of health behavior.

Predictors of Health Behaviors

As outlined earlier, self-affirmation seems to play a role in the processing of threats to the self-system. Applied to health behavior theories, these threats are mainly understood as risk perceptions. Consequently, many studies examining the effects of self-affirmation on predictors of health behavior change have examined risk perceptions either directly or via

TABLE 5.1 Published Self-Affirmation Effects on Health Behaviors With Subgroup-Specific Effects (Moderators) and Mediators Where Available

Health behavior	Study	Population	Effects on behavior	Moderators of effects (if available)	Mediators of effects (if available)
Alcohol consumption	Armitage et al. (2014)	Adolescents	Self-affirmed participants consumed less alcohol after health message		
	Armitage and Arden (2016)	University staff and students	Self-affirmed participants consumed less alcohol after health message on wine bottle		
	Armitage, Harris, and Arden (2011)	Retailer employees	Self-affirmed participants consumed less alcohol after health message		
	Harris and Napper (2005)	Female undergraduates	No significant main effects of self-affirmation on behavior (alcohol consumption)		
	Meier et al. (2015)	Undergraduate students	No significant main effects of self-affirmation on behavior (alcohol consumption)		
	Norman and Wrona-Clarke (2016)	University students	No significant main effects of self-affirmation on behavior (alcohol consumption)	No significant moderation by forming implementation intentions	
	Scott et al. (2013)	Undergraduate students	No significant main effects of self-affirmation on behavior (alcohol consumption)	Moderated indirect effects via intentions in heavier drinkers	Mediation via intention

(Continued)

TABLE 5.1   Published Self-Affirmation Effects on Health Behaviors With Subgroup-Specific Effects (Moderators) and Mediators Where Available (*cont.*)

Health behavior	Study	Population	Effects on behavior	Moderators of effects (if available)	Mediators of effects (if available)
Caffeine consumption	Reed and Aspinwall (1998)	Female undergraduate students	No significant main effects of self-affirmation on behavior (caffeine consumption)	Self-affirmed participants with higher baseline consumption reduced their consumption significantly more than controls and those with lower baseline consumption	
Smoking	Armitage et al. (2008)	Adult UK smokers with low SES	Self-affirmed smokers were more likely to obtain quitting information		Message acceptance and intentions to quit
	Harris et al. (2007)	Undergraduate students	No significant main effects of self-affirmation on behavior (smoking)		
	Memish, Schüz, Frandsen, Ferguson, and Schüz (2016)	Community sample	No significant main effects of self-affirmation on smoking	Self-affirmed smokers with higher baseline smoking (>20 cigarettes/day) reported significant reduction in smoking	
	Persoskie et al. (2015)	Smokers in US health survey	Smokers higher in self-affirmation had more quit attempts	Stronger effects in smokers living in US states with more comprehensive antismoking legislation	

Physical Activity			
Charlson et al. (2014)	Cardiovascular patients	More increases in physical activity following a combined positive affect/self-affirmation intervention	
Cooke et al. (2014)	University students	Self-affirmed participants reported higher activity levels after health message	No mediation via intentions or attitudes
Düring and Jessop (2015)	University students	No significant main effects of self-affirmation on behavior (physical activity)	
Falk et al. (2015)	Community sample of sedentary adults	Self-affirmed participants recorded significantly less sedentary time after health message	Mediation via activity in ventromedial prefrontal cortex
Good et al. (2015)	Adolescents	No significant main effects of self-affirmation on behavior (physical activity)	
Jessop et al. (2014); study 1	Convenience facebook sample	Self-affirmed participants without implementation intentions exercised more often than nonaffirmed participants without implementation intentions	

(Continued)

TABLE 5.1 Published Self-Affirmation Effects on Health Behaviors With Subgroup-Specific Effects (Moderators) and Mediators Where Available (cont.)

Health behavior	Study	Population	Effects on behavior	Moderators of effects (if available)	Mediators of effects (if available)
	Jessop et al. (2014); study 2	Undergraduate students	Self-affirmed participants with implementation intentions exercised less often than nonaffirmed participants with implementation intentions	Implementation intentions in addition to self-affirmation decrease exercise	
	Mancuso et al. (2012)	Asthma patients	No significant main effects of self-affirmation on behavior (physical activity)		
Diet	Epton and Harris (2008)	Female university students	Self-affirmed participants consumed significantly more fruit and vegetables than nonaffirmed participants		
	Fielden et al. (2016)	Undergraduate students and mothers with low SES	Self-affirmed participants consumed significantly more fruit and vegetables than nonaffirmed participants	Participants with lower baseline fruit and vegetable consumption showed the largest increase if self-affirmed. Low SES mothers consumed more fruit and vegetables if self-affirmed.	

	Study	Sample			
	Harris et al. (2014)	University staff and students	Self-affirmed participants consumed significantly more fruit and vegetables than nonaffirmed participants	Implementation intentions in addition to self-affirmation further increased fruit and vegetable consumption	Intentions to eat fruit and vegetables mediated the interaction effect of self-affirmation and involvement on behavior
	Pietersma and Dijkstra (2011)	Undergraduate students	No significant main effects of self-affirmation on behavior (fruit and vegetable consumption)	Involvement moderated the effects such that moderately involved participants consumed more vegetables when self-affirmed	
	van Koningsbruggen et al. (2014)	Female participants in a university online study	Self-affirmed participants consumed recommended levels of fruit and vegetables on significantly more days than nonaffirmed participants		Serial mediation via anticipated regret and behavioral intentions
Safe sex behaviors	Blanton et al. (2013)	Undergraduate students	No significant main effects of self-affirmation on behavior (ordering condoms)	Self-affirmed participants who completed a coping-focused exercise ordered significantly more condoms than those focusing on risk	
	Ko and Kim (2010); study 2	Undergraduate students	No significant main effects of self-affirmation on behavior (picking up STD brochures)		

(Continued)

TABLE 5.1 Published Self-Affirmation Effects on Health Behaviors With Subgroup-Specific Effects (Moderators) and Mediators Where Available (*cont.*)

Health behavior	Study	Population	Effects on behavior	Moderators of effects (if available)	Mediators of effects (if available)
	Sherman et al. (2000)	Undergraduate students	Self-affirmed participants purchased significantly more condoms and took significantly more HIV education brochures than nonaffirmed participants		
Sun protection	Jessop et al. (2009)	Opportunity sample of sunbathers	Self-affirmed participants were significantly more likely to take a free sunscreen sample	Significant effects for positive traits affirmation condition only	
	Schüz et al. (2013)	Opportunity sample University Open Day	Self-affirmed participants reported significantly less unprotected sun exposure than nonaffirmed participants after UV photograph	Nonaffirmed high risk participants receiving UV photo increased risk behavior, self-affirmed participants in the same condition did not.	
Diagnostic tests	Klein et al. (2010)	Random-digit dialed general population members	No significant main effects of self-affirmation on behavior (colorectal cancer screening)		
	van Koningsbruggen and Das (2009)	Participants in a university online study	No significant main effects of self-affirmation on behavior (taking online Type II Diabetes test)	Self-affirmed participants at high risk for type II diabetes were significantly more likely to take a test, self-affirmed participants at low risk significantly less likely	

Self-Management Behaviors	Logel and Cohen (2012)	University women	Significantly higher weight loss in affirmed compared to nonaffirmed participants	Working memory mediated weight loss in affirmed participants
	Wileman et al. (2014)	Hemodialysis patients	Self-affirmed participants had significantly lower serum phosphate levels (indicative of better adherence to phosphate binder medication)	
	Wileman et al. (2015)	Hemodialysis patients	Self-affirmed participants had significantly lower levels of interdialytic weight gain (indicative of adherence to fluid management recommendations)	

indirect predictors, such as attentional bias toward risk messages or the defensive processing of health messages (derogation). For example, Klein, Harris, Ferrer, and Zajac (2011) found that participants who were given the possibility to self-affirm by writing a short paragraph about the value most important to them rated their susceptibility for breast cancer higher after reading health information linking alcohol consumption beyond safe limits to breast cancer than participants not self-affirming (by writing about their least important value and why it might be important to someone else). However, as will be discussed later, these effects are also subject to moderation by risk status. Griffin and Harris (2011) note this as a "calibration" effect by which in particular risk message recipients at high risk for negative consequences would increase their risk perceptions as a result of self-affirmation, whereas recipients at low risk would mainly reduce their concerns about the risk communicated. Similar effects on risk perceptions have been shown for personalized risk feedback, that is, risk feedback that was tailored to participants objective risk status, such as UV photographs of participants' faces highlighting skin areas that have had high levels of sun exposure and were thus at higher risk for skin ageing and skin cancer (Schüz et al., 2013).

There is also substantial evidence for the effects of self-affirmation on the precursors of risk perception, in particular defensive responses and attentional processes. Both defensive responses and attentional processes are crucial processes in the response to health warnings, as they predict whether the content of a health warning is attended to and encoded in corresponding cognitions. Further, these processes might be interrelated—attentional biases away from threatening message content could make message derogation more likely. Klein and Harris (2009) found that self-affirmed participants displayed an attentional bias toward the threatening words they previously read in a health message linking alcohol consumption to cancer, whereas nonaffirmed participants showed an attentional bias away from these words. These findings on risk perceptions suggest that self-affirmation might enable participants to more openly process the risk information contained in health messages. Accordingly, many studies report that participants who self-affirmed prior to viewing a health message responded less defensively to this message, for example, by reporting less message derogation (doubting the quality of the health message, noting that the message might be overblown; van Koningsbruggen & Das, 2009; van Koningsbruggen, Das, & Roskos-Ewoldsen, 2009), or by greater message acceptance (overall small effect sizes in a metaanalysis; Epton et al., 2015).

The effects of self-affirmation on self-efficacy however appears to be less clear-cut. While some studies report increases in self-efficacy beliefs after a self-affirmation manipulation (e.g., Epton & Harris, 2008; Jessop, Simmonds, & Sparks, 2009; Morgan & Harris, 2015) that then could predict changes in health behaviors, other studies find no effects of self-affirmation on self-efficacy (e.g., Wileman et al., 2014, 2015) or find that effects of self-affirmation on behavior are not mediated by self-efficacy (e.g., Armitage, Rowe, Arden, & Harris, 2014).

As noted earlier, two recent reviews (Epton et al., 2015; Sweeney & Moyer, 2015) find small (d = .14 in Epton et al., 2015; d = .26 in Sweeney & Moyer, 2015) but reliable effects of self-affirmation on intentions to change health behavior. In accordance with the moderator assumptions outlined earlier, some studies (e.g., Harris & Napper, 2005; Pavey & Sparks, 2012) find that effects of self-affirmation on intentions are stronger in participants at higher risk for negative health consequences (e.g., heavier drinkers as opposed to light drinkers in both studies). However, the evidence for intentions as mediators of self-affirmation effects is meagre, some studies (e.g., van Koningsbruggen & Das, 2009) found the effects to be mediated by intentions, another study (Scott, Brown, Phair, Westland, & Schüz, 2013) found that intentions to reduce drinking mediated the effect between self-affirmation and reduced drinking, but this effect was moderated by drinking so that mainly stronger drinkers increased their intentions as a result of self-affirming and accordingly reduced their alcohol intake.

These findings suggest that self-affirmation might have small to medium-sized effects on some evidence-based predictors of health behaviors, but how about the effects on actual health behavior change?

Effects on Health Behaviors

The systematic reviews mentioned earlier suggest significant, but small (d = .32 in Epton et al., 2015; d = .27 in Sweeney & Moyer, 2015) effects of self-affirmation on health behavior. This chapter does not aim at reiterating these reviews; rather, in this section, we would like to review the effects of self-affirmation on different types of health behavior. To do so, we have conducted a systematic literature search in which we updated the two aforementioned systematic reviews with the substantial number of studies examining self-affirmation effects on health behaviors in 2014–16. In addition, we have focused on published research only in order to allow the reader to access the original literature. In addition to the 19 published studies with effects of self-affirmation on health behavior reported in Epton et al. (2015) and Sweeney & Moyer (2015), we have identified an additional 14 studies published in the meantime applying the same search strategy. We have organized these studies according to health risk behaviors (alcohol consumption, caffeine consumption, and smoking), health promoting behaviors (physical activity, healthy diet, and sun protection), as well as self-management behaviors (taking diagnostic tests, self-management) in Table 5.1.

A look at the table suggests that the effects of self-affirmation on health behavior might be more pronounced for health promotion behaviors, such as fruit and vegetable consumption (Epton & Harris, 2008; Harris et al., 2014; van Koningsbruggen et al., 2014), hemodialysis self-management (Wileman et al., 2015; Wileman et al., 2014), and physical activity (Cooke, Trebaczyk, Harris, & Wright, 2014; Jessop, Sparks, Buckland, Harris, & Churchill, 2014) compared with health risk behaviors, such as smoking (Harris, Mayle, Mabbott, & Napper, 2007) or alcohol consumption (Harris & Napper, 2005). For example, Harris and Napper (2005) found that self-affirmation did not reduce alcohol consumption in a sample of university students (health risk behavior), whereas Epton and Harris (2008) found that self-affirming promoted fruit and vegetable consumption in university students (health promotion behavior). Similarly, while Cooke et al. (2014) found that self-affirmation increased reported physical activity, Harris et al. (2007) found that self-affirmation did not reduce cigarette consumption. These differences may be due to the impact of self-affirmation or may reflect the reality that people find it easier to increase health promoting behaviors than decrease health risk behaviors. Risk behaviors tend to be experienced as more central to a person's identity than behaviors that are specifically engaged in to promote health—for example, smokers perceive smoking to be a central part of "who they are," even after cessation (Vangeli, Stapleton, & West, 2010). Additionally, risk behaviors are typically performed more frequently than promotion behaviors. Thus, in any intervention study, it may be easier to increase an infrequently performed health promoting behavior (e.g., fruit and vegetable consumption) than decrease a frequently performed health risk behavior (e.g., smoking). However, it should be noted that the Sweeney and Moyer (2015) metaanalysis found no moderator effects of health-promoting versus health risk behavior on the effects of self-affirmation on intention and behavior. Firm conclusions regarding this moderator, however, are difficult to draw because of the small number of tests in this metaanalysis. We therefore believe this issue needs more research attention, in particular since knowing which type of behavior attracts larger effects of self-affirmation is crucial information for the design of effective health behavior change interventions.

In sum, the studies reviewed suggest that self-affirmation in conjunction with providing health information has small but positive effects on health behaviors. This is consistent with the idea that self-affirmation restores the persuasive impact of health information that is otherwise undermined by self-integrity concerns, and hence, thus primarily indirectly promotes healthier behavior (Cohen & Sherman, 2014). While most self-affirmation and health studies presented participants with some kind of health message, there are some experimental and nonexperimental studies showing that self-affirmation might also have direct effects on behavior.

For instance, Logel and Cohen (2012) found that self-affirmed participants lost more weight than nonaffirmed participants without reading a specific health message promoting weight loss or warning against detrimental health consequences of overweight. With regard to nonexperimental studies, Taber et al. (2015) showed that people who had a higher disposition to spontaneously (i.e., without instruction or manipulation) self-affirm were more likely to be willing to learn results from genetic sequencing for preventable and unpreventable diseases, which would enable them to take precautionary action. Persoskie et al. (2015) similarly show that smokers with a higher disposition to self-affirm are more likely to make a quit attempt and stay smoke-free if they lived in US federal states with stricter antismoking legislation.

Moderators of Self-Affirmation Effects

Risk Level

Studies often find that self-affirmation does not consistently work for everybody. A variety of personal, social, behavioral, and environmental factors can influence the processes at work, so that beneficial effects of self-affirmation are only found under certain conditions or for some people but not for others. In general, it seems that self-affirmation is mainly of benefit where individuals are faced with an acute threat of high relevance that triggers a self-evaluative process. Self-affirmation theory states that defensive reactions are more likely if threatening information relates to important aspects of the self-system. Consequently, the effects of self-affirmation as a buffer of defensive reactions should be more pronounced in individuals for whom the threatened aspect is particularly important, such as people who frequently engage in risk behaviors and receive risk feedback that challenges their behavior. Accordingly, one of the most frequently studied moderators of self-affirmation effects is risk level, that is, any behavioral or conceptual measure that can serve as an indicator of personal relevance of the threat. For example, in studies looking at the combined effects of self-affirmation and cigarette warning labels, risk level is usually operationalized via the number of cigarettes smoked per day or smoker self-concept (Dillard, McCaul, & Magnan, 2005; Harris et al., 2007). A variety of studies showed that individuals at higher risk levels benefit more from self-affirmation interventions than low-risk individuals. For example, after reading an antismoking message and being self-affirmed, heavier smokers reported a steeper increase in message acceptance and intention to quit than lighter smokers (Armitage, Harris, Hepton, & Napper, 2008), and after being exposed to cigarette warning labels, heavier, self-affirmed smokers reported higher personal relevance of the messages and higher intentions to quit than lighter and nonaffirmed smokers (DiBello, Neighbors, & Ammar, 2015; Harris et al., 2007).

Similar moderating effects of risk level have been found in the sun protection domain (Schüz et al., 2013), for diabetes screening (van Koningsbruggen & Das, 2009), and with regard to alcohol (Pavey & Sparks, 2012; Scott et al., 2013), coffee (Sherman, Nelson, & Steele, 2000; van Koningsbruggen et al., 2009), and food consumption (Griffin & Harris, 2011). However, the moderating effect of risk level is not consistent across studies, with some studies reporting a nonsignificant self-affirmation by risk level interaction on outcomes like intention, severity, or effectiveness ratings (e.g., Dillard et al., 2005; Epton & Harris, 2008), or even showing that a significant interaction effect was due to low-risk smokers engaging in more detrimental cognitions after being self-affirmed, with largely nonsignificant effects for high-risk smokers (Zhao, Peterson, Kim, & Rolfe-Redding, 2014). In line with these findings, a metaanalysis did not find message relevance (i.e., the percentage of the sample meeting the behavioral guidelines highlighted in the health message at baseline) to be a significant moderator of the effects of self-affirmation (Epton et al., 2015). However, in terms of perceived threat, meeting certain health guidelines (e.g., for physical activity or fruit and vegetable intake) may conceptually be very different from engaging in risky behaviors, such as heavy drinking or smoking, thus effects of this potential moderator may have become blurred in the metaanalysis. Moreover, some studies found that the moderating effect of risk level is highest among individuals placed in the middle of the risk continuum, for example, self-affirmed, moderate drinkers directed more attention toward the threatening parts of a message than nonaffirmed and heavy drinkers (Klein & Harris, 2009). More research regarding the potential moderating role of risk level is thus warranted, especially because health education efforts that might want to integrate self-affirmation based interventions are likely to target people that vary in their risk level for the targeted health behavior (Zhao et al., 2014).

Self-Esteem

Another construct that is often studied in conjunction with self-affirmation is self-esteem. While self-esteem is sometimes conceptualized to function as a mediator of the self-affirmation effects (self-affirmation may boost self-esteem which in turn may facilitate adaptive message processing, see later), some studies have tested the moderation hypothesis that self-affirmation is particularly beneficial in individuals with low self-esteem, as these individuals do not possess as many threat management resources, such as positive self-feelings as their high-esteem counterparts, thus their self-system is more easily threatened by external messages. There has been some support for the moderating role of self-esteem in Social Psychology (Creswell et al., 2005; Holland, Meertens, & Van Vugt, 2002; Spencer, Fein, & Lomore, 2001; van Dijk, van Koningsbruggen, Ouwerkerk, & Wesseling, 2011), but only few studies have tested this in the health behavior area. While Dijkstra and van Asten (2014) did not find an interaction effect of self-affirmation and self-esteem on intention to eat more fruit and vegetables, Düring and Jessop (2015) found interactions between self-affirmation and self-esteem on attitudes and intentions toward physical activity, as well as message derogation, so that self-affirmed, low self-esteem individuals reached similar levels on these cognitions as high self-esteem participants. This study also suggests that there is little benefit in providing high self-esteem individuals with a self-affirmation manipulation, as there were no differences in attitudes, intention, and message derogation between the control and the self-affirmation condition for these participants.

Other Potential Moderators

The two metaanalyses reporting on self-affirmation effects on intentions and health behavior found only little summary evidence for tested moderators. Sweeney and Moyer (2015) reported nonsignificant effects for type of health behavior, proximal versus distal measures of behavior, and type of self-affirmation manipulation on intention and behavior, while Epton et al. (2015) found that self-affirmation effects on behavior changes were higher when the hazard was proximal, the manipulation was a values essay, and samples included smaller percentages of white participants. There is a long list of other potential moderators of self-affirmation effects, which have been tested in Social and Health Psychology contexts. These include factors relating to the manipulation, such as the timing of the self-affirmation intervention, awareness of the manipulation and message strength/argument quality; social and cultural factors, such as belonging to a negatively stereotyped group, gender, individualist versus collective cultural background; as well as intrapersonal factors, such as trait defensiveness, perceived ambiguity of the health message, and mood. In short, self-affirmation seems to be more effective when introduced prior to a threat (or more precisely, before someone has had a chance to engage in defensive processing with regard to the threat; Critcher et al., 2010). Moreover, if individuals are unaware of the fact that they are engaging in self-affirmation, effects are larger than when self-affirmation happens consciously (Sherman, Bunyan, Creswell, & Jaremka, 2009; Sherman & Cohen, 2006). Furthermore, intervention designers are advised to pay careful attention when developing the content of their advisory health messages as argument quality was shown to be an important moderator of self-affirmation effects (Brinol, Petty, Gallardo, & DeMarree, 2007; Klein et al., 2011), only when provided with a strong argument, did self-affirmed participants engage in adaptive processing of threatening messages—an effect that is potentially due to the greater diligence with which threatening messages are processed when self-affirming. In line with the notion that self-affirmation works best when people feel threatened, engaging in a self-affirmation task was shown to be particularly benefi-cial for members of negatively stereotyped groups (e.g., when comparing academic performance of black students versus white students or female students' versus male students' performance at a math test; Shnabel, Pur-die-Vaughns, Cook, Garcia, & Cohen, 2013). This finding is corroborated by another study showing a significant effect of self-affirmation only for female but not for male participants (Sherman et al., 2000). In terms of individual difference variables, perhaps not surprisingly, self-affirmation was shown to be particularly beneficial for those individuals who habitu-ally engage in high levels of defensive processing (Griffin & Harris, 2011). Moreover, self-affirmation was shown to be particularly suited to increase message acceptance in participants perceiving high levels of ambigu-ity in the messages (Klein, Hamilton, Harris, & Han, 2015). In terms of mood, a study testing the effects of self-affirmation on implementation intentions showed that self-affirmation only promoted the formation of implementation intentions in individuals who reported positive affect af-ter encountering the health message (Ferrer, Shmueli, Bergman, Harris, & Klein, 2012). To our knowledge, no studies exist testing for the moderating role of mood on more conventional outcomes like health message deroga-tion, intention, or behavior.

Mediators of Self-Affirmation Effects

It seems as if more is known about the circumstances under which self-affirmation does and does not work than why exactly self-affirmation is working. Accordingly, the evidence-base for mediators of self-affirmation effects is much sparser than that for moderator effects. As mentioned pre-viously, one commonly studied mediator of self-affirmation effects is self-esteem. While Napper, Harris, and Epton (2009) and Armitage and Rowe (2011) did not find any evidence for the mediating role of self-esteem—or in fact, that self-affirming was associated with higher levels of self-esteem than a control task—another study by Armitage (2012) suggested that rather than affecting overall levels of self-esteem, self-affirmation may change the specific domain a person's self-esteem is derived from. The study showed that instead of deriving their self-esteem from body shape and weight, girls in the self-affirmation condition were more likely to de-rive self-esteem from other domains.

Mood/positive affect has been discussed as a potential mediator (McQueen & Klein, 2006), but there is currently only very limited evidence that self-affirmation affects mood at all (e.g., Dillard et al., 2005; Napper et al., 2009; Sherman et al., 2000). More promisingly, mediating effects have been found for message acceptance (Armitage et al., 2008) and message derogation (van Koningsbruggen & Das, 2009), as well as intentions (van Koningsbruggen & Das, 2009), feelings of vulnerability (Klein et al., 2011), and response efficacy (Epton & Harris, 2008). Feeling love/connectedness was also shown to mediate self-affirmation effects on health message acceptance (Crocker, Niiya, & Mischkowski, 2008). One recent study further showed that self-affirmed participants experienced higher levels of anticipated regret in response to a health message (suggesting reduced defensiveness), which, in turn, was related to greater intentions to adopt the recommended behavior and these greater intentions predicted participants' healthier behavior after 1 week (van Koningsbruggen et al., 2014). This evidence that anticipated regret and intentions acted as serial mediators of the impact of self-affirmation on health behavior also nicely illustrates the earlier discussed proposition that self-affirmation is assumed to indirectly facilitate healthier behavior after processing relevant health information (Cohen & Sherman, 2014).

More recently, Critcher and Dunning (2015) have suggested that a more viable way to conduct self-affirmation research is to ask the question how self-affirmation may undo a self-threat rather than trying to test a variety of mediators and thus focusing on what affirmation does instead of on what affirmation interrupts. In a series of four experiments, they provide evidence suggesting that self-affirmation restores self-worth by facilitating broader self-views, a greater perspective on negative feedback mediates the effects of self-affirmation on reduced defensiveness, and that an exercise broadening participants' perspective reduces defensiveness in a manner equivalent to a self-affirmation manipulation. In general, this suggests that self-affirmation may work by placing the threat in a broader context, thus limiting its detrimental effect on the self-system (also see Sherman, 2013).

SELF-AFFIRMATION IN INTERVENTIONS TO CHANGE HEALTH BEHAVIORS

Before we talk about the role of self-affirmation in interventions to change health-related behavior, we thought it prudent to establish at which point in health behavior change self-affirmation might play a role. Self-affirmation has been characterized as a motivational technique (Epton & Harris, 2008), as most effects on theory-based predictors of health behavior change are documented on risk perceptions and their precursors. These processes in turn have been identified as factors impacting on individual motivation to change health behavior, and research generally finds that motivational techniques alone are insufficient to promote health behavior change (e.g., Zhang & Cooke, 2012). Being motivated is often seen as the first step toward behavior change (Heckhausen, 1991), and is thought to lead to the formation of positive goal intentions to initiate behavior change. However, as noted by Sheeran (2002), there is often an intention-behavior gap such that individuals fail to translate their positive intentions into action.

This suggests that there is a second step beyond possessing high motivation to engage in behavior change. This step has been labeled the volitional step (Heckhausen, 1991) and involves translating motivation into action. Goal-setting techniques, such as implementation intentions (Gollwitzer, 1999), which help individuals to plan how to perform behavior by specifying when, where, and how to complete behavior, have been shown to promote behavior change.

Goal-setting has also been shown to work in combination with motivational interventions to promote health behavior change. For example, Zhang and Cooke (2012) demonstrated that university students who received a motivational intervention and completed an implementation intention engaged in significantly more physical activity than students who either received only the leaflet or who received nothing.

Thus, if self-affirmation is a motivational technique it would seem plausible that combining self-affirmation with goal-setting in an intervention should lead to greater health behavior change relative to either intervention alone. However, research to date, does not support this proposal. Although Harris et al. (2014) found that individuals who self-affirmed and formed implementation intentions reported higher fruit and vegetable consumption at 1 week follow-up, by 3 months follow-up this effect had disappeared. Moreover, Jessop et al. (2014) showed in two studies that there were detrimental effects of combining self-affirmation and implementation intentions to promote physical activity, with participants who completed both techniques engaging in *less* physical activity than individuals who self-affirmed but did not complete implementation intentions. In the alcohol field, on the other hand, there is some evidence that self-affirmation combines with implementation intentions to promote a reduction in alcohol consumption (Armitage, Harris, & Arden, 2011; Armitage et al., 2014), although a recent paper shows that combining self-affirmation with implementation intentions did not reduce alcohol consumption in a sample of university students (Norman & Wrona-Clarke, 2016).

What would interventions to manipulate self-affirmation in practice look like? After all, most research to date has employed laboratory-based self-affirmation manipulations, such as writing about a cherished personal value (Reed & Aspinwall, 1998), filling in a self-affirming questionnaire that asks participants to apply positively values to themselves (Napper et al., 2009), or complete self-affirming implementation intentions in which participants make implementation intentions to think about positive aspects of themselves when threatened (Armitage et al., 2011; Armitage & Arden, 2016). Participants in self-affirmation studies were asked to complete these means *before* being exposed to health messages, with changes in cognitions and behavior typically assessed afterward. These settings require the context of a research study, as without this context, it could be difficult to get potential readers of health messages to self-affirm prior to viewing such messages. Currently, there has only been little research examining the potential for self-affirmation manipulations to be upscaled for public health use, with probably only a few exemptions.

Dillard et al., 2005 combined text-based cigarette health warnings with brief messages that were designed to affirm the smokers exposed to them—such as "You are a kind person" or "You are an honest person." However, this study found no effects of the manipulation on less defensive processing or higher risk perceptions in smokers. More encouraging results have been reported by Jessop et al. (2009) who integrated a brief self-affirmation task in a health promotion leaflet about skin cancer and sun safety. Sunbathers were asked to indicate, using a short checklist, whether eight general positive traits (e.g., open-minded, hardworking) were true of them before continuing to read the health leaflet. This brief reflection on positive traits successfully promoted sunbathers' requests for a free sample of sunscreen. Another study that embedded a personalized value-based self-affirmation task in a comprehensive set of online health-promoting measures for undergraduate students (Epton et al., 2014) found lower prevalence of smoking in the intervention compared to the control arm after 6 months. Perhaps the idiosyncratic nature of self-affirmation might be a crucial feature of this process—affirming core personal values will probably be easier and more effective if participants choose personally relevant domains for affirmation rather than reading prechosen affirming statements as in the study of Dillard et al. (2005). A recent study (Arpan, Lee, & Wang, 2016) supports this idea—here, participants were presented with a short value-affirming message within the logo banner of a website when being shown a health-promoting message, with effects similar to conventional self-affirmation.

However, research on the parameters determining the effective inclusion of self-affirmation in comprehensive health promotion interventions is still in its infancy. Finding ways of including idiosyncratic means of affirming the self that can be embedded in health messages without being distractive, incoherent ("Why should I think about what a great person I am when I read this health promotion booklet?"), or ineffective will be a challenge for future research. Compared to more traditional media (e.g., health leaflets), digital media possibilities may also make it easier to integrate self-affirmation interventions in applied settings (e.g., online health interventions, mobile applications). However, future research efforts might also conclude that the use of self-affirmation based interventions might be more applicable and effective in smaller, interpersonal intervention settings than in larger-scaled interventions (e.g., mass communications).

CONCLUSIONS

Even though there are many questions to be answered in the context of self-affirmation and health education, we think this chapter has outlined that there is the potential for this seemingly esoteric concept to make health messages more effective by avoiding defensive responses. It seems that encouraging people to focus on positive aspects of their self-concept makes them less prone to reject health messages. Given the the prominence and ubiquity of health messages and health-oriented public service announcement, this is a promising feature of self-affirmation that could lead to more effective health messages.

More high-quality research on the determinants of self-affirmation effects and on the durability of behavior changes induced by self-affirmation will determine whether we will see more of this concept in future research seeking to change health behavior (we do hope so).

References

Studies marked with * are included in the review.

Armitage, C. J. (2012). Evidence that self-affirmation reduces body dissatisfaction by basing self-esteem on domains other than body weight and shape. *Journal of Child Psychology and Psychiatry, 53*(1), 81–88.

*Armitage, C. J., & Arden, M. A. (2016). Enhancing the effectiveness of alcohol warning labels with a self-affirming implementation intention. *Health Psychology.* (In press).

*Armitage, C. J., Harris, P. R., & Arden, M. A. (2011). Evidence that self-affirmation reduces alcohol consumption: randomized exploratory trial with a new, brief means of self-affirming. *Health Psychology, 30*(5), 633–641.

*Armitage, C. J., Harris, P. R., Hepton, G., & Napper, L. (2008). Self-affirmation increases acceptance of health-risk information among UK adult smokers with low socioeconomic status. *Psychology of Addictive Behaviors, 22*(1), 88–95.

Armitage, C. J., & Rowe, R. (2011). Testing multiple means of self-affirmation. *British Journal of Psychology, 102*, 535–545.

*Armitage, C. J., Rowe, R., Arden, M. A., & Harris, P. R. (2014). A brief psychological intervention that reduces adolescent alcohol consumption. *Journal of Consulting and Clinical Psychology, 82*(3), 546–550.

Arpan, L. M., Lee, Y. S., & Wang, Z. (2016). Integrating self-affirmation with health risk messages: effects on message evaluation and response. *Health Communication,* 1–11.

*Blanton, H., Gerrard, M., & McClive-Reed, K. P. (2013). Threading the needle in health-risk communication: increasing vulnerability salience while promoting self-worth. *Journal of Health Communication, 18*(11), 1279–1292.

Brinol, P., Petty, R. E., Gallardo, I., & DeMarree, K. G. (2007). The effect of self-affirmation in nonthreatening persuasion domains: timing affects the process. *Personality and Social Psychology Bulletin, 33*(11), 1533–1546.

*Charlson, M. E., Wells, M. T., Peterson, J. C., Boutin-Foster, C., Ogedegbe, G. O., Mancuso, C. A., & Isen, A. M. (2014). Mediators and moderators of behavior change in patients with chronic cardiopulmonary disease: the impact of positive affect and self-affirmation. *Translational Behavioral Medicine, 4*(1), 7–17.

Cohen, G. L., Aronson, J., & Steele, C. M. (2000). When beliefs yield to evidence: reducing biased evaluation by affirming the self. *Personality and Social Psychology Bulletin, 26*(9), 1151–1164.

Cohen, G. L., & Sherman, D. K. (2014). The psychology of change: self-affirmation and social psychological intervention. *Annual Review of Psychology.*, *65*, 333–371.

*Cooke, R., Trebaczyk, H., Harris, P., & Wright, A. J. (2014). Self-affirmation promotes physical activity. *Journal of Sport and Exercise Psychology*, *36*(2), 217–223.

Creswell, J. D., Welch, W. T., Taylor, S. E., Sherman, D. K., Gruenewald, T. L., & Mann, T. (2005). Affirmation of personal values buffers neuroendocrine and psychological stress responses. *Psychological Science*, *16*(11), 846–851.

Critcher, C. R., & Dunning, D. (2015). Self-Affirmations provide a broader perspective on self-threat. *Personality and Social Psychology Bulletin*, *41*(1), 3–18.

Critcher, C. R., Dunning, D., & Armor, D. A. (2010). When self-affirmations reduce defensiveness: timing is key. *Personality and Social Psychology Bulletin*, *36*(7), 947–959.

Crocker, J., Niiya, Y., & Mischkowski, D. (2008). Why does writing about important values reduce defensiveness? Self-affirmation and the role of positive other-directed feelings. *Psychological Science*, *19*(7), 740–747.

Department of Health (Australia) (2014). Introduction of Tobacco Plain Packaging in Australia. Available from: http://www.health.gov.au/internet/main/publishing.nsf/content/tobacco-plain

DiBello, A. M., Neighbors, C., & Ammar, J. (2015). Self-affirmation theory and cigarette smoking warning images. *Addictive Behaviors*, *41*(0), 87–96.

Dijkstra, A., & van Asten, R. (2014). The eye movement desensitization and reprocessing procedure prevents defensive processing in health persuasion. *Health Communication*, *29*(6), 542–551.

Dillard, A. J., McCaul, K. D., & Magnan, R. E. (2005). Why is such a smart person like you smoking? Using self-affirmation to reduce defensiveness to cigarette warning labels. *Journal of Applied Biobehavioral Research*, *10*(3), 165–182.

Dunlop, S. M., Dobbins, T., Young, J. M., Perez, D., & Currow, D. C. (2014). Impact of Australia's introduction of tobacco plain packs on adult smokers' pack-related perceptions and responses: results from a continuous tracking survey. *BMJ Open*, *4*(12).

*Düring, C., & Jessop, D. C. (2015). The moderating impact of self-esteem on self-affirmation effects. *British Journal of Health Psychology*, *20*(2), 274–289.

*Epton, T., & Harris, P. R. (2008). Self-affirmation promotes health behavior change. *Health Psychology*, *27*(6), 746–752.

Epton, T., Harris, P. R., Kane, R., van Koningsbruggen, G. M., & Sheeran, P. (2015). The impact of self-affirmation on health-behavior change: a meta-analysis. *Health Psychology*, *34*(3), 187–196.

Epton, T., Norman, P., Dadzie, A. S., Harris, P. R., Webb, T. L., Sheeran, P., & Shah, I. (2014). A theory-based online health behaviour intervention for new university students (U@Uni): results from a randomised controlled trial. *BMC Public Health*, *14*(1).

*Falk, E. B., O'Donnell, M. B., Cascio, C. N., Tinney, F., Kang, Y., Lieberman, M. D., & Strecher, V. J. (2015). Self-affirmation alters the brain's response to health messages and subsequent behavior change. *Proceedings of the National Academy of Sciences of the United States of America*, *112*(7), 1977–1982.

Ferrer, R. A., Shmueli, D., Bergman, H. E., Harris, P. R., & Klein, W. M. P. (2012). Effects of self-affirmation on implementation intentions and the moderating role of affect. *Social Psychological and Personality Science*, *3*(3), 300–307.

*Fielden, A. L., Sillence, E., Little, L., & Harris, P. R. (2016). Online self-affirmation increases fruit and vegetable consumption in groups at high risk of low intake. *Applied Psychology: Health and Well-Being*, *8*, 3–18.

Gollwitzer, P. M. (1999). Implementation intentions: strong effects of simple plans. *American Psychologist*, *54*(7), 493–503.

*Good, A., Harris, P. R., Jessop, D., & Abraham, C. (2015). Open-mindedness can decrease persuasion amongst adolescents: the role of self-affirmation. *British Journal of Health Psychology*, *20*(2), 228–242.

Griffin, D. W., & Harris, P. R. (2011). Calibrating the response to health warnings: limiting both overreaction and underreaction with self-affirmation. *Psychological Science*, 22(5), 572–578.

*Harris, P. R., Brearley, I., Sheeran, P., Barker, M., Klein, W. M. P., David Creswell, J., & Bond, R. (2014). Combining self-affirmation with implementation intentions to promote fruit and vegetable consumption. *Health Psychology*, 33(7), 729–736.

*Harris, P. R., Mayle, K., Mabbott, L., & Napper, L. (2007). Self-affirmation reduces smokers' defensiveness to graphic on-pack cigarette warning labels. *Health Psychology*, 26(4), 437–446.

*Harris, P. R., & Napper, L. (2005). Self-Affirmation and the biased processing of threatening health-risk information. *Personality and Social Psychology Bulletin*, 31(9), 1250–1263.

Heckhausen, H. (1991). *Motivation and action*. Berlin, Heidelberg, New York: Springer.

Holland, R. W., Meertens, R. M., & Van Vugt, M. (2002). Dissonance on the road: Self-esteem as a moderator of internal and external self-justification strategies. *Personality and Social Psychology Bulletin*, 28(12), 1713–1724.

Jemmott, J. B., Croyle, R. T., & Ditto, P. H. (1988). Common sense epidemiology: self-based judgments from laypersons and physicians. *Health Psychology*, 7(1), 55–73.

*Jessop, D. C., Simmonds, L. V., & Sparks, P. (2009). Motivational and behavioural consequences of self-affirmation interventions: a study of sunscreen use among women. *Psychology & Health*, 24(5), 529–544.

*Jessop, D. C., Sparks, P., Buckland, N., Harris, P. R., & Churchill, S. (2014). Combining self-affirmation and implementation intentions: evidence of detrimental effects on behavioral outcomes. *Annals of Behavioral Medicine*, 47(2), 137–147.

Kessels, L. T. E., Ruiter, R. A. C., & Jansma, B. M. (2010). Increased attention but more efficient disengagement: neuroscientific evidence for defensive processing of threatening health information. *Health Psychology*, 29(4), 346–354.

Klein, W. M. P., Hamilton, J. G., Harris, P. R., & Han, P. K. J. (2015). Health messaging to individuals who perceive ambiguity in health communications: the promise of self-affirmation. *Journal of Health Communication*, 20(5), 566–572.

Klein, W. M. P., & Harris, P. R. (2009). Self-affirmation enhances attentional bias toward threatening components of a persuasive message. *Psychological Science*, 20(12), 1463–1467.

Klein, W. M. P., Harris, P. R., Ferrer, R. A., & Zajac, L. E. (2011). Feelings of vulnerability in response to threatening messages: effects of self-affirmation. *Journal of Experimental Social Psychology*, 47(6), 1237–1242.

*Klein, W. M. P., Lipkus, I. M., Scholl, S. M., McQueen, A., Cerully, J. L., & Harris, P. R. (2010). Self-affirmation moderates effects of unrealistic optimism and pessimism on reactions to tailored risk feedback. *Psychology & Health*, 25(10), 1195–1208.

*Ko, D. M., & Kim, H. S. (2010). Message framing and defensive processing: a cultural examination. *Health Communication*, 25(1), 61–68.

Kunda, Z. (1990). The case for motivated reasoning. *Psychological Bulletin*, 108(3), 480–498.

Loeber, S., Vollstädt-Klein, S., Wilden, S., Schneider, S., Rockenbach, C., Dinter, C., & Kiefer, F. (2011). The effect of pictorial warnings on cigarette packages on attentional bias of smokers. *Pharmacology Biochemistry and Behavior*, 98(2), 292–298.

*Logel, C., & Cohen, G. L. (2012). The role of the self in physical health: Testing the effect of a values-affirmation intervention on weight loss. *Psychological Science*, 23(1), 53–55.

*Mancuso, C. A., Choi, T. N., Westermann, H., Wenderoth, S., Hollenberg, J. P., Wells, M. T., & Charlson, M. E. (2012). Increasing physical activity in patients with asthma through positive affect and self-affirmation: a randomized trial. *Archives of Internal Medicine*, 172(4), 337–343.

McQueen, A., & Klein, W. M. P. (2006). Experimental manipulations of self-affirmation: a systematic review. *Self and Identity*, 5(4), 289–354.

*Memish, K. E., Schüz, N., Frandsen, M., Ferguson, S. G., & Schüz, B. (2016). Using self-affirmation to increase the effects of emotive health warnings on smoking: a randomised exploratory trial. *Nicotine & Tobacco Research*, ntw167.

*Meier, E., Miller, M. B., Lechner, W. V., Lombardi, N., Claborn, K. R., & Leffingwell, T. R. (2015). The inability of self-affirmations to decrease defensive bias toward an alcohol-related risk message among high-risk college students. *Journal of American College Health*, *63*(5), 324–329.

Morgan, J. I., & Harris, P. R. (2015). Evidence that brief self-affirming implementation intentions can reduce work-related anxiety in downsize survivors. *Anxiety, Stress and Coping*, *28*(5), 563–575.

Napper, L., Harris, P. R., & Epton, T. (2009). Developing and testing a self-affirmation manipulation. *Self & Identity*, *8*(1), 45–62.

*Norman, P., & Wrona-Clarke, A. (2016). Combining self-affirmation and implementation intentions to reduce heavy episodic drinking in university students. *Psychology of Addictive Behaviors*, *30*(4), 434–441.

Pavey, L. J., & Sparks, P. (2012). Autonomy and defensiveness: experimentally increasing adaptive responses to health-risk information via priming and self-affirmation. *Psychology & Health*, *27*(3), 259–276.

*Persoskie, A., Ferrer, R. A., Taber, J. M., Klein, W. M. P., Parascandola, M., & Harris, P. R. (2015). Smoke-free air laws and quit attempts: evidence for a moderating role of spontaneous self-affirmation. *Social Science & Medicine*, *141*, 46–55.

*Pietersma, S., & Dijkstra, A. (2011). Do behavioural health intentions engender health behaviour change? A study on the moderating role of self-affirmation on actual fruit intake versus vegetable intake. *British Journal of Health Psychology*, *16*(4), 815–827.

*Reed, M. B., & Aspinwall, L. G. (1998). Self-affirmation reduces biased processing of health-risk information. *Motivation and Emotion*, *22*(2), 99–132.

Schüz, N., Eid, M., Schüz, B., & Ferguson, S. G. (2016). Immediate effects of plain packaging health warnings on quitting intention and potential mediators: results from two ecological momentary assessment studies. *Psychology of Addictive Behaviors*, *30*, 220–228.

*Schüz, N., Schüz, B., & Eid, M. (2013). When risk communication backfires: randomized controlled trial on self-affirmation and reactance to personalized risk feedback in high-risk individuals. *Health Psychology*, *32*(5), 561–570.

*Scott, J. L., Brown, A. C., Phair, J. K., Westland, J. N., & Schüz, B. (2013). Self-affirmation, intentions and alcohol consumption in students: a randomised exploratory trial. *Alcohol and Alcoholism*, *48*(4), 458–463.

Sheeran, P. (2002). Intention-behaviour relations: a conceptual and empirical review. In M. Hewstone, & W. Stroebe (Eds.), *European Review Of Social Psychology* (pp. 1–36). (12). New York: Wiley.

Sherman, D. K. (2013). Self-affirmation: understanding the effects. *Social and Personality Psychology Compass*, *7*, 834–845.

Sherman, D. K., Bunyan, D. P., Creswell, J. D., & Jaremka, L. M. (2009). Psychological vulnerability and stress: the effects of self-affirmation on sympathetic nervous system responses to naturalistic stressors. *Health Psychology*, *28*(5), 554–562.

Sherman, D. K., & Cohen, G. L. (2006). The psychology of self-defense: self-affirmation theory. *Advances in Experimental Social Psychology*, *38*, 183–242.

*Sherman, D. K., Nelson, L. D., & Steele, C. M. (2000). Do messages about health risks threaten the self? Increasing the acceptance of threatening health messages via self-affirmation. *Personality and Social Psychology Bulletin*, *26*(9), 1046–1058.

Shnabel, N., Purdie-Vaughns, V., Cook, J. E., Garcia, J., & Cohen, G. L. (2013). Demystifying values-affirmation interventions: writing about social belonging is a key to buffering against identity threat. *Personality and Social Psychology Bulletin*, *39*(5), 663–676.

Spencer, S. J., Fein, S., & Lomore, C. D. (2001). Maintaining one's self-image vis-à-vis others: the role of self-affirmation in the social evaluation of the self. *Motivation and Emotion*, *25*(1), 41–65.

Steele, C. M. (1988). The psychology of self-affirmation: sustaining the integrity of the self. In L. Berkowitz (Ed.), *Advances in Experimental Social Psychology* (pp. 261–302). (Vol. 21). San Diego, CA, US: Academic Press.

Steele, C. M., & Liu, T. J. (1983). Dissonance processes as self-affirmation. *Journal of Personality and Social Psychology, 45*(1), 5–19.

Süssenbach, P., Niemeier, S., & Glock, S. (2013). Effects of and attention to graphic warning labels on cigarette packages. *Psychology & Health, 28*(10), 1192–1206.

Sweeney, A. M., & Moyer, A. (2015). Self-affirmation and responses to health messages: a meta-analysis on intentions and behavior. *Health Psychology, 34*(2), 149–159.

Taber, J. M., Klein, W. M. P., Ferrer, R. A., Lewis, K. L., Harris, P. R., Shepperd, J. A., & Biesecker, L. G. (2015). Information avoidance tendencies, threat management resources, and interest in genetic sequencing feedback. *Annals of Behavioral Medicine, 49*(4), 616–621.

van't Riet, J., & Ruiter, R. A. C. (2013). Defensive reactions to health-promoting information: an overview and implications for future research. *Health Psychology Review, 7*(Suppl 1), S104–S136.

van Dijk, W. W., van Koningsbruggen, G. M., Ouwerkerk, J. W., & Wesseling, Y. M. (2011). Self-esteem, self-affirmation, and schadenfreude. *Emotion, 11*(6), 1445–1449.

van Koningsbruggen*, G. M., & Das, E. (2009). Don't derogate this message! Self-affirmation promotes online type 2 diabetes risk test taking. *Psychology & Health, 24*(6), 635–649.

van Koningsbruggen, G. M., Das, E., & Roskos-Ewoldsen, D. R. (2009). How self-affirmation reduces defensive processing of threatening health information: evidence at the implicit level. *Health Psychology, 28*(5), 563–568.

van Koningsbruggen, G. M., Harris, P. R., Smits, A. J., Schüz, B., Scholz, U., & Cooke, R. (2014). Self-Affirmation Before Exposure to Health Communications Promotes Intentions and Health Behavior Change by Increasing Anticipated Regret. *Communication Research,* 0093650214555180.

Vangeli, E., Stapleton, J., & West, R. (2010). Residual attraction to smoking and smoker identity following smoking cessation. *Nicotine and Tobacco Research, 12,* 865–869.

*Wileman, V., Chilcot, J., Armitage, C. J., Farrington, K., Wellsted, D. M., Norton, S., & Almond, M. (2015). Evidence of improved fluid management in patients receiving haemodialysis following a self-affirmation theory-based intervention: a randomised controlled trial. *Psychology & Health, 31*(1), 100–114.

*Wileman, V., Farrington, K., Chilcot, J., Norton, S., Wellsted, D. M., Almond, M. K., & Armitage, C. J. (2014). Evidence that self-affirmation improves phosphate control in hemodialysis patients: a pilot cluster randomized controlled trial. *Annals of Behavioral Medicine: a Publication of the Society of Behavioral Medicine, 48*(2), 275–281.

Zhang, Y., & Cooke, R. (2012). Using a combined motivational and volitional intervention to promote exercise and healthy dietary behaviour among undergraduates. *Diabetes Research and Clinical Practice, 95*(2), 215–223.

Zhao, X., Peterson, E. B., Kim, W., & Rolfe-Redding, J. (2014). Effects of self-affirmation on daily versus occasional smokers' responses to graphic warning labels. *Communication Research, 41*(8), 1137–1158.

6

Behavior Change Interventions for Cybersecurity

P. Briggs*, D. Jeske**, L. Coventry*

*Northumbria University, Newcastle upon Tyne, United Kingdom;
**Edinburgh Napier University, Edinburgh, United Kingdom

INTRODUCTION

In recent years there has been a great deal of interest in the ways in which models of behavior can help engineer behavior change. Some models originate in the field of behavioral economics, where books such as Thaler and Sunstein's (2008) *Nudge: Improving Decisions About Health, Wealth and Happiness* or Kahneman's (2011) *Thinking, Fast and Slow* have popularized the idea that behaviors can be designed into a system, influencing choice at the point of interaction. These contrast with traditional psychology models of behavior that describe the relationship between attitude and behavior, with many originating from Fishbein and Ajzen's (1975) Theory of Reasoned Action or Ajzen's (1991) Theory of Planned Behavior.

In this chapter, we begin with an introduction to the former and show how various behavioral nudges have been explored in relation to cybersecurity before describing MINDSPACE (Dolan, Hallsworth, Halpern, King, & Metcalfe, 2012) a behavior change framework that describes nine *behavioral influencers* that can be exploited in a behavior change paradigm. We provide an overview of the nine "influencers" and describe research exploring the influencer's role in security-related decision making and behavior.

We then introduce some of the more popular theoretical models of behavior change with a focus on Protection Motivation Theory (PMT; Rogers, 1975) as a model that explicitly deals with the ways in which individuals appraise a cybersecurity threat (in terms of both its severity

Behavior Change Research and Theory. http://dx.doi.org/10.1016/B978-0-12-802690-8.00004-9

and their vulnerability to that threat), but also appraise their ability to cope with that threat, a known problem in cybersecurity research. We propose that PMT offers a model that is useful in the cybersecurity context as we are interested in encouraging people to better *protect* their cyber assets from cyber threats such as malware or malicious actors including insiders, hackers, and fraudsters. We outline how the use of this model may help understand influencing factors and how they interconnect.

Finally, in trying to bridge the two approaches, we ask how PMT and MINDSPACE can be effectively linked in order to provide a more integrated framework that could be used to shape the design and implementation of longer term behavior change strategies. This framework can be applied within organizations, thus providing an important insight to managers and practitioners involved in cybersecurity efforts.

BEHAVIORAL ECONOMICS AND CHOICE ARCHITECTURE

Behavioral Economics sits at the intersection of Economics and Psychology. Standard economic theory builds on the assumption that individuals are fully rational, completely selfish, forward-thinking decision makers. However analytical models built on this assumption have failed to reliably predict how people will behave. Behavioral economics provides numerous principles to account for less rational behavioral choices and argues that this irrationality can be predicted (Ariely, 2008). While traditionally focusing on economic behaviors, application of behavioral economics has become more widespread, partly as a result of a hugely popular policy-oriented publication by Thaler and Sunstein (2008) which investigates how predictable deviations from rational behavior can be used to "nudge" people into socially desirable directions.

The application of behavioral economics is most commonly seen in the health domain, where a range of successful interventions have induced us to *inter alia* buy healthier foods, stop smoking, drink more water, or take more exercise. Such interventions or nudges are best employed where individuals need to make quick decisions by selecting the best possible choice among several options (e.g., in the supermarket) but they have been deployed in a range of different contexts. The approach has gained popularity in Britain, with the creation of a UK Government Behavioural Insights Team (2013), colloquially known as the "Nudge Unit" which has the task of using insights from behavioral sciences to inform public policy. The name arises from the team's use of nudges to influence decision-making behavior across a variety of domains, including health (Burgess, 2012; Michie & West, 2013), and retirement planning and voting participation (Glynn, Huge, & Lunney, 2009), however the team is probably best known for the development of the MINDSPACE framework which documents a set of influencers on human behavior, and this is described in more detail in the next section.

A set of behavioral nudges can be designed into a system or environment creating a "choice architecture" (Johnson, Egelman, & Bellovin, 2012). There is essentially no "neutral" way to present choices, but a choice architecture will deliberately privilege some choices over others. A nudge, then, can be defined as any aspect of the overall choice architecture that alters people's behavior in a predictable way without forbidding any options or significantly changing their economic incentives. Design tools exist that can nudge people to make particular choices (Münscher, Vetter, & Scheuerle, 2015). Typically these tools will include the use of default settings, simplified notices that make certain choices more "salient," social nudges that induce people to conform to type and a range of other message manipulations that simply make some choices seem easier or more desirable than others. In general, such choice architectures are more successful in circumstances in which people make swift decisions, relying on fast decision heuristics (described by Kahneman, 2011 as system 1) rather than conduct a slower and more detailed analysis of the available evidence (system 2).

Choice architectures have been utilized in a range of health care interventions (Michie & West, 2013; for a recent review see Skov, Lourenço, Hansen, Mikkelsen, & Schofield, 2013). This includes helping individuals make healthier food choices by using color codes to identify healthier options (Hakim & Meissen, 2013; Levy, Riis, Sonnenberg, Barraclough, & Thorndike, 2012; Lunt & Staves, 2011; Thorndike, Sonnenberg, Riis, Barraclough, & Levy, 2012). Interventions based on choice architecture have also been implemented to increase patient engagement (Nease, Glave Frazee, Zarin, & Miller, 2013) and improve optimal prescription choices in medical settings (Charani, Cooke, & Holmes, 2010). Within the workplace, Aharony, Pan, Ip, Khayal, and Pentland (2011) have shown that carefully designed interventions can help improve physical activities via personal rewards and incentivized buddy support.

The Cybersecurity Context

Cybersecurity interventions take place within the broad context of human–computer interaction, which in turn can be characterized as a series of interactions, and moment-to-moment decisions. This means that the existing interaction structure can be readily adopted as a choice architecture, for example, by simply manipulating a default setting or the order in which a set of menu choices appears. Thus system designers can "improve" user behavior without relying on or even requiring any deliberation from the decision maker (Nease et al., 2013). Note that it is a particular characteristic of choice architectures and nudge interventions that they do not typically seek to engineer a change of mind, but typically work directly to engineer a change in behavior or to prime a particular decision (Lunt & Staves, 2011). Choice architectures can thus affect choice without first having to convince a user of the merit of that choice (Dolan et al., 2012) and this has proved somewhat controversial (Yeung, 2012). However such an approach is considered useful in the cybersecurity context, where a user may not feel confident or be able to evaluate different options.

To date, nudges have been used in a range of cybersecurity settings in order to influence user decision making, particularly in relation to mobile devices (Balebako et al., 2011; Choe, Jung, Lee, & Fisher, 2013). For example, Van Bruggen et al. (2013) used messages based on morality, deterrence, and incentives to nudge users to lock smartphones, while Raja, Hawkey, Hsu, Wang, and Beznosov (2011) found that messages that conveyed information about risks and about safer online behaviors could improve participants' understanding of how firewalls work and the consequences of their actions. A third example of nudging in security is described in the work by Choe et al. (2013). These authors tried to nudge users away from privacy-invasive mobile phone applications using message framing (positive or negative) and different visual privacy ratings (colors and symbols). They found that framing had small effects, while visualized privacy indicators seemed to play a more significant role in nudging individuals away from or toward installation (Choe et al., 2013).

MINDSPACE: An Overview of Behavioral Influencers

The MINDSPACE framework was developed to assist in policy making (Dolan et al., 2012) and is associated with the UK Government's Behavioural Influences Unit. It concisely documents the academic research on the underlying processes, mental constraints, and cognitive biases of behavior change, pulling these into a set of nine influences, described in following sections, upon which choice architectures can be built. These influencers collectively capture the environmental, social, and personal influencers of behavior.

Messenger Effects

Messenger effects address the extent to which the communicator of a message will affect the influence that message has on subsequent behavior. Messenger effects have been known for some time and are frequently used in the advertising industry, where millions are spent on the recruitment of "key opinion leaders" or celebrities to endorse a product. Surprisingly, there have been only limited investigations of messenger effects in the cybersecurity sphere, despite the large number of studies that have demonstrated that people are more willing to trust information when it comes from a credible source (Ben-Naim, Bonnefon, Herzig, Leblois, & Lorini, 2013; De Sordi, Meireles, & Carvalho de Azevedo, 2014; Zhou & Sun, 2009).

One of the known problems in cybersecurity is that "experts" are sometimes seen as enforcers of unrealistic security policy. This means that employees don't always turn to IT or cybersecurity experts for information and advice, but will, instead, approach peers or immediate line managers as these people are seen as more useful as a source of unofficial but practical cybersecurity knowledge (Blythe, Coventry, & Little, 2015). This practice—of developing a trusted peer network—is common in other fields and gives rise to the development of a "shadow security" system within organizations (Kirlappos, Parkin, & Sasse, 2015).

Incentives

Incentives can also be used to shape cybersecurity behavior, however, the literature here gives a rather mixed message. Incentives or rewards do not always work as well as sanctions, although this may depend on the situation. In a survey-based study, Siponen, Pahnila, and Mahmood (2010) found that sanctions could be an effective way of improving compliance with an organization's cybersecurity policy, provided poor behavior was detected reliably and sanctions enforced early. Rewards for compliance were less effective. These findings are only partially consistent with an earlier study by Herath and Rao (2009), who found that penalties for failure to comply with security policy could be an effective deterrent where employees were reasonably sure they would be discovered, but *only* if they also believed that the policies were reasonable and effective, that is, that the policies would work to improve the overall performance and security of the company. Additionally, the most severe sanctions actually reduced future intention to comply with policy (Herath & Rao, 2009).

This is one of a set of findings around the ways in which excessive control can backfire and lead to a breakdown in the psychological contract (Raghu, Jayaraman, & Rao, 2004). Certainly employees can tend to perceive pressure to conform as job interference and may consequently choose nonconformity as a form of rebellion. Again, we are reminded of recent findings that employees make their own decisions about what is reasonable and try to enact a limited form of compliance as a sufficing strategy.

Norms

Norms are the behaviors that group members see as desirable or appropriate within a setting. In several of the studies cited previously, employees quickly agree upon appropriate behavioral norms and are highly influenced by their colleagues in this respect. For example, in both the Herath and Rao (2009) and Siponen et al. (2010) studies, "normative beliefs" was the single largest predictor of employees' intention to comply with information security policy. The importance of the perceived norm is such that it has led to a number of "social proof" interventions, designed to improve security behavior. For example, Das, Dabbish, Hong, and Kramer (2014) used social interventions to increase the adoption of three security features: Login Notifications, Login Approvals, and Trusted Contacts. This finding is in line with other studies showing the impact of social norms upon various forms of cybersecurity behavior (Chang & Ho, 2006; Godlove, 2012; Ion, Langheinrich, Kumaraguru, & Capkun, 2010).

Defaults

Default settings are important across a range of cybersecurity contexts as it is rare for users to change default settings, even when given expert advice to do so (Shah & Sandvig, 2008). Examples of both "good" and "bad" security defaults exist, thus a default might automatically configure a user's privacy setting on SNS (Fank & LeFevre, 2010). Defaults are also used to force users to select stronger passwords featuring specific characteristics (Florencio & Herley, 2010). In some instances, defaults are not always helpful when users are trying to prioritize security (Felt et al., 2012) or deal with insider threat on social media such as Facebook (Johnson et al., 2012).

Salience

There have been a number of successful interventions that have relied upon making the impact of certain actions more salient. For example, Turland, Coventry, Jeske, Briggs, and van Moorsel (2015) used menu order and color coding to make the "safe" choices around wireless network selection more obvious, while Maurer, De Luca, and Kempe (2011) used display warnings to stop users entering critical data on websites that had been associated with fraudulent activity or phishing attacks. A range of privacy nudges have been developed that help to make users aware of the unintended recipients of a message, before it is actually sent (Brockish, Lowery, Soave, & Tao, 2013; Wang et al., 2013, 2014) or that confront users with the consequences of app usage on mobile devices in order that they more closely examine privacy consequences (Shklovski, Mainwaring, Skuladottir, & Borghthorsson, 2014). Some interventions simply alert the user to possible privacy violations, for example, by providing immediate feedback when an app makes unreasonable permission requests for location-sharing services (Jedrzejczyk, Price, Bandara, & Nuseibeh, 2010). Such interventions generally rely on visual cues or warnings to improve the salience of certain choices, making the consequences clear for the user.

Priming

Our acts are often influenced by the cues around us and these cues can act outside of conscious awareness. In the original MINDSPACE literature (Dolan et al., 2012) priming was seen as a largely unconscious process, whereby subliminal cues such as happy or sad faces, emotional words or colors could be shown to influence subsequent behavior (Kliger & Gilad, 2012). There are only very limited studies of this form of "unconscious" priming in a cybersecurity context, although Turland et al. (2015) have shown that red (warning), green (safe) color priming can nudge users toward the selection of a secure wireless network. However, priming in the more generally understood sense of the term (i.e., mentally preparing people for an event) has been shown to be effective. For example, people who are primed to expect a phishing email are certainly more able to detect that email (Parsons, McCormac, Pattinson, Butavicius, & Jerram, 2015).

Affect

Affect or emotion is an important human response and can be harnessed as a powerful tool when influencing behavior. Obviously, designers have, for many years, tried to engineer a "hedonic" or pleasurable response to a product or system, but negative affect in the form of fear appeals is more commonly used as a campaigning tool and certainly fear has been shown to be a predictor of password strength in ecommerce activity (Zhang & McDowell, 2009). In the cybersecurity context, most studies have explored fear appeals or have elicited negative emotions. For example, negative affect was used in warnings to users engaged in risky behavior (Shepherd, Archibald, & Ferguson, 2014); to shame users into complying more closely with security (Harris & Furnell, 2012); to elicit anticipatory regret in social media users (Wang et al., 2011), and to encourage users to lock smartphones (Van Bruggen et al., 2013).

Commitment

A number of behavior change techniques rely on the reinforcement of an initial commitment by the participant, often making that commitment public in order to minimize the chances that they will subsequently back down on their stated "promise" to change. In some studies (Liao & Wang, 2011), this commitment gets translated into a particular form of behavior change, often via a series of more detailed "implementation intentions." In the cybersecurity sphere, this sense of commitment often gets obfuscated with the question of where the responsibility for security in the workplace lies. Those with poor technical know-how, for example, are less likely to show a commitment to cybersecurity (Jenkins, Durcikova, Ross, & Nunamaker, 2010) and many employees show a strong reluctance to take any meaningful responsibility for security in the workplace, believing it to be the duty of others who are more technically skilled (Blythe et al., 2015).

Ego

People are naturally driven to adopt more of those behaviors that make them feel better about themselves and less of those behaviors that make them feel worse. In other words, people strive to present a positive and consistent self-image (Dolan et al., 2012). This plays out in the cybersecurity domain in a number of ways. First, employees are more likely to behave securely when they receive managerial support for this behavior (Jenkins et al., 2010; Straub & Welke, 1998). Second, employees will behave securely in circumstances in which they can be *both* productive *and* secure (i.e., when they do not have to make sacrifices in one domain in order to excel in another). Finally, people are more likely to protect themselves online when they actually believe that they can succeed and so interventions that boost self-belief or self-efficacy can have a beneficial effect on security (He, Yuan, & Tian, 2014; Wirth, Rifon, LaRose, & Lewis, 2007).

THEORETICAL MODELS OF BEHAVIOR AND CHANGE

MINDSPACE essentially offers a pragmatic approach; the influencers are simply a set of levers that are believed to directly affect behavior. The relationship between these influencers and the underlying psychological constructs is not typically explored in any detail. In contrast, a variety of psychological models of behavior exist which address the interplay of attitudes and behaviors, recognize the importance of user's knowledge and experience as well as psychological traits and stable attitudes and beliefs. Many of these models were inspired by Fishbein and Ajzen's (1975) Theory of Reasoned Action and Ajzen's (1991) Theory of Planned Behavior, in the sense that they reflect the various factors that can influence an individual's attitude to a threat and the ways in which attitude influences behavioral intentions.

The Theory of Reasoned Action identifies two factors that determine behavioral intention: attitudes and subjective norms. An attitude is a person's opinion about whether a behavior will lead to a positive or negative outcome, while a subjective norm is a perceived social pressure arising from one's perception. A subjective norm refers to beliefs about what others including experts think, as well as motivation to perform or not perform a specific behavior. Together, attitudes and subjective norms determine behavioral intention, which then predicts behavior. The Theory of Reasoned Action assumes that behavior can be completely controlled, but this is not always the case and so the Theory of Planned Behavior differentiates between perceived behavioral control and actual behavioral control.

Many of the models also include explicit assessments of the likely success of that behavioral intention, in terms of both the efficacy of the behavior and an individual's belief in their own ability to deliver that behavior. Relevant models of behavior, based upon this premise, include Protection Motivation Theory (PMT); the Extended Parallel Process Model (EPPM; Witte, 1992)—generally considered as a development of PMT—and the Trans-Theoretical Model of Behavior Change, where the various stages involved in a change process are defined. This is a very complex field, with over 80 available models of behavior change in current circulation (Michie, West, Campbell, Brown, & Gainforth, 2014).

A recent literature review focused on relevant psychological models for cybersecurity policy compliance (Sommestad, Hallberg, Lundholm, & Bengtsson, 2014) and identified 60 different psychological constructs, drawn from a large number of established theories that included General Deterrence Theory (Straub & Welke, 1998), PMT (Rogers & Prentice-Dunn, 1997), the Theory of Reasoned Action (Fishbein & Ajzen, 1975), the Theory of Planned Behavior (Ajzen, 1991), Neutralization Theory (Siponen & Vance, 2010), Social Control Theory (Nye, 1958; Wiatrowski, Griswold, & Roberts, 1981), and Kohlberg's (1973) Theory of Moral Decision-Making. We will focus here on PMT as a relevant framework for interventions as it is one of the more widely used behavior change models in the cybersecurity field, due largely to its emphasis on behavior in the face of threat.

The use of Protection Motivation Theory in cybersecurity

PMT (Rogers & Prentice-Dunn, 1997) was developed to bring clarity to the understanding of fear as a motivator for certain behaviors, and later extended to look more broadly at the psychological mechanisms underlying persuasive communication. PMT has been used in many different domains, but most markedly in relation to understanding health behaviors (Block & Keller, 1998). In its simplest form, PMT proposes that individuals engage in two appraisals when making decisions (Rippetoe & Rogers, 1987). The first is the assessment of a threat (*threat appraisal*), a judgment that in turn takes in both the perceived severity of the threat and the individual's perceived vulnerability to the threat. The second is an assessment of the individual's ability to cope with the threat (*coping appraisal*). This also takes two subcomponents, requiring an individual to both assess their ability to respond effectively to a threat, but also assess the cost of making that response. To date, PMT has featured in several studies on cybersecurity-related behaviors (Chenoweth, Minch, & Gattiker, 2009; LeFebvre, 2012; Kim, Yang, & Park, 2014; Mutchler, 2012; Siponen, Mahmood, & Pahnila, 2014; Shillair et al., 2015; Tu & Yuan, 2012; Yoon, Hwang, & Kim, 2012). In line with the original theory we propose that threat and coping appraisals in the security setting break down into further clusters, described in more detail as follows.

Threat Appraisals

Threat appraisal is an important construct for cybersecurity (Dinev & Hu, 2007). In a review of the security compliance literature (Sommestad et al., 2014), threat appraisal was found to be the strongest predictor of a positive attitude toward security policy compliance (i.e., had the largest effect size) with data drawn from studies by both Herath and Rao (2009) and Pahnila, Siponen, and Mahmood (2007), although the effect size was lower in relation to actual intention to comply (Siponen et al., 2010). Two related constructs—perceived severity and perceived vulnerability—were also shown to predict intention (Ifinedo, 2012; Li, Zhang, & Sarathy, 2010; Vance, 2010). This distinction is useful for cybersecurity and is an important component of PMT.

Perceived severity is a function of both individual understanding and experience (i.e., reflective of the particular mental models an individual may have developed around cybersecurity), which in turn is likely to reflect normative beliefs and personal experience across a range of threat contexts. Expertise may thus play an important role in the assessment of perceived severity. One would expect that chief information security officers, protection officers, and other high level managers responsible for network and data security would be more qualified to assess threats and have better calibrated threat perceptions (see also work by Albrechtsen & Hovden, 2009). The environment in which a threat occurs may also play an important role in shaping threat awareness. Organizations that have designated IT departments may delegate responsibility for assessing threats to these units, with the unintended consequence that individual workers may abrogate any responsibility for assessing or responding to threat (Blythe et al., 2015). Thus the *organizational environment* in which a threat occurs may play an important role in shaping employee threat awareness as well as perceived responsibility to respond to a threat.

Perceived vulnerability (or susceptibility) reflects the extent to which an individual believes that they will be affected by that threat. It is interesting to note that users who can be relatively carefree about personal risk can still be called to action by critical incidents, an example being the Heartbleed security incident. According to a survey conducted by the Pew Research Institute (Rainie & Duggan, 2014), 39% of Internet users changed their passwords or cancelled various accounts following the announcements about the breach, behaviors which signaled a change in vulnerability perceptions.

Perceived vulnerability is influenced by individual differences in personality, attitudes, values, and beliefs. For example, an individual who uses a work device for a range of nonwork, commercial, and social activities may engage in various forms of insecure behavior that may leave him or her vulnerable to attack, individuals may still exhibit individual differences in their perceptions of vulnerability. Personality traits such as introversion, conscientiousness, impulsivity, and openness to experience can influence both perceptions of vulnerability and security behaviors. For example, users who rank high in openness to experience are unlikely to concern themselves with privacy threats and, as a consequence, they are more open to attack (Halevi, Lewis, & Memon, 2013), while introverts are likely to show greater general caution in their online behavior (Kraut et al., 1998). Behavior change interventions that recognize these personal elements of threat appraisal are likely to be more effective than a "one-size-fits-all" approach (Rasul & Hollywood, 2012). In other words, interventions that can ensure more realistic perceptions of threat or that are tailored to individual concerns and misperceptions may be more likely to be effective.

Coping Appraisals

Two factors—response efficacy and response cost—are influential in relation to coping appraisals. Response efficacy is a personal appraisal of one's own ability to cope in terms of knowing what secure behaviors are appropriate and understanding how to execute them, while response cost is more attuned to a users' willingness to sacrifice productivity in other areas in order to attend to a security threat. Turning again to Sommestad et al.'s (2014) metaanalysis of those factors likely to affect compliance with organizational security policy, we see that both of these constructs are important (Bulgurcu, Cavusoglu & Benbasat, 2010; Ifinedo, 2012; Siponen, 2010; Vance, 2010).

Response Efficacy

It is clear that many users are unaware of the appropriate responses to make in terms of a cybersecurity threat. For example, many users find it difficult to know how and when to install and use virus protection and users are often unable to detect or report a phishing attack (Bursztein et al., 2014). In recent studies, it has been shown that while employees may care about protecting their organization in the face of a cybersecurity attack, they do not understand the actions they should take and will often develop a "shadow security" culture (see also Kirlappos et al., 2015) wherein they adopt a range of behaviors that they believe will offer some protection, without sacrificing too much time and effort into maintaining unrealistic practices (see "Response costs").

Self-efficacy addresses an individual's beliefs about their competence to cope with a task and more generally exercise influence over the events that affect their lives (Bandura, 1977) Those individuals with low self-efficacy generally have poor self-belief in relation to their ability to manage threat. Thus we see a relationship between self-efficacy and virus protection behaviors (Lee, LaRose, & Rifon, 2008), using a personal firewall (Ng & Rahim, 2005), being cautious with email attachments (Ng, Kankanhalli, & Xu, 2009), antispyware adoption (Gurung, Luo, & Liao, 2009; Lee & Kozar, 2008; Liang & Xue, 2010; Sriramachandramurthy,

Balasubramanian, & Hodis, 2009), enabling security measures on home wireless networks (Woon, Tan, & Low, 2005), and complying with password guidelines (Mwagwabi, McGill, & Dixon, 2014).

Rhee, Kim, and Ryu (2009) found that experiences of security incidents had a negative relationship with self-efficacy suggesting that experience of a security threat may lower individuals' levels of self-efficacy for security. They found that self-efficacy was a significant determinant of students' use of security protection software, engagement in security conscious care behavior, and intention to strengthen their security efforts (e.g., learn more about security, add additional security measures). Overall, the existing research suggests that self-efficacy is an important determinant of security behavior in consumers and within the workplace.

Response cost

Response cost is more attuned to a users' willingness to sacrifice productivity in other areas in order to attend to a security threat. Turning again to Sommestad et al.'s (2014) metaanalysis of those factors likely to affect compliance with organizational security policy, we see that this construct is important (Bulgurcu et al., 2010; Ifinedo, 2012; Siponen, 2010; Vance, 2010). If an employee is unwilling to sacrifice productivity for security, this becomes a *response cost* issue as the user may not be able to devote the time and effort into understanding and executing the responses demanded of their organization. Response costs have been widely debated within the security literature and there is no clear understanding of their role in security behaviors. However, most security actions require that users step away from their primary task and devote unrealistic amounts of time and effort into protection (Inglesant & Sasse, 2010). Such solutions are not considered productive and can in fact cost an organization both time and money. There is a clear issue here, then, in terms of the extent to which organizations signal the importance of cybersecurity measures to employees. Those organizations with clear and well-communicated policies and that motivate good security behavior (typically via the threat of sanctions) are more likely to reduce risk, but may be in danger of also reducing productivity (Bulgurcu et al., 2010; D'Arcy, Hovav, & Galletta, 2009; Herath & Rao, 2009; Pahnila et al., 2007; Siponen & Vance, 2010; Straub, 1990). It is also important to explore productive security, that is, ways of reducing the productivity impact of security behaviors.

AN INTEGRATED APPROACH TO THE DESIGN OF CYBERSECURITY INTERVENTIONS

Earlier we reviewed a range of nudges and influencers described within the MINDSPACE framework (Dolan et al., 2012) before considering a theoretical model for understanding when and why people will respond to a cybersecurity threat. In practice these two approaches are not neatly divided and in a cybersecurity context it is beneficial to consider *both* the underlying model and the influencing tools available when designing an intervention. This is typically a very complex process, as the influences do not always map neatly onto the underlying cognitive components of the model. However, we can take the two overarching elements of PMT—threat appraisal and coping appraisal—and consider a range of reported interventions or nudges that have been effective in (1) enhancing perceptions of risk and vulnerability, while building (2) better response efficacy and minimizing response costs. We also map the relationship between these two approaches (the constructs of PMT and the nudges or interventions of MINDSPACE) in Fig. 6.1.

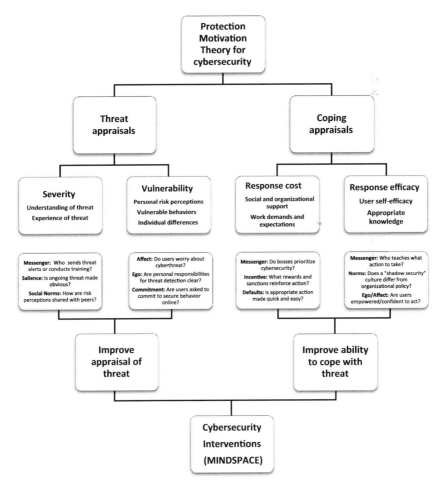

FIGURE 6.1 **A PMT approach to cybersecurity and associated interventions from the MINDSPACE framework.**

Changing Threat Appraisals

One thing that has become obvious from the cybersecurity research literature is that many campaigns are designed to scare the user into adopting more secure behaviors (affect). However, such approaches seldom work and indeed, some produce a maladaptive response where people cope with the fear appeal by denying the existence of the threat. It has been claimed that while threat awareness is necessary, it is by no means a sufficient means of inducing secure behavior (Dodge, Carver, & Ferguson, 2007; Furnell, Bryant, & Phippen, 2007; Lee & Kozar, 2005; Rhee, Ryu, & Kim, 2005; Stanton, Stam, Mastrangelo, & Jolton, 2005; Vroom & von Solms, 2004; Weirich & Sasse, 2001).

Interestingly, people do not experience threat unless they have some bond to the thing that is threatened, that is, some ownership of the object under attack (Anderson & Agarwal, 2010). Where the threat seems personal (and highly salient) as was the case with the Heartbleed virus, then people were highly motivated to protect themselves by changing passwords. But such acute threat perceptions are unlikely to percolate throughout a workplace unless the employee feels a strong need to protect his or her organization. Leach (2003) has argued that successful interventions should work to build a strong psychological contract between worker and workplace so as to keep employees committed to the cybersecurity agenda at work. It is certainly true that in those workplaces characterized by strong organizational commitment (norms), employees are more likely to comply with that organization's security policy.

These are longer term solutions, but many interventions designed to change threat appraisals operate in the shorter term. Typically, such interventions have focused upon redesigning threat messages (changing defaults and making particular actions more salient). Examples include manipulating the language, duration, or timing of a warning for better effect of message (Ormond & Warkentin, 2015). Other interventions manipulate the credibility of the messenger ("messenger" effects, see Zhou & Sun, 2009), use "tailoring" or personalization to make messages more salient (Davinson & Sillence, 2010), or provide various incentives or (affect and ego) appeals to "morality" (Van Bruggen et al., 2013). This is not a simple landscape and the various manipulations are not easily understood in terms of an overall framework. The efficacy of a low versus high threat message has been found to be moderated by individual differences in "avoidance orientation" (Van t Riet, Ruiter, & de Vries, 2011).

One area of enquiry has been in the design of dialogue boxes (in terms of salience or affect) as a means of highlighting the dangers associated with an interaction. Examples of this kind of approach include the privacy dialogues designed to "nudge" better privacy behaviors, designs to make social media users "think again" before sending a post (Wang et al., 2013) or the redesign of malware warnings such that they become more "usable" (Bauer,

Bravo-Lillo, Cranor, & Fragkaki, 2013) or more effectively convey a sense of threat. For example, in a study by Modic and Anderson (2014), the most effective malware warnings were those that very clearly defined the extent of risk that an individual faced if they ignored the warning, although they also found an influence of authority (a messenger effect in MINDSPACE terms) as well as a social effect of in-group opinion (with, rather surprisingly, Facebook friends carrying more weight than regular friends). The authors conclude that warning effectiveness could be improved by providing a clear, concrete, and nontechnical description of the threat and by using social influence via reference to authority or to a social group.

Changing Coping Appraisals

People will only engage in an action if they believe that action will be effective, that is, will work to mitigate a cybersecurity threat (Woon et al., 2005). This raises the obvious issue of what kinds of interventions can be introduced that would improve the motivation to act on a threat while also reducing the perceived cost of that action. One obvious issue to consider here—certainly in terms of the *desire* to act—is the extent to which that action may be incentivized, either extrinsically (by the organization or social group) or intrinsically (an ego effect). Organizational rewards for cybersecurity behaviors are rather sparse. Indeed, we are more likely to see sanctions for poor security-related behavior, than rewards for good behavior. While it is true that some sanctions are effective in motivating employees to (1) read and (2) follow a cyber security policy, they may only work in the short term. Interestingly, social rewards in the form of peer recognition (ego, positive affect) can be highly influential. Similarly, shame or embarrassment (negative affect) can be influential in motivating behavior. For example, users may become socially embarrassed by the knowledge that they have assisted in the spread of a virus and may subsequently lose their social standing within an organization or group (Weirich & Sasse, 2001).

If we now consider issues around the perceived capability to act, we might also consider the social context of interaction in terms of both messenger effects and group norms. We noted earlier, that messenger effects could be used to influence behavior in this space. For example, recognizing that peers or line managers might be considered more approachable in terms of offering information and local advice about how to cope with a particular threat (Blythe et al., 2015).

CONCLUSIONS

The work in this area is only just starting and there is still much to learn about the design of interventions that will improve both threat and coping appraisals and result in a shifting of the behavioral pendulum from inaction to action. An effective behavior change approach is likely to combine the analytical strength of a behavioral model with an understanding of how different influencers may be acting as barriers or facilitators to the desired behavior, but will also build upon a more nuanced understanding of those interventions that have worked in the past.

We have attempted to show how a number of known influencers (from MINDSPACE) relate to the different dimensions of a behavioral model (PMT), but this is just the beginning. Successful adoption of a more integrated framework for behavior change in the cybersecurity sphere is likely to rest on a number of key principles. First, that there is a careful consideration of the extent to which a target behavior is realistic and achievable with the target audience. Much of the work on PMT has focused upon compliance with security policy but sometimes these policies are simply unrealistic for employees who are juggling a range of work demands. Second, the target behavior needs to be fully understood and supported by a consistent message. In contrast to the health domain, where important health messages such as "give up smoking" or "drink more water" are both succinct and well supported across health professionals, the cybersecurity domain is fraught with conflicting messages about ideal behaviors. Third, it is useful to consider the fit between the underlying behavioral model and the behavior change being engineered. In this chapter we have considered PMT but different behavior change models have different strengths. Fourth, it is useful to analyze the *current* choice architecture framework in order to understand why people may not carry out the desired behavior, paying particular attention to the underlying but sometimes hidden incentives and influencers at work. Finally, there are typically many alternative solutions available when redesigning a choice architecture and the literature is fraught with design failures that didn't build appropriately on previous work. A better and more coherent body of evidence in this space would be extremely useful.

References

Aharony, N., Pan, W., Ip, C., Khayal, I., & Pentland, A. (2011). The social fMRI: measuring, understanding, and designing social mechanisms in the real world. In: *Proceedings of UbiComp*, September 17–21. Beijing, China.

Ajzen, I. (1991). Theory of planned behavior. *Organizational Behavior and Human Decision Processes*, 50, 179–211.

Albrechtsen, E., & Hovden, J. (2009). The information security digital divide between information security managers and users. *Computers & Security*, 28(6), 476–490.

Anderson, C. L., & Agarwal, R. (2010). Practicing safe computing: a multimedia empirical examination of home computer user security behavioral intentions. *MIS Quarterly*, 34(3), 613–643.

Ariely, D. (2008). *Predictably irrational: The hidden forces that shape our decisions*. USA: Harper Collins.

Balebako, R., Leon, P. G., Almuhlmedi, H., Kelly, P. G., Mugan, J., Acquisti, A., Cranor, L., & Sadeh, N. (2011). Nudging users towards privacy on mobile phones. In: *Proceedings of the second international workshop on Persuasion, Influence, Nudge & Coercion through mobile devices* (PINC2011), May 8. Vancouver, BC.

Bandura, A. (1977). Self-efficacy: toward a unifying theory of behavioral change. *Psychological Review, 84*(2), 191.

Bauer, L., Bravo-Lillo, C., Cranor, L. F., Fragkaki, E. (2013). Warning design guidelines. CMUCyLab-13-002.

Behavioural Insights Team. (2013). Blog. Available from http://blogs.cabinetoffice.gov.uk/behavioural-insights-team/category/uncategorized/

Ben-Naim, J., Bonnefon, J. F., Herzig, A., Leblois, S., & Lorini, E. (2013). Computer-mediated trust in self-interested expert recommendation. In S. J. Cowley, & F. Vallée-Tourangeau (Eds.), *Cognition beyond the brain: Interactivity, computation and human artifice.* Dordrecht: Springer.

Block, L. G., & Keller, P. A. (1998). Beyond protection motivation: an integrative theory of health appeals. *Journal of Applied Social Psychology, 28*(17), 1584–1608.

Blythe, J. M., Coventry, L., & Little, L. (2015). Unpacking security policy compliance: the motivators and barriers of employees' security behaviors. In: *Proceedings of the 11th Symposium On Usable Privacy and Security* (SOUPS). USENIX Association.

Brockish, L., Lowery, L., Soave, M., & Tao, J. (2013). Playing the part: introducing Facebook roles. For HCDE 505 at the University of Washington.

Bulgurcu, B., Cavusoglu, H., & Benbasat, I. (2010). Information security policy compliance: an empirical study of rationality-based beliefs and information security awareness. *MIS Quarterly, 34*(3), 523–548.

Burgess, A. (2012). 'Nudging' healthy lifestyles: the UK experiments with the behavioural alternative to regulation and the market. *European Journal of Risk Regulation, 1*, 3–16.

Burstein, E., Benko, B., Margolis, D., Pietraszek, T., Archer, A., Aquino, A., & Savage, S. (2014). Handcrafted fraud and extortion: manual account hijacking in the wild. In: *Proceedings of the 2014 conference on Internet Measurement Conference*, November (pp. 347–358).

Chang, S. E., & Ho, C. B. (2006). Organizational factors to the effectiveness of implementing information security management. *Industrial Management & Data Systems, 106*(3), 345–361.

Charani, E., Cooke, J., & Holmes, A. (2010). Antibiotic stewardship programmes—what's missing? *The Journal of Antimicrobial Chemotherapy, 65*(11), 2275–2277.

Chenoweth, T., Minch, R., & Gattiker, T. (2009). Application of protection motivation theory to adoption of protective technologies. In: *Proceedings of the 42nd Hawaii International Conference on System Sciences* (pp. 1–10).

Choe, E. K., Jung, J., Lee, B., & Fisher, K. (2013). Nudging people away from privacy-invasive mobile apps through visual framing. In: *Proceedings of 14th INTERACT international conferences*, September 2–6. Cape Town, South Africa.

D'Arcy, J., Hovav, A., & Galletta, D. (2009). User awareness of security countermeasures and its impact on information systems misuse: a deterrence approach. *Information Systems Research, 20*(1), 79–98.

Das, S., Dabbish, L. A., Hong, J. I., & Kramer, A. D. I. (2014). Increasing security sensitivity with social proof: a large-scale experimental confirmation. In: *Proceedings of the ACM conference on computer and communications security*, November 3 (pp. 739–749).

Davinson, N., & Sillence, E. (2010). It won't happen to me: promoting secure behaviour among Internet users. *Computers in Human Behaviour, 26*, 1739–1747.

De Sordi, J. O., Meireles, M., & Carvalho de Azevedo, M. (2014). Information selection by managers: priorities and values attributed to the dimensions of information. *Online Information Review, 38*(5), 661–679.

Dinev, T., & Hu, Q. (2007). The centrality of awareness in the formation of user behavioral intention toward protective information technologies. *Journal of the Association of Information Systems, 8*(7), 386–408.

Dodge, R. C., Jr., Carver, C., & Ferguson, A. J. (2007). Phishing for user security awareness. *Computers & Security*, *26*, 73–80.

Dolan, P., Hallsworth, M., Halpern, D., King, D., & Metcalfe, R. (2012). Influencing Behaviour: the MINDSPACE way. *Journal of Economic Psychology*, *33*, 264–277.

Fank, L., & LeFevre, K. (2010). Privacy wizards for social networking sites. In: *Proceedings of WWW2010*, April 26–30. Raleigh, NC.

Felt, A. P., Ha, E., Egelman, S., Haney, A., Chin, E., & Wagner, D. (2012). Android permissions: user attention, comprehension, and behaviour. In: *Proceedings of Symposium on Usable Privacy and Security* (SOUPS).

Fishbein, M., & Ajzen, I. (1975). *Belief, attitude, intention, and behavior: An introduction to theory and research*. Reading, MA: Addison-Wesley.

Florencio, D., & Herley, C. (2010). Where do security policies come from? In: *Proceedings of Symposium on Usable Privacy and Security* (SOUPS).

Furnell, S. M., Bryant, P., & Phippen, A. D. (2007). Assessing the security perceptions of personal Internet users. *Computers & Security*, *26*, 410–417.

Glynn, C. J., Huge, M. E., & Lunney, C. A. (2009). The influence of perceived social norms on college students' intention to vote. *Political Communication*, *26*(1), 48–64.

Godlove, T. (2012). Examination of the factors that influence teleworkers' willingness to comply with information security guidelines. *Information Security Journal*, *21*(4), 216–229.

Gurung, A., Luo, X., & Liao, Q. (2009). Consumer motivations in taking action against spyware: an empirical investigation. *Information Management & Computer Security*, *17*(3), 276–289.

Hakim, S. M., & Meissen, G. (2013). Increasing consumption of fruits and vegetables in the school cafeteria: the influence of active choice. *Journal of Health Care for the Poor and Underserved*, *24*(Suppl. 2), 145–157.

Halevi, T., Lewis, J., & Memon, N. (2013). A pilot study of cyber security and privacy related behavior and personality traits. In: *Proceedings of the 22nd international conference on World Wide Web companion* (pp. 737–744).

Harris, M., & Furnell, S. (2012). Routes to security compliance: be good or be shamed? *Computer Fraud & Security*, *2012*(12), 12–20.

He, W., Yuan, X., & Tian, X. (2014). The self-efficacy variable in behavioral information security research. In: *Proceedings of the second international conference on enterprise systems* (pp. 28–32).

Herath, T., & Rao, H. R. (2009). Encouraging information security behaviors in organizations: role of penalties, pressures and perceived effectiveness. *Decision Support Systems*, *47*, 154–165.

Ifinedo, P. (2012). Understanding information systems security policy compliance: an integration of the theory of planned behavior and the protection motivation theory. *Computers & Security*, *31*(1), 83–95.

Inglesant, P. G., & Sasse, M. A. (2010). The true cost of unusable password policies: password use in the wild. In: *Proceedings of the SIGCHI conference on human factors in computing systems*, April (pp. 383–392).

Ion, I., Langheinrich, M., Kumaraguru, P., & Capkun, S. (2010). Influence of user perception, security needs, and social factors on device pairing method choices. In: *Proceedings of Symposium on Usable Privacy and Security* (SOUPS).

Jedrzejczyk, L., Price, B. A., Bandara, A. K., & Nuseibeh, B. (2010). On the impact of real-time feedback on users' behaviour in mobile location-sharing applications. In: *Proceedings of Symposium on Usable Privacy and Security* (SOUPS).

Jenkins, J. L., Durcikova, A., Ross, G., & Nunamaker, J. F. Jr., (2010). Encouraging users to behave securely: examining the influence of technical, managerial, and educational controls on users' secure behavior. In: *Proceedings of ICIS 2010*. Paper 150. Available from http://aisel.aisnet.org/icis2010_submissions/150

Johnson, M., Egelman, S., & Bellovin, S. M. (2012). Facebook and privacy: it's complicated. In: *Proceedings of Symposium on Usable Privacy and Security* (SOUPS).

Kahneman, D. (2011). *Thinking, fast and slow*. London: Penguin Books Ltd.

Kim, S. H., Yang, K. H., & Park, S. (2014). An integrative behavioral model of information security policy compliance. *The Scientific World Journal*, Article ID463870.

Kirlappos, I., Parkin, S., & Sasse, M. A. (2015). Shadow security as a tool for the learning organization. *Computers & Society*, 45(1), 29–37.

Kliger, D., & Gilad, D. (2012). Red light, green light: color priming in financial decisions. *Journal of Behavioral and Experimental Economics*, 41(5), 738–745.

Kohlberg, L. (1973). The claim to moral adequacy of a highest stage of moral judgment. *The Journal of Philosophy*, 70(18), 630–646.

Kraut, R., Patterson, M., Lundmark, V., Kiesler, S., Mukophadhyay, T., & Scherlis, W. (1998). Internet paradox: a social technology that reduces social involvement and psychological well-being? *American Psychologist*, 53(9), 1017.

Leach, J. (2003). Improving user security. *Computers & Security*, 22(8), 685–692.

Lee, Y., & Kozar, K. A. (2005). Investigating factors affecting the adoption of anti-spyware systems. *Communications of the ACM*, 48(8), 72–77.

Lee, Y., & Kozar, K. (2008). An empirical investigation of anti-spyware software adoption: a multitheoretical perspective. *Information & Management*, 45(2), 109–119.

Lee, D., Larose, R., & Rifon, N. (2008). Keeping our network safe: a model of online protection behaviour. *Behaviour & Information Technology*, 27(5), 445–454.

LeFebvre, R. (2012). The human element in cyber security: a study on student motivation to act. In: *Proceedings of InfoSecCD*, October 12–13. Kennesaw, GA.

Levy, D. E., Riis, J., Sonnenberg, L. M., Barraclough, S. J., & Thorndike, A. N. (2012). Food choices of minority and low-income employees: a cafeteria intervention. *American Journal of Preventive Medicine*, 43(3), 240–248.

Li, H., Zhang, J., & Sarathy, R. (2010). Understanding compliance with Internet use policy from the perspective of rational choice theory. *Decision Support Systems*, 48(4), 635–645.

Liang, H., & Xue, Y. (2010). Understanding security behaviors in personal computer usage: a threat avoidance perspective. *Journal of the Association for Information Systems*, 11(7), 394–413.

Liao, G. Y., & Wang, C. M. (2011). Exploring the influences of implementation intention on information security behaviors. In: *Proceedings of the American Conference on Information Systems* (AMCIS), Paper 473.

Lunt, J., & Staves, M. (2011). Nudge, nudge. Think, think. *Safety & Health Practitioner*, 29(11), 41–44.

Maurer, M. -E., De Luca, A., & Kempe, S. (2011). Using data type based security alert dialogs to raise online security awareness. In: *Proceedings of Symposium on Usable Privacy and Security* (SOUPS), July 20–22. Pittsburgh, PA.

Michie, S., & West, R. (2013). Behaviour change theory and evidence: a presentation to government. *Health Psychology Review*, 7(1), 1–22.

Michie, S., West, R., Campbell, R., Brown, J., & Gainforth, H. (2014). *ABC of behaviour change theories (ABC of behavior change): An essential resource for researchers, policy makers and practitioners*. Surrey, UK: Silverback Publishing (Silverback IS).

Modic, D., & Anderson, R. (2014). Reading this may harm your computer: the psychology of malware warnings. *Computers in Human Behavior*, 41, 71–79.

Münscher, R., Vetter, M., & Scheuerle, T. (2015). A review and taxonomy of choice architecture techniques. *Journal of Behavioral Decision Making*.

Mutchler, L. A. (2012). *Expanding protection motivation theory: The role of individual experience in information security policy compliance*. PhD dissertation, Mississippi State University, US.

Mwagwabi, F., McGill, T., & Dixon, M. (2014). Improving compliance with password guidelines: how user perceptions of passwords and security threats affect compliance with guidelines. In: *Proceedings of the 47th Hawaii International Conference on System Sciences*, January 6–9. Waikoloa, HI.

Nease, R. F., Glave Frazee, S., Zarin, L., & Miller, S. B. (2013). Choice architecture is a better strategy than engaging patients to spur behavior change. *Health Affairs, 32*(2), 242–249.

Ng, B. -Y., Kankanhalli, A., & Xu, Y. (2009). Studying users' computer security behavior: a health belief perspective. *Decision Support Systems, 46*(4), 815–825.

Ng, B. Y., & Rahim, M. (2005). A socio-behavioral study of home computer users' intention to practice security. In: *Proceedings of PACIS*, (p. 20).

Nye, F. I. (1958). *Family relationships and delinquent behavior*. Oxford, England: John Wiley.

Ormond, D., & Warkentin, M. (2015). Is this a joke? The impact of message manipulations on risk perceptions. *Journal of Computer Information Systems, 55*(2), 9–19.

Pahnila, S., Siponen, M., & Mahmood, A. (2007). Employees' behavior towards IS security policy compliance. In: *Proceedings of the 40th annual Hawaii International Conference on System Sciences*, January 3–6. Big Island, HI.

Parsons, K., McCormac, A., Pattinson, M., Butavicius, M., & Jerram, C. (2015). The design of phishing studies: challenges for researchers. *Computers & Security, 52*, 194–206.

Raghu, T. S., Jayaraman, B., & Rao, H. R. (2004). Toward an integration of an agent and activity centric approaches in organizational process modeling: incorporating incentive mechanisms. *Information Systems Research, 15*(4), 316–335.

Rainie, L., & Duggan, M. (2014). *Heartbleed's Impact*. Pew Research Center. Report. Available from http://www.pewinternet.org

Raja, F., Hawkey, K., Hsu, S., Wang, K. -L. C., & Beznosov, K. (2011). A brick wall, a locked door, and a bandit: a physical security metaphor for firewall warnings. In: *Proceedings of Symposium on Usable Privacy and Security* (SOUPS), July 20–22. Pittsburgh, PA.

Rasul, I., & Hollywood, D. (2012). Behavior change and energy use: is a 'nudge' enough? *Carbon Management, 3*(4), 349–351.

Rhee, H. S., Ryu, Y., & Kim, C. T. (2005). I am fine but you are not: optimistic bias and illusion of control on information security. In: *Proceedings of the ICIS*. Paper 32. Available from http://aisel.aisnet.org/icis2005/32

Rhee, H. S., Kim, C., & Ryu, Y. U. (2009). Self-efficacy in information security: Its influence on end users' information security practice behavior. *Computers & Security, 28*(8), 816–826.

Rippetoe, P. A., & Rogers, R. W. (1987). Effects of components of protection-motivation theory on adaptive and maladaptive coping with a health threat. *Journal of Personality and Social Psychology, 52*(3), 596–604.

Rogers, R. W. (1975). A protection motivation theory of fear appeals and attitude change. *Journal of Psychology, 91*, 93–114.

Rogers, R. W., & Prentice-Dunn, S. (1997). Protection motivation theory. In D. S. Gochman (Ed.), *Handbook of health behavior research I: Personal and social determinants* (pp. 113–132). New York, NY: Plenum Press.

Shah, R. C., & Sandvig, C. (2008). Software defaults as de facto regulation. The case of the wireless Internet. *Information Communication & Society, 11*(1), 25–46.

Shepherd, L. A., Archibald, J., & Ferguson, R. I. (2014). Reducing risky security behaviours: utilising affective feedback to educate users. *Future Internet, 6*, 760-722.

Shillair, R., Cotton, S. R., Tsai, H. -Y. S., Alhabash, S., LaRose, R., & Rifon, N. J. (2015). Online safety beings with you and me: convincing Internet users to protect themselves. *Computers in Human Behavior, 48*, 199–207.

Shklovski, I., Mainwaring, S. D., Skuladottir, H. H., & Borghthorsson, H. (2014). Leakiness and creepiness in app space: Perceptions of privacy and mobile app use. In: *Proceedings of CHI*. Toronto, ON.

Siponen, M. T. (2010). A conceptual foundation for organizational information security awareness. *Information Management & Computer Security, 8*(1), 31–41.

Siponen, M., Mahmood, M. A., & Pahnila, S. (2014). Employees' adherence to information security policies: an exploratory field study. *Information & Management, 51*, 217–224.

Siponen, M., Pahnila, S., & Mahmood, M. A. (2010). Compliance with information security policies: an empirical investigation. *IEEE Computer, February*, 64–71.

Siponen, M., & Vance, A. (2010). Neutralization: new insights into the problem of employee information systems security policy violations. *MIS Quarterly, 34*(3), 487–502.

Skov, L. R., Lourenço, S., Hansen, G. L., Mikkelsen, B. E., & Schofield, C. (2013). Choice architecture as a means to change eating behaviour in self-service settings: a systematic review. *Obesity Reviews, 14*(3), 187–196.

Sommestad, T., Hallberg, J., Lundholm, K., & Bengtsson, J. (2014). Variables influencing information security policy compliance. *Information Management & Computer Security, 22*(1), 42–75.

Sriramachandramurthy, R., Balasubramanian, S. K., & Hodis, M. A. (2009). Spyware and adware: how do Internet users defend themselves? *American Journal of Business, 24*(2), 41–52.

Stanton, J. M., Stam, K. R., Mastrangelo, P., & Jolton, J. (2005). Analysis of end user security behaviors. *Computers & Security, 24*(2), 124–133.

Straub, D. W. (1990). Effective IS security: an empirical study. *Information Systems Research, 1*(3), 255–276.

Straub, D. W., & Welke, R. J. (1998). Coping with systems risk: security planning models for. management decision-making. *MIS Quarterly, 22*(4), 441–469.

Thaler, R. H., & Sunstein, C. R. (2008). *Nudge. Improving decisions about health, wealth and happiness.* New York: Penguin Books.

Thorndike, A. N., Sonnenberg, L., Riis, J., Barraclough, S., & Levy, D. E. (2012). A 2-phase labeling and choice architecture intervention to improve healthy food and beverage choices. *American Journal of Public Health, 102*(3), 527–533.

Tu, Z., & Yuan, Y. (2012). Understanding user's behaviors in coping with security threat of mobile device loss and theft. In: *Proceedings of the 45th Hawaii International Conference on System Sciences* (pp. 1393–1402).

Turland, J., Coventry, L., Jeske, D., Briggs, P., & van Moorsel, A. (2015). Nudging towards security: developing an application for wireless network selection for android phones. In: *Proceedings of the 2015 British HCI Conference*, July (pp. 193–201).

Van Bruggen, D., Liu, S., Kajzer, M., Striegel, A., Crowell, C. R., & D'Arcy, J. (2013). Modifying smartphone user locking behavior. In: *Proceedings of SOUPS*, July 24–26. Newcastle, UK.

Van't Riet, J., Ruiter, R. A. C., & de Vries, H. (2011). Avoidance orientation moderates the effect of threatening messages. *Journal of Health Psychology, 17*(1), 14–25.

Vance, A. (2010). Why do employees violate IS security policies: Insightes from multiple theoretical perspectives. PhD Thesis. Oulu: The University of Oulu.

Vroom, C., & von Solms, R. (2004). Towards information security behavioural compliance. *Computers & Security, 23*, 191–198.

Wang, Y., Leon, P. D., Acquisti, A., Cranor, L. F, Forget, A., & Sadeh, N. (2014). A field trial of privacy nudges for Facebook. In: *Proceedings of the SIGCHI Conference on Human Factors in Computing Systems* (CHI) (pp. 2367–2376). New York, NY.

Wang, Y., Leon, P. D., Scott, K. Chen, X., Acquisti, A. & Cranor, L. F. (2013). Privacy nudges for social media: an exploratory Facebook study. In: *Proceedings of the 22nd international conference on World Wide Web Companion* (WWW Companion) (pp. 763–770). Switzerland.

Wang, Y., Norcie, G., Komanduri, S., Acquisti, A., Leon, P. G., & Cranor, L. F. (2011). "I regretted the minute I pressed share": a qualitative study of regrets on Facebook. In: *Proceedings of SOUPS.*

Weirich, D., & Sasse, M. A. (2001). Pretty good persuasion: a first step towards effective password security in the real world. In: *Proceedings of the 2001 workshop on new security paradigms*, September (pp. 137–143). ACM.

Wiatrowski, M. D., Griswold, D. B., & Roberts, M. K. (1981). Social control theory and delinquency. *American Sociological Review, 46*(5), 525–541.

Wirth, C. B., Rifon, N. J., LaRose, R., & Lewis, M. L. (2007). Promoting teenage online safety with an i-safety intervention: enhancing self-efficacy and protective behaviors. In: *Proceedings of the Annual Meeting of the International Communication Association*. Montreal, QUE.

Witte, K. (1992). Putting the fear back into fear appeals: the extended parallel process model. *Communications Monographs, 59*(4), 329–349.

Woon, I. M. Y., Tan, G. W., & Low, R. T. (2005). A protection motivation theory approach to home wireless security. In: *Proceedings of the twenty-sixth international conference on information systems* (pp. 367–380). Las Vegas, NV.

Yeung, K. (2012). Nudge as fudge. *The Modern Law Review, 75*(1), 122–148.

Yoon, C., Hwang, J.-W., & Kim, R. (2012). Exploring factors that influence students' behaviors in information security. *Journal of Information Systems Education, 23*(4), 407–415.

Zhang, L., & McDowell, W. C. (2009). Am I really at risk? Determinants of online users' intentions to use strong passwords. *Journal of Internet Commerce, 8*(3–4), 180–197.

Zhou, T. & Sun, Y. (2009). An Empirical analysis of online consumer initial trust building based on ELM. In: *Proceedings of the international conference on networks security, wireless communications and trusted computing*, April, Vol. 2 (pp. 59–62).

7

Automatic Tracking of Behavior With Smartphones: Potential for Behavior Change Interventions

L. Piwek, A. Joinson

School of Management, University of Bath, Bath, United Kingdom

INTRODUCTION

In the following chapter, we review recent work on harnesses the sensors embedded in smartphones to understand individuals, and consider how such techniques might be used in behavior change interventions, and the ethical and practical issues such techniques might bring about.

Worldwide, mobile broadband users (who typically use smartphones) numbered approximately 370 million in 2009, 720 million in 2011, and will increase to 2 billion in 2015 (Portio Research, 2011). By 2025, a majority of the projected 8 billion people in the world will carry a smartphone (Portio Research, 2011). However, calling the device in our pockets a "smartphone" is slightly misleading. It could more properly be described as a digital camera, a photo book, a video recorder, a music player, a radio, a voice recorder, a GPS navigator, a handheld games console, a digital television, an Internet browser, an email manager, a weather forecaster, a watch, an alarm clock, a calendar, a calculator, and so much more (Miller, 2012). This ingenious device continuously records numerous variables every few seconds; from location and levels of movement to the number of calls we make, the number of letters we type when sending text messages, or the proximity to other similar devices that we pass on our way to work.

Alongside the growth in capabilities provided by smartphones, we have also seen them become an integral part of people's lives. For instance, Oulasvirta, Rattenbury, Ma, and Raita (2012) found that users check their

Behavior Change Research and Theory. http://dx.doi.org/10.1016/B978-0-12-802690-8.00005-0

phones 34 times a day, not necessarily because they really need to check them that many times, but because it has simply become a habit. A more recent estimate shows that people use their smartphones up to 85 times/day on average (Andrews, Ellis, Shaw, & Piwek, 2015). Such frequent, pervasive and multidimensional connectivity results in large quantities of "personal big data" being generated by users. This data represents the digital footprint that users leave behind every time they interact, or simply carry, a smartphone (Kosinski, Stillwell, & Graepel, 2013). The question we pose in this chapter is, "how can these capabilities be harnessed to support behavior change interventions?"

From the perspective of behavior change, such digital footprints may hold the key to decoding complex patterns of behavior, emotional status, user context, stress levels, and decision patterns made by users. Critically, for those interested in behavior change, such cues may also enable designers to tailor interventions to be both appropriate and timely. For instance, imagine if an exercise encouragement app could tailor the intervention based on their users' current location, activity level during the day, outside weather, calendar, and current psychological state. Or, perhaps a program aimed at sustainable travel could draw on a person's plans for the day, the weather forecast, local travel conditions, and the calories consumed and used the previous day. In either case, the opportunity for designing behavior change interventions that are tailored toward a specific individual massively improves.

In fact, a large number of studies already show that such inference is possible. When you take the smartphone from your pocket and activate the screen to simply check the time, you have just recorded a digital trace of this activity. Such a small trace already tells a simple story about you. In this split-second interaction with your smartphone, you are likely to record your detailed location with a timestamp, the current battery life of the phone, the mobile antennas it is connected to, the other Bluetooth devices or Wi-Fi hotspots that surround you, and a digital trace of every phone call you make. This data is collected automatically and some of it is immediately relayed back to the mobile providers network servers, while some is stored locally on your phone. Such automatic data upload is possible thanks to the complexity and sophistication of the sensors embedded within a smartphone, the processing power of microprocessors and the ever-expanding system of mobile telecommunication networks. On its own, such raw data has little value, but the modern advances in computer science and machine learning enable new insights in data extraction, synthesis, and analysis. Fig. 7.1 shows a summary of the typical sensors and components found in modern smartphones as well as the potential data that these sensors can track or collect.

The present review focuses on the potential for using smartphones as a tool for making inferences about user behavior and psychological state

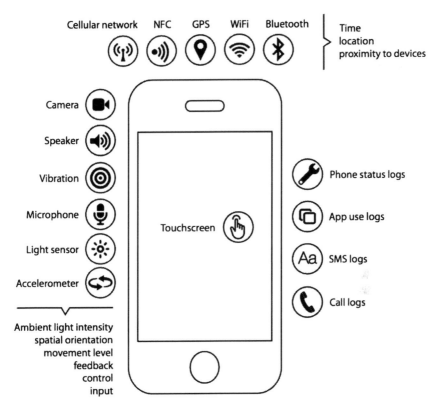

FIGURE 7.1   Illustration of the sensors and tracking features commonly found in modern smartphones with the potential data that these sensors can track or collect.

using the data passively collected by the device. By passive inference we mean that there is no input or user interaction or engagement with the smartphone, but rather the smartphone samples behavior passively, in the background, using onboard sensors and data collection services (Fig. 7.1). We focus on the potential for passively collected information because we believe that the power of sensor-enabled smartphone interventions comes from the ability to harness the in-built capabilities of a smartphone to collect data, combine it with behavioral science insights, and then produce an intervention at the level of user awareness. To our mind, there is little advantage to getting users to explicitly enter data into an "app" that could be inferred using the in-built technology of the phone.

To this end, we reviewed 45 relevant studies from a broad range of disciplines such as engineering, computer science, Bayesian statistics, machine learning, and cognitive psychology (Table 7.1). We used research literature databases, including Web of Knowledge and Google Scholar to search for keywords such as "automatic tracking smartphone,"

TABLE 7.1 Summary of All Reviewed Studies

References	Phone used	Sensors/data	Behavior predictions	Study length	Sample	Accuracy (%)
Onnela et al. (2007)	Any	Call logs	Social tie strength	4.5 months	7 million	NA
Eagle et al. (2009a)	Any	Call logs SMS logs Cell tower data	Dynamics of rural versus urban societies	48 months	1.5 million	NA
Song et al. (2010)	Any	Cell tower data	Location Mobility patterns	3 months	50,000	93
de Montjoye et al. (2013a)	Any	Cell tower data	Location Mobility patterns	15 months	1.5 million	95
Eagle et al. (2009b)	Nokia 6600	Call logs Bluetooth Cell tower data App use logs Phone status	Social communication patterns Type of social contact	9 months	94	95
Eagle and Pentland (2006)	Nokia 6600	Bluetooth Call logs	Location Activities	9 months	100	NA

Reference	Device	Data sources	Outcomes	Setting/Duration		
Do and Gatica-Perez (2014)	Nokia N95	Cell tower data App use logs Phone status GPS	Mobility patterns App use patterns Proximity in social interactions Location	17 months	71	NA
Min et al. (2013)	Android	App use logs Bluetooth SMS logs Call logs Call logs SMS logs	App use patterns Social communication patterns Type of social contact	6 months	40	90
Osmani et al. (2014)	HTC Desire HTC Desire S Samsung Nexus S HTC Nexus One	Bluetooth Wi-Fi	Proximity in social interactions Proximity in crowds	Lab	7	85
Morrison et al. (2009)	Any	Bluetooth GPS	Crowd density estimation Visitor flow maps	Natural	2,572	NA

(Continued)

TABLE 7.1 Summary of All Reviewed Studies (*cont.*)

References	Phone used	Sensors/data	Behavior predictions	Study length	Sample	Accuracy (%)
Versichele et al. (2012)	Any	Bluetooth	Crowd density estimation	Natural	80,828	NA
			Returning visitors			
			Visitor flow maps			
Shepard et al. (2011)	iPhone	App use logs	Future app use logs	3 months	25	NA
Pan et al. (2011)	iPhone	Bluetooth	Future app use logs/installation	5 months	55	45
		App use logs				
		Call logs				
Weppner and Lukowicz (2013)	Any	Bluetooth	Crowd density estimation	Natural	5,000	75
Kostakos (2008)	Any	Bluetooth	Public transport usage	1 month	1,000	NA
Hermersdorf et al. (2006)	Any	Bluetooth	Socially significant locations	10 days	1,299	NA
Rachuri et al. (2010)	Nokia Symbian	Microphone	Emotion identification	Lab/10 days	10	70
Lathia et al. (2013)	Android	Accelerometer	Speaker identification		18	90
		Bluetooth	Level of movement			
		GPS	Proximity in social interactions			
			Location			

			Emotion identification	Lab/2 weeks	1	77–87
Lee and Park (2012)	Android	Twitter client				
		SMS logs				
		Call logs				
		Phone status				
		GPS				
LiKamWa et al. (2013)	iPhone	SMS logs	Mood detection	2 months	32	93
		Call logs				
		Usage patterns				
		GPS				
Lu et al. (2012)	Android	Microphone	Stress detection indoor	Lab	14	76–81
			Stress detection outdoor			
Bogomolov et al. (2013)	Android	Call logs	Happiness	17 months	117	90
		SMS logs				
		Bluetooth				
Bogomolov et al. (2014)		SMS logs	Stress	6 months	117	72
MacKerron and Mourato (2013)	iPhone	Microphone	Happiness	6 months	21,947	NA
		GPS				
		Ambient light				

(Continued)

TABLE 7.1 Summary of All Reviewed Studies (*cont.*)

References	Phone used	Sensors/data	Behavior predictions	Study length	Sample	Accuracy (%)
Chittaranjan et al. (2013)	Nokia N95	Call logs SMS logs GPS Bluetooth App use logs	Personality traits	17 months	117	NA
de Montjoye et al. (2013b)	Android	Call logs SMS logs GPS	Personality traits	15 months	63	49–63
Yakoub et al. (2015)	Any	Call logs SMS logs SMS text	Personality traits	NA	NA	70
Seneviratne et al. (2014)	Android	App use logs App profiles	Religion Relationship status Spoken languages Parenting Country of origin	Lab	200	70–90

Burns et al. (2011)	Android	GPS Wi-FI Bluetooth Call logs SMS logs Accelerometer Ambient light	Depressive symptoms Mood Emotions Activities Environmental context Social context	2 months	8	NA
Grünerbl et al. (2012)	Android	GPS Accelerometer Call logs	Bipolar symptoms	2 months Lab	10	NA
Muaremi et al. (2014)	Android	Microphone	Bipolar symptoms	NA	NA	82
Khalil and Glal (2009)	Nokia N95 Nokia N97 Nokia 5800	Accelerometer	Walking	Lab	20	93
Wu et al. (2012)	iPhone	Accelerometer	Stair walking Jogging Level walking Sitting	Lab	16	52–94

(Continued)

TABLE 7.1 Summary of All Reviewed Studies (*cont.*)

References	Phone used	Sensors/data	Behavior predictions	Study length	Sample	Accuracy (%)
He and Li (2013)	Samsung Nexus S	Accelerometer	Jumping Running Walking Lying Sitting	Lab	NA	90–98
Gao et al. (2009)	HTC Touch	Accelerometer	Walking Running	Lab	NA	90–100
Schiel et al. (2010)	NA	Accelerometer	Walking	4 days	30	NA
Schiel et al. (2011)	Sony Ericksson	Accelerometer	Running Cycling Car driving	3 days	16	NA
Ketabdar and Lyra (2010)	iPhone	Accelerometer	Walking Running Resting No activity	Lab	4	92

Mattila et al. (2009)	NA	Accelerometer	Exercise intensity Walking Running	Lab	2	NA
Lee et al. (2011)	iPod	Accelerometer	Standing Sitting Lying Walking Running Falling	Lab	6	98
Stuckey et al. (2013)	Blackberry	Accelerometer	Exercise intensity	2 months	25	NA
Case et al. (2015)	iPhone Android Moves App HealthMate App	Accelerometer	Walking	NA	14	95
Arora et al. (2014)	LG Optimus S	Accelerometer	Parkinson's disease symptoms	Lab	20	97
Natale et al. (2012)	iPhone	Accelerometer	Sleep estimation	Lab	13	87
Chen et al. (2013)	Android iPhone	Microphone Ambient light Accelerometer	Sleep estimation	1 week	8	85

"smartphone behavior," "smartphone emotion," "smartphone personality," and "mHealth." Our criterion for study inclusion in this review was that the study used a primarily automatic (i.e., passive data collection) approach by using smartphones for behavioral tracking, although some studies had a mixed approach where they cross-referenced automatic tracking with self-reports for validation purposes. We break the review into four major sections that broadly cover the potential for automatic behavior detection with smartphones. We begin with section "Predicting User Activities and Social Interactions" where we describe studies that focus on the automatic prediction of user activities, context, and social interactions from smartphone tracking. This section includes small-scale studies as well as a big data project that used millions of data points to infer large-scale behavioral patterns. Section "Emotions, Mood, and Well-Being" focuses on the detection of psychological constructs such as emotions, mood, levels of stress, happiness, and general well-being. Section "Personality" describes studies that attempt to use smartphone activity to automatically detect the users' personality traits. Section "Health Behavior and Physical Activity" refers to a number of studies from the field of "mobile health" where smartphones have been tested to automatically detect or diagnose disorders or to detect various aspects of physical activity. We conclude with a discussion on the reliability and validity of the reviewed studies as well as issues related to the security and privacy of data collected by smartphones, and potential uses in behavior change interventions.

AUTOMATIC TRACKING OF BEHAVIOR

Predicting User Activities and Social Interactions

To what degree is human behavior predictable? In principle, humans are creatures of routines with regular and repeatable behaviors such as work activities, travel journeys, shopping habits, or the use of specific services. However, from the perspective of an outside observer who is unaware of our motivations and schedules, our activity pattern can easily appear to be random and unpredictable. In statistics, constructing predictive models of human behavior has long been a topic of interest in the area of recommendation systems (Quercia, Lathia, Calabrese, Di Lorenzo, & Crowcroft, 2010), context-aware services (Gu, Pung, & Zhang, 2005), and personalized and adaptive interfaces (Bridle & McCreath, 2006). Smartphones clearly emerged as a potentially convenient option for tracking and mining user behavior in daily life because they are usually placed in close proximity to the users, are utilized with high frequency, and contain many sensors that can record contextual and activity cues, including location, application usage, and calling behavior. This information can be considered as both the input and output of a prediction framework, in which the future values of some variables (e.g., next place) are predicted on the basis of the current context (current place, time, etc.).

Indeed, the application of smartphones for the prediction of human activity has already been demonstrated in a number of projects. In an already "classical" study, Onnela et al. (2007) examined 18 weeks of call records obtained from mobile operators involving 7 million users. This enormous data set allowed Onnela et al. (2007) to simultaneously study the local and global structure of a society-wide communication network. Whereas a single call between two individuals over an 18-week period did not carry much information, reciprocal calls of a long duration between two users served as a signature of some work-, family-, leisure-, or service-based relationship. The authors observed a coupling between the interaction strengths and the network's local structure, with the counterintuitive consequence that social networks are robust in the removal of the strong ties but fall apart after a phase transition if the weak ties are removed.

Eagle, de Montjoye, and Bettencourt (2009) used calls and SMS logs combined with cellular tower data to analyze the behavioral dynamics of rural and urban societies. The authors used 4 years of mobile phone data from 1.4 million subscribers within a small country to characterize attributes such as socioeconomic status and region. They showed that rural and urban communities differ dramatically, not only in terms of personal network topologies, but also in terms of inferred behavioral characteristics such as travel. In another landmark study, Song, Qu, Blumm, and Barabsi (2010) explored the predictability of human dynamics by studying the mobility patterns of anonymized mobile phone users. The authors used a 3 month–long record from mobile cell towers to capture the mobility patterns of 50,000 individuals chosen from 10 million anonymous mobile phone users. By measuring the entropy of each individual's trajectory, they found a 93% potential predictability in user mobility across the whole user base. Despite the significant differences in the travel patterns, Song et al. (2010) found a remarkable lack of variability in predictability, which is largely independent of the distance users cover on a regular basis. Their results indicate that when it comes to processes driven by human mobility, the development of accurate predictive models is a scientifically grounded possibility. At a more fundamental level, they also indicate that, despite our deep-rooted desire for change and spontaneity, our daily mobility is, in fact, characterized by a deep-rooted regularity. In a similar approach, de Montjoye, Hidalgo, Verleysen, and Blondel (2013) examined 15 months of human mobility data from mobile cell towers for 1.5 million individuals. The authors found that human mobility traces are unique. In a data set where the location of an individual is specified hourly, only four spatiotemporal points were enough to uniquely identify 95% of the individuals. de Montjoye, Quoidbach, Robic, and

Pentland (2013) developed a formula based on Bayesian modeling, showing that even coarse data sets provide little anonymity.

User context has also been explored in a more user-centered approach. Over a course of 9 months, Eagle, Pentland, and Lazer (2009) collected a set of longitudinal behavioral data from 94 participants using Nokia phones for tracking call logs, Bluetooth devices in proximity, cell tower IDs, application usage, and phone status. The authors compared the automatically collected data from mobile phones to standard self-report survey data. They found that the information from these two data sources was overlapping but distinct. They demonstrated that it is possible to accurately infer 95% of friendships based on the observational data alone, where friend dyads demonstrated distinctive temporal and spatial patterns in their physical proximity and calling patterns. In a corresponding study, Do and Gatica-Perez (2014) conducted a large-scale longitudinal smartphone investigation to predict the next location of a user, and which application he/she would use, based on the current context consisting of location, time, app usage, Bluetooth proximity, and communication logs. The authors experimented with data from 71 users over a 17-month period. In the case of predicting location, they found that Bluetooth proximity was an important contextual cue along with location and time. This finding again confirms the dependency between human mobility and social interactions.

Min, Wiese, Hong, and Zimmerman (2013) used call and text message logs collected from 40 users over a 6-month period to classify contacts according to life facet (i.e., family, work, social). They extracted various features such as communication intensity, regularity, medium, and temporal tendency, and they classified the relationships using machine learning techniques. Their results showed that life facets could be classified with up to 90% accuracy with the most relevant features being call duration, channel selection, and time of day of the communication. In a related study, Shepard, Rahmati, Tossell, Zhong, and Kortum (2011) examined how app usage is dependent on contextual variables such as location, time of day, and day of week; researchers have used these contextual variables to predict users' future app usage. Pan, Aharony, and Pentland (2011) demonstrated that smartphone usage logs (e.g., app installation logs, call logs, Bluetooth logs) together with externally collected information such as friendship and affiliation can be used to predict future app installation behavior of users.

A number of studies have examined the use of Bluetooth sensors in smartphones in the detection, classification, and prediction of group behavior and social interaction patterns. The core idea is that a reading of Bluetooth traces should enable one to determine whether a person is in the presence of (many) other people, or is alone. Osmani, Carreras, Matic, and Saar (2014) focused on proximity detection, specifically the ability of a system to recognize the colocation of two or more individuals and infer interpersonal distances. Osmani et al. developed Comm2Sense, a mobile platform to detect proximity among users with Wi-Fi hotspots and Wi-Fi receivers. They tested it on seven smartphones including four different models, namely HTC Desire, HTC Desire S, Samsung Nexus S, and HTC Nexus One with modified firmware to allow for adjustment of transmitting power. The results showed the ability of Comm2Sense to detect proximity with a median error of 0.5 m over a wide range of environments, both indoor and outdoor. These results were sufficient to detect social interaction distances and public space distances with an accuracy of 86 and 84%, respectively. Bluetooth signals have also been used to examine crowd density estimation in stadium-based sporting events (Morrison, Bell, & Chalmers, 2009; Versichele, Neutens, Delafontaine, & Van de Weghe, 2012; Weppner & Lukowicz, 2013), passenger journeys in public transportation (Kostakos, 2008), to infer relationships (Eagle & Pentland, 2006), and to identify socially significant locations (Hermersdorf et al., 2006).

Emotions, Mood, and Well-Being

Emotions can be described as a discrete and consistent response to internal or external events that have a particular significance for the organism (Nesse, 1990; Scherer, 2005). Emotions are brief in duration and consist of a coordinated set of responses, which may include verbal, physiological, behavioral, and neural mechanisms (Fox, 2008). Emotional classification, detection, and expression have been among the most intensively studied topics in cognitive psychology and neuroscience. While there is some controversy surrounding the classification of emotions (Frijda, 1986; Gray, 1982; Ortony & Turner, 1990), most theorists agree with Ekman and Friesen (1978) notion of "basic" emotions (i.e., joy, sadness, surprise, fear, anger, disgust, and contempt) that are a baseline for other expressions.

It has been well established that most emotions have clear behavioral characteristics. For example, anger has behavioral signals that are expressed via the voice (high level of pitch with its broad variability, fast tempo, high volume; Scherer, 1986), the face (typically lower brow, raised upper lid, tightened lid and lip; Ekman & Friesen, 2003), and body movement (high speed in the use of arm gestures; Pollick, Paterson, Bruderlin, & Sanford, 2001). Such well-studied "behavioral signatures" for emotional expressions provide a good baseline for detecting those expressions with smartphone sensors.

Rachuri et al. (2010) and Lathia et al. (2013) developed and tested EmotionSense, a passive monitoring smartphone app that uses a microphone to automatically capture emotive, behavioral, and social signals from smartphone owners. To achieve such automatic classification, researchers used machine learning techniques (to "teach" applications to detect a voice from silence) and data from the Emotional Prosody Speech and Transcripts library (Liberman, Davis, Grossman, Martey, & Bell, 2002) (a standard benchmark library in emotion and speech processing research). Using the library, the authors selected "five broad" emotions: anger, fear, happiness, neutrality, and sadness. They later evaluated the EmotionSense system through several microbenchmark tests and 18 participants who were asked to record their emotions in a daily diary. The results showed that EmotionSense achieved over 70% accuracy for broad emotion recognition. The studies by Rachuri et al. (2010) and Lathia et al. (2013) are among the most comprehensive illustrations of how emotions can be automatically detected by means of classifiers running locally on off-the-shelf mobile phones, and how speaking and interactions can be correlated with activity measures.

Lee and Park (2012) adopted a different approach to emotion detection; they gathered, analyzed and classified device usage patterns such as typing speed, maximum text length, erased text length, touch count, device shake count, luminance, location, and time. The authors also developed a social network service client integrated with Twitter for Android to collect self-reports of emotional context and to build a Bayesian Network classifier for emotion recognition. Lee and Park's (2012) system was then used to classify user emotions such as happiness, surprise, anger, disgust, sadness, fear, and neutrality with an accuracy ranging from 77% to 87%.

Another approach to emotion detection with smartphones is to infer the mood of the user based on contextual information. A mood is typically less specific, less intense, and less likely to be triggered by a particular stimulus or event compared to emotions, feelings, or affect (Beedie, Terry, & Lane, 2005). Moods are generally more internal (while emotions are more visible to others) and have either a positive or negative valence. In other words, people typically speak of being in a good mood or a bad mood. In this context, LiKamWa, Liu, Lane, and Zhong (2013) created a smartphone app MoodScope to collect and analyze phone usage history such as phone calls, email messages, SMS, application usage, web browsing histories, and location changes. Using this broad communication information, the authors statistically inferred a user's daily average mood with an initial accuracy of 66%, which gradually improved to an accuracy of 93% after a 2-month personalized training period.

MacKerron and Mourato (2013) developed a smartphone app *Mappiness* to study subjective well-being. Mappiness prompted participants at random moments, presenting a brief questionnaire while using GPS to determine geographical coordinates. The authors collected over 1 million responses from more than 20,000 participants. They combined GPS locations with objective spatial data, and estimated a model relating land cover to momentary subjective well-being using only the within-individual variation, while controlling for weather, daylight, activity, companionship, location type, time, day, and any response trend. They found that the study participants were significantly and substantially happier outdoors in all green or natural habitat types (i.e., "rural") than they were in urban environments.

Smartphones have also been used in the automatic detection of stress. Stress is a specific type of emotional response; it is the tension one experiences in response to a threat (Schneiderman, Ironson, & Siegal, 2005). When a person is able to cope successfully with stress, they experience eustress, the opposite of distress. Stress can therefore have positive or negative outcomes, depending on a person's coping ability and the severity of the stressor (Schneiderman et al., 2005). Stressors may be real or imagined; an event that produces stress for one individual may have no affect on another. There are a number of studies on modeling and detecting stress from voice amplitude, fundamental frequency, pitch, energy, spectral characteristics, and speaking rate (Hecker, 1968; Zhou, Hansen, & Kaiser, 2001; Fernandez & Picard, 2003). Lu et al. (2012) averaged those findings to develop *StressSense* in order to unobtrusively recognize stress from the human voice using the microphones in smartphones. By applying model adaptation, Lu et al. (2012) demonstrated that it is feasible to customize a universal stress model to different users and different scenarios using only a few new data observations and at a low computational overhead. *StressSense* achieved 81 and 76% accuracy for indoor and outdoor environments, respectively. In a separate study, Bogomolov, Lepri, Ferron, Pianesi, and Pentland (2014) proposed a system that recognized daily stress based on data obtained from 117 individuals by tracking call logs, SMS logs, Bluetooth proximity data, and self-reported information about daily stress, together with "background" indicators such as the weather factor and personality traits. They used a multifactorial statistical model and obtained an accuracy score of 72% for daily stress recognition. The same approach and data set has also been used by Bogomolov, Lepri, and Pianesi (2013) to track happiness; they used a machine learning model and obtained an accuracy score of 80% for daily happiness recognition.

Personality

The American Psychological Association defines personality as "individual differences in characteristic patterns of thinking, feeling and behaving" (APA, 2015). The most widespread and generally accepted model of personality is the five-factor model of personality (FFM; Goldberg, 1993). FFM was shown to include most known personality traits, and it is claimed to represent the basic structure underlying the variations in human behavior and preferences, providing a nomenclature and a conceptual framework that unifies much of the research findings in the psychology of individual differences (Lambiotte & Kosinski, 2015). FFM includes the following traits: extraversion, agreeableness, conscientiousness, emotional stability, and openness to experience.

Research has shown that personality correlates with many aspects of life, including job success (Judge, Higgins, Thoresen, & Barrick, 1999), attractiveness (Byrne, Griffitt, & Stefaniak, 1967), drug use (Roberts, Chernyshenko, Stark, & Goldberg, 2005), marital satisfaction (Kelly & Conley, 1987), and happiness (Ozer & Benet-Martinez, 2006). One of the major insights offered by big social data research relates to the predictability of individuals' personality from their web-based digital footprints (Kosinski et al., 2013). As smartphones generate a large quantity of such digital footprints, a question arises as to whether we can automatically infer the users' personality traits from their mobile activity too.

Chittaranjan, Blom, and Gatica-Perez (2013) conducted a large study investigating the relationship between automatically extracted behavioral characteristics derived from rich smartphone data and self-reported FFM personality traits. They sampled data from the smartphones of 117 Nokia N95 users collected over a continuous period of 17 months. The collected data included anonymized call logs, SMS logs, Bluetooth scans, calling profiles, and application usage. From the analysis, the authors showed that several aggregated features obtained from smartphone usage data could be indicators of the Big Five traits. For instance, extraverts, who are characterized by talkativeness and their outgoing nature, were more likely to receive calls and spend more time on them. Agreeableness among women was associated with an increase in the number of incoming calls, while agreeable men were found to communicate with a higher number of unique contacts through voice calls. On the other hand, conscientiousness was associated with higher usage of the Mail app, which could be used in a professional context, and with lower usage of the YouTube application, which is likely to be used for entertainment purposes. Based on these results, Chittaranjan et al. (2013) also showed that a machine learning framework based on a supervised learning method can effectively classify an unknown user's Big Five trait measures as belonging to either the higher half or lower half of the population.

In a similar study, de Montjoye et al. (2013b) used a custom Android app installed on the smartphones of 62 participants to capture mobile logs in order to predict personality traits. The carriers' logs included such information as number of calls, number of texts, active user behaviors (e.g., number of calls initiated, time to answer a text), location, regularity, (e.g., temporal calling routine, call, and text intertime), and diversity (call entropy, number of interactions by number of contacts ratio). de Montjoye et al. (2013b) were able to predict users' personality with a mean accuracy across traits of 42% better than random, reaching up to 61% accuracy on a three-class problem. Among the most useful features to predict personality traits were daily distance traveled (neuroticism), entropy of text contacts (extraversion and agreeableness), variance of call time (conscientiousness), and average texting time (openness).

Yakoub, Zein, Yasser, Adl, and Hassanien (2015) also derived smartphone usage logs and the language used in text messages, and used supervised machine learning methods and text mining techniques to find correlations between text messages and predications of users' personality traits. The results provided an overview of how text messages and smartphone logs represent user behavior; they chew over the user personality traits with an accuracy of up to 70%.

Seneviratne, Seneviratne, Mohapatra, and Mahanti (2014) collected data from over 200 smartphone users to investigate how user traits can be inferred by observing only a single snapshot of the installed apps. Using supervised learning methods and minimal external information, the authors showed that user traits such as religion, relationship status, spoken languages, countries of interest, and whether or not the user is a parent of small children, could be predicted with 70–90% precision.

Health Behavior and Physical Activity

Smartphones have long been used as a secondary tool for providing interventions in health care. Many of these interventions have been categorized as mobile health or "mHealth" which is broadly defined as a range of medical and public health practices supported by mobile devices (Tomlinson, Rotheram-Borus, Swartz, & Tsai, 2013). Applications of mHealth range from the use of mobile phones to improve point of service data collection (Tomlinson et al., 2009), care delivery (Rotheram-Borus et al., 2011), and patient communication (Siedner, Haberer, Bwana, Ware, & Bangsberg, 2012), to the use of alternative wireless devices for real-time medication monitoring and adherence support (Haberer et al., 2012). Within the mHealth category, automatic detection of behavior has also emerged as a way of diagnosing or monitoring symptoms, although its adoption has been relatively slow.

Burns et al. (2011) developed a smartphone app *Mobilyze!* in which machine learning models predicted patients' mood, emotions, cognitive states, activities, environmental context, and social context. Contextual data collected from smartphones included GPS, Wi-Fi, Bluetooth detection of other wireless devices (e.g., personal computers, some video game consoles), the accelerometer, ambient light, as well as time and activities of the phone's operating system (e.g., recent calls, active phone apps). The authors enrolled eight adults with major depressive symptoms in a pilot study to receive the app and complete clinical assessments for 8 weeks. Accuracy rates varied broadly between 60% and 91% in predicting categorical contextual states such as location, but for states rated on scales (e.g., mood), predictive capability was poor.

Grünerbl et al. (2012) extracted data on location, motion, and phone call patterns and showed that mildly depressed people exhibit an increased desire to talk, quantified by an increase in length and number of phone calls. Similarly, Muaremi, Gravenhorst, Grünerbl, Arnrich, and Tröster (2014) used phone call statistics, speaking parameters derived from phone conversations and emotional acoustic features to build and test user-specific classification models. The authors showed that the phone call length, the harmonics-to-noise ratio, the number of short turns and the variance of voice pitch fundamental frequency (F0) were the most important variables for predicting bipolar disorder episodes with an average score of 82%.

One of the most distinctive and commonly used sensors in smartphones is the accelerometer (Fig. 7.1). Accelerometers (and gyroscopes) have been used to enable screen rotation and image stabilization for the phone's camera as well as providing a motion-based gaming interface. Historically, the accelerometer has been used as a stand-alone device in sport sciences for detection of gait, posture, and levels of physical activity (Aminian et al., 1999; Mathie, Coster, Lovell, & Celler, 2004; Chen & Bassett, 2005; Ward, Evenson, Vaughn, Rodgers, & Troiano, 2005). It is therefore not surprising that the accelerometer quickly became a sensor that has been exploited for recognizing and quantifying physical activity with smartphones. Bort-Roig, Gilson, Puig-Ribera, Contreras, and Trost (2014) reviewed a large number of studies that used smartphone apps linked with an accelerometer or a gyroscope to measure:

- accuracy of classifying types of physical activity such as walking or jogging with various intensity levels (Khalil & Glal, 2009; Wu, Dasgupta, Ramirez, Peterson, & Norman, 2012; He & Li, 2013);
- accuracy of classifying physical activity using popular apps (Case, Burwick, Volpp, & Patel, 2015);
- accuracy of recognizing daily living activities such as sitting, lying, or standing, including the transitioning between these activities (He & Li, 2013);
- accuracy and application as a part of the intervention and prevention of obesity and diabetes (Gao, Kong, & Tan, 2009; Schiel et al., 2010; Schiel, Thomas, Kaps, & Bieber, 2011), remote monitoring (Ketabdar & Lyra, 2010), exercise programs (Mattila, Ding, Mattila, & Särelä, 2009), metabolic syndrome, and cardiovascular disease (Lee, Kim, Jee, & Yoo, 2011; Stuckey, Kiviniemi, & Petrella, 2013).

Bort-Roig et al. (2014) found that those studies that did report on measurement properties found average-to-excellent levels of accuracy for different physical activity-related behaviors. However, intervention effects reported in the extant literature are modest at best and Bort-Roig et al. (2014) concluded that future studies need to utilize randomized controlled trial research designs, larger sample sizes, and longer study periods to better explore the physical activity measurement and intervention capabilities of smartphones.

Arora et al. (2014) described a system for the high accuracy discrimination of the symptoms of Parkinson's disease using the accelerometers on smartphones. The authors objectively measured and quantified the severity of the key movement symptoms of the disease by extracting a range of different features based on the time and frequency-domain properties of the acceleration time series. They compared the underlying differences in the gait and postural sway accelerations between Parkinson's disease participants and controls. The authors demonstrated an average sensitivity of 98.5% and an average specificity of 97.5% in discriminating Parkinson's disease participants from controls. The smartphone accelerometer can also be used to automatically assess sleep/wake behavior such as sleep patterns, circadian rhythms, and sleep duration. Measuring sleep patterns and quality from movement is based on actigraphy which has been broadly described as an equally accurate, less expensive, and less cumbersome alternative to traditional polysomnography (Van De Water, Holmes, & Hurley, 2011). Several review papers have concluded that actigraphy can approximate sleep versus wake status over 24 h and have noted that it has been used to monitor insomnia, circadian sleep/wake disturbances, and periodic limb movement disorder (Ancoli-Israel et al., 2003). The use of motion-based sleep evaluation has also been tested with smartphones, although the evidence here is so far mixed. A study by (Natale et al., 2012) compared the accuracy of a medical-grade actigraph to iPhone accelerometer in sleep estimation. They showed that the agreement between iPhone and the actigraph was satisfactory for such sleep parameters as total sleep time, wake after sleep onset, and sleep efficiency. However, the authors stressed that future studies should necessarily use polysomnography as a "gold standard" reference point to fully evaluate the accuracy of smartphones in detecting sleep. Chen, Lin, and Chen (2013) developed an algorithm that could predict sleep duration by exploiting a collection of soft hints that tie sleep duration to various smartphone usage patterns such as the time and length of smartphone usage, recharge events, silence, darkness, and movement. The authors showed that their algorithms could infer sleep duration with an error margin of around 40 min using a completely automatic approach that could cope with the natural variation in users' sleep routines and environments.

Behar, Roebuck, Domingos, Gederi, and Clifford (2013) conducted a comprehensive review of the majority of available smartphone apps that make use of the phone accelerometer and sound recorder, and answers to various questionnaires, to provide feedback to the users on how well they were sleeping. The idea behind the Behar et al. (2013) review was to establish how useful such apps are for clinical application related to sleep problems (such as insomnia or sleep apnea). However, the authors found that with the exception of some of the sleep scales, none of the apps provided any scientifically validated feedback. Moreover, none of these apps used the combination of the different signals along with the patient information provided by the questionnaire.

DISCUSSION

People use smartphones continuously on a daily basis and a broad range of studies have shown that it is now possible to infer a wide range of behaviors and activities using different indicators of activity from mobile sensors. The key technologies in each described study are typically sophisticated mathematical algorithms: decision trees, Bayesian methods, fuzzy logic, anomaly analysis, or neural networks that can already be applied to turn "big data" of mobile digital footprints into predictions about behavior (Avci & Bosch, 2010). This includes:

- prediction of user location and patterns of mobility (i.e., where they are likely to go);
- detection of type and strength of social ties, patterns of social interaction, and proximity to other people indoor and in public spaces;
- identification of emotional state, stress, mood, and general well-being;
- prediction of personality traits and personal traits such as religion, relationship status, or country of origin;
- diagnosis of depressive and bipolar symptoms, and Parkinson's disease symptoms;
- recognition of physical activity type (e.g., walking, jumping, running) and intensity;
- sleep estimation.

Table 7.1 provides a summary of all the studies we reviewed with the type of sensors used, behaviors identified, as well as the estimated accuracy of the detection of specific behaviors, study length, and sample sizes used in the study. Those studies represent a broad range of promising computational, mathematical, and statistical approaches to automatically infer complex patterns of behaviors from mobile activity. However, there are clear limitations that emerge as a result of our review.

The core issue is the validity, reliability, and applicability of various solutions described in this review. For example, Gravenhorst et al. (2014) point out that the automatic analysis in the mental health context is still in its infancy. More controlled laboratory studies are required before the results can be adapted to real-life studies based on smartphone applications. This applies to a broader context; many of the studies we have described have only been validated with a very small sample size in a laboratory context (Table 7.1) and have not been validated for real-life deployment. Therefore, the existing solutions we reviewed should be treated as early prototypes rather than ready-to-deploy products.

Another serious challenge is posed by the fast pace of progress in the domain of mobile technology. The evolution of smartphones is very rapid and therefore a large number of the solutions we reviewed are likely to become obsolete, or technically difficult to replicate, within a very short time. This already applies to the studies by Eagle et al. (2009b), Rachuri et al. (2010), and Lathia et al. (2013) that used Nokia Symbian operating system (which has already become defunct technology). Even the most popular mobile operating systems such as Android or iOS platforms (as of 2015) evolve very rapidly and the new versions of the systems are not always compatible with older smartphone models. The worry is that many of the solutions for automatic detection developed in the reviewed studies may require revalidation from scratch if they are ever to be used with the new phone models in real-life deployment.

While the literature on automatic detection of behavior with smartphones is rich in the domain of computer science, there is a shortage of studies evaluating the application of smartphone detection in the social and behavioral sciences. This issue has already been raised by Miller (2012) regarding the use of smartphones in psychological research. However, it signals a wider problem of slow adoption of their deployment in behavior change, and wider social science studies. While computer scientists develop the toolboxes rapidly, they become "proof-of-concept showcases" without the real-world, practical application in the field of behavior change behavioral detection. The exception are large-scale studies that use complex network analysis models to understand social dynamics (Onnela et al., 2007; Song et al., 2010; de Montjoye et al., 2013b), but these studies use a large data approach rather than a person-centered approach which is a key domain in behavior change. Hypothetically speaking, this is one of the areas where interdisciplinary collaboration between computer scientists and social scientists is critical but this is not yet happening on a scale that would signal a revolution in practices.

In general, the majority of the studies use custom apps that need installation on mobile devices, making the use of these solutions a semiautomatic process; they only enable data gathering if there is willingness to install an app on a participant's phone. The only exception are studies using large-scale data sets derived from mobile providers such as cell tower information (Song et al., 2010; de Montjoye et al., 2013b) or call records (Onnela et al., 2007). Another issue is the presence of self-reports and experience sampling in many of the described studies. The use of self-report data is inevitable due to the need to provide a validation baseline for the creation of automatic tracking algorithms. Nevertheless, it poses a challenge, as the systems were typically not tested without such reference data so their validity for application in the real world may be somewhat limited.

These preliminary reviews are not overly optimistic; there are major issues with the reliability and validity of the developed apps. Regulatory bodies struggle to incorporate smartphone apps and tracking solutions into health care and behavior change, with reports indicating that there are loopholes and problems in validating the mechanisms, which may lead to acceptance of unreliable or even harmful apps. In general, health care is lagging behind the fast pace of smartphone developments with mHealth being more synonymous with using SMS as an intervention rather than the deployment and prescription of app-based interventions on smartphones. This leads to another large issue regarding automatic tracking—the *privacy* of individuals in the smartphone era.

Our review illustrates that digital traces of continuous mobile activity can reveal our identities (de Montjoye et al., 2013a), user contexts (Lathia et al., 2013), physical activities (Lane et al., 2011), emotions (Rachuri et al., 2010), and stress (Lu et al., 2012). Moreover, we can make highly accurate predictions about the personality traits of users by analyzing the linguistic content of text messages (Yakoub et al., 2015) or by examining the average time users spend calling or texting (Chittaranjan et al., 2013). It is clear that such "personal big data" generated by smartphones magnifies the uniqueness of individuals and brings challenges to privacy. If an individual's patterns of behavior and activity are unique enough, outside information can be used to link the data back to that individual. For instance, in one study, a medical database was successfully combined with an electoral roll to extract the health record of the governor of Massachusetts (Sweeney, 2002). In another, mobile phone data has been reidentified using users' top locations (Zang & Bolot, 2011). All together, the ubiquity of smartphone-generated data sets, the uniqueness of human traces and the information that can be inferred from them highlight the importance of understanding the privacy bounds. Behavior change interventions based around the data collected from smartphones must take user privacy and the security of data seriously if the promise of smartphone behavior change is to be fully realized.

References

Aminian, K., Robert, P., Buchser, E. E., Rutschmann, B., Hayoz, D., & Depairon, M. (1999). Physical activity monitoring based on accelerometry: validation and comparison with video observation. *Medical & Biological Engineering & Computing, 37*, 304–308.

Ancoli-Israel, S., Cole, R., Alessi, C., Chambers, M., Moorcroft, W., & Pollak, C. P. (2003). The role of actigraphy in the study of sleep and circadian rhythms. *Sleep, 26*, 342–392.

Andrews, S., Ellis, D. A., Shaw, H., & Piwek, L. (2015). Beyond self-report: what s going on (and off) with smartphones? *PLoS One, 10*(10), e0139004.

APA. (2015). Personality. Available from http://www.apa.org/topics/personality/

Arora, S., Venkataraman, V., Donohue, S., Biglan, K. M., Dorsey, E. R., & Little, M. A. (2014). High accuracy discrimination of Parkinson's disease participants from healthy controls using smartphones. In: *2014 IEEE International Conference on Acoustics, Speech and Signal Processing* (ICASSP) (pp. 3641–3644). IEEE.

Avci, A., & Bosch, S. (2010). Activity recognition using inertial sensing for healthcare, well-being and sports applications: a survey. In: *23rd international conference on Architecture of Computing Systems* (ARCS) (pp. 1–10).

Beedie, C., Terry, P., & Lane, A. (2005). Distinctions between emotion and mood. *Cognition & Emotion, 19*, 847–878.

Behar, J., Roebuck, A., Domingos, J. a. S., Gederi, E., & Clifford, G. D. (2013). A review of current sleep screening applications for smartphones. *Physiological Measurement, 34*, R29–R46.

Bogomolov, A., Lepri, B., Ferron, M., Pianesi, F., & Pentland, A. S. (2014). Daily stress recognition from mobile phone data, weather conditions and individual traits. In: *Proceedings of the ACM International Conference on Multimedia*, MM (pp. 477–486). New York, NY: ACM Press.

Bogomolov, A., Lepri, B., & Pianesi, F. (2013). Happiness recognition from mobile phone data. In: *2013 international conference on social computing* (pp. 790–795). IEEE.

Bort-Roig, J., Gilson, N. D., Puig-Ribera, A., Contreras, R. S., & Trost, S. G. (2014). Measuring and influencing physical activity with smartphone technology: a systematic review. *Sports Medicine, 44*, 671–686.

Bridle, R., & McCreath, E. (2006). Inducing shortcuts on a mobile phone interface. In: *Proceedings of the 11th international conference on Intelligent User Interfaces*, IUI (p. 327). New York, NY: ACM Press.

Burns, M. N., Begale, M., Duffecy, J., Gergle, D., Karr, C. J., Giangrande, E., & Mohr, D. C. (2011). Harnessing context sensing to develop a mobile intervention for depression. *Journal of Medical Internet Research, 13*, e55.

Byrne, D., Griffitt, W., & Stefaniak, D. (1967). Attraction and similarity of personality characteristics. *Journal of Personality and Social Psychology, 5*, 82–90.

Case, M., Burwick, H., Volpp, K., & Patel, M. (2015). Accuracy of smartphone applications and wearable devices for tracking physical activity data. *JAMA, 313*, 10–11.

Chen, K. Y., & Bassett, D. R. (2005). The technology of accelerometry-based activity monitors: current and future. *Medicine & Science in Sports & Exercise, 37*, S490–S500.

Chen, Z., Lin, M., & Chen, F. (2013). Unobtrusive sleep monitoring using smartphones. In: *Pervasive computing technologies for healthcare* (PervasiveHealth) (pp. 145–152).

Chittaranjan, G., Blom, J., & Gatica-Perez, D. (2013). Mining large-scale smartphone data for personality studies. In: Personal and ubiquitous computing, Vol. 17 (pp. 433–450).

de Montjoye, Y. A., Hidalgo, C. a., Verleysen, M., & Blondel, V. D. (2013a). Unique in the crowd: the privacy bounds of human mobility. *Scientific Reports, 3*, 1376.

de Montjoye, Y. A., Quoidbach, J., Robic, F., & Pentland, A. S. (2013b). Predicting personality using novel mobile phone-based metrics. In A. M. Greenberg, W. G. Kennedy, & N. D. Bos (Eds.), *Social computing, behavioral-cultural modeling and prediction* (pp. 48–55). Berlin, Heidelberg: Springer.

Do, T. M. T., & Gatica-Perez, D. (2014). Where and what: using smart-phones to predict next locations and applications in daily life. *Pervasive and Mobile Computing, 12*, 79–91.

Eagle, N., de Montjoye, Y. A., & Bettencourt, L. M. (2009a). Community computing: comparisons between rural and urban societies using mobile phone data. In: *2009 International Conference on Computational Science and Engineering* (pp. 144–150).

Eagle, N., & Pentland, A. S. (2006). Reality mining: sensing complex social systems. *Personal and Ubiquitous Computing, 10*, 255–268.

Eagle, N., Pentland, A. S., & Lazer, D. (2009b). Inferring friendship network structure by using mobile phone data. *Proceedings of the National Academy of Sciences, 106*, 15274–15278.

Ekman, P., & Friesen, W. (1978). *Facial action coding system: A technique for the measurement of facial movement*. Palo Alto, CA: Consulting Psychologists Press.

Ekman, P., & Friesen, W. (2003). *Unmasking the face: A guide to recognizing emotions from facial clues*. New York, NY: Malor Books.

Fernandez, R., & Picard, R. W. (2003). Modeling drivers speech under stress. *Speech Communication, 40*, 145–159.

Fox, E. (2008). *Emotion science: An integration of cognitive and neuroscientific approaches.* New York, NY: Palgrave Macmillan.

Frijda, N. H. (1986). *The emotions.* New York, NY: Cambridge University Press.

Gao, C., Kong, F., & Tan, J. (2009). HealthAware: tackling obesity with health aware smart phone systems. In: *2009 IEEE International Conference on Robotics and Biomimetics* (ROBIO) (pp. 1549–1554). IEEE.

Goldberg, L. R. (1993). The structure of phenotypic personality traits. *The American Psychologist, 48,* 26–34.

Gravenhorst, F., Muaremi, A., Bardram, J., Grünerbl, A., Mayora, O., Wurzer, G., Frost, M., Osmani, V., Arnrich, B., Lukowicz, P., & Tröster, G. (2014). Mobile phones as medical devices in mental disorder treatment: an overview. *Personal and Ubiquitous Computing, 19,* 335–353.

Gray, J. A. (1982). *The neuropsychology of anxiety.* Oxford: Oxford University Press.

Grünerbl, A., Oleksy, P., Bahle, G., Haring, C., Weppner, J., & Lukowicz, P. (2012). Towards smart phone based monitoring of bipolar disorder. In: *Proceedings of the Second ACM Workshop on Mobile Systems, Applications, and Services for HealthCare,* mHealthSys (p. 1). New York, NY: ACM Press.

Gu, T., Pung, H. K., & Zhang, D. Q. (2005). A service oriented middle-ware for building context aware services. *Journal of Network and Computer Applications, 28,* 1–18.

Haberer, J. E., Robbins, G. K., Ybarra, M., Monk, A., Ragland, K., Weiser, S. D., Johnson, M. O., & Bangsberg, D. R. (2012). Real-time electronic adherence monitoring is feasible, comparable to unannounced pill counts, and acceptable. *AIDS and Behavior, 16,* 375–382.

He, Y., & Li, Y. (2013). Physical activity recognition utilizing the built-in kinematic sensors of a smartphone. *International Journal of Distributed Sensor Networks, 2013,* 1–10.

Hecker, M. H. L. (1968). Manifestations of Task-Induced Stress in the Acoustic Speech Signal. *The Journal of the Acoustical Society of America, 44,* 993.

Hermersdorf, M., Nyholm, H., Salminen, J., Tirri, H., Perkio, J., Tuulos, V. (2006). Sensing in rich Bluetooth environments. In: *Proceedings of WSW'06 at SenSys'06.* New York, NY: ACM Press.

Judge, T. A., Higgins, C. A., Thoresen, C. J., & Barrick, M. R. (1999). The Big Five personality traits, general mental ability, and career success across the life span. *Personnel Psychology, 52,* 621–652.

Kelly, E. L., & Conley, J. J. (1987). Personality and compatibility: a prospective analysis of marital stability and marital satisfaction. *Journal of Personality and Social Psychology, 52,* 27–40.

Ketabdar, H., & Lyra, M. (2010). System and methodology for using mobile phones in live remote monitoring of physical activities. In: *2010 IEEE international symposium on technology and society* (pp. 350–356). IEEE.

Khalil, A., & Glal, S. (2009). StepUp: step counter mobile application to promote healthy lifestyle. In: *2009 international conference on the Current Trends in Information Technology* (CTIT) (pp. 1–5). IEEE.

Kosinski, M., Stillwell, D., & Graepel, T. (2013). Private traits and attributes are predictable from digital records of human behavior. *Proceedings of the National Academy of Sciences of the United States of America, 110,* 5802–5805.

Kostakos, V. (2008). Using Bluetooth to capture passenger trips on public transport buses. arXiv preprint arXiv:0806.0874, 1–13.

Lambiotte, B. R., & Kosinski, M. (2015). Tracking the digital footprints of personality. *Proceedings of the Institute of Electrical and Electronics Engineers, 102,* 1934–1939.

Lane, N., Mohammod, M., Lin, M., Yang, X., Lu, H., Ali, S., Doryab, A., Berke, E., Choudhury, T., & Campbell, A. (2011). BeWell: a smartphone application to monitor, model and promote wellbeing. In: *Proceedings of the fifth International ICST conference on pervasive computing technologies for healthcare* (p. 8). IEEE.

Lathia, N., Pejovic, V., Rachuri, K. K., Mascolo, C., Musolesi, M., & Rentfrow, P. J. (2013). Smartphones for large-scale behavior change interventions. *IEEE Pervasive Computing*, *12*, 66–73.

Lee, M. H., Kim, J., Jee, S. H., & Yoo, S. K. (2011). Integrated solution for physical activity monitoring based on mobile phone and PC. *Healthcare Informatics Research*, *17*, 76.

Lee, H., & Park, I. P. (2012). Towards unobtrusive emotion recognition for affective social communication. In: *2012 IEEE Consumer Communications and Networking Conference* (CCNC) (pp. 260–264).

Liberman, M., Davis, K., Grossman, M., Martey, N., & Bell, J. (2002). *Emotional prosody speech and transcripts LDC2002S28. DVD*. Philadelphia, PA: Linguistic Data Consortium.

LiKamWa, R., Liu, Y., Lane, N. D., & Zhong, L. (2013). MoodScope: Building a mood sensor from smartphone usage patterns. In *Proceeding of the 11th annual international conference on Mobile systems, applications, and services*, MobiSys (p. 389). New York, NY: ACM Press.

Lu, H., Frauendorfer, D., Rabbi, M., Mast, M. S., Chittaranjan, G. T., Campbell, A. T., Gatica-Perez, D., & Choudhury, T. (2012). StressSense: detecting stress in unconstrained acoustic environments using smartphones. In: *Proceedings of the 2012 ACM Conference on Ubiquitous Computing*, UbiComp (p. 351). New York, NY: ACM Press.

MacKerron, G., & Mourato, S. (2013). Happiness is greater in natural environments. *Global Environmental Change*, *23*, 992–1000.

Mathie, M. J., Coster, A. C. F., Lovell, N. H., & Celler, B. G. (2004). Accelerometry: providing an integrated, practical method for long-term, ambulatory monitoring of human movement. *Physiological Measurement*, *25*, R1–R20.

Mattila, J., Ding, H., Mattila, E., & Särelä, A. (2009). Mobile tools for home-based cardiac rehabilitation based on heart rate and movement activity analysis. In: *Proceedings of the 31st Annual International Conference of the IEEE Engineering in Medicine and Biology Society: Engineering the Future of Biomedicine*, EMBC (pp. 6448–6452).

Miller, G. (2012). The smartphone psychology manifesto. *Perspectives on Psychological Science*, *7*, 221–237.

Min, J. k., Wiese, J., Hong, J. I., & Zimmerman, J. (2013). Mining smartphone data to classify life-facets of social relationships. In: *Proceedings of the 2013 conference on Computer Supported Cooperative Work*, CSCW (p. 285). New York, NY: ACM Press.

Morrison, A., Bell, M., & Chalmers, M. (2009). Visualisation of Spectator Activity at Stadium Events. In: *2009 13th International Conference Information Visualisation* (pp. 219–226). IEEE.

Muaremi, A., Gravenhorst, F., Grünerbl, A., Arnrich, B., & Tröster, G. (2014). Assessing bipolar episodes using speech cues derived from phone calls. In P. Cipresso, G. Lopez, A Matic (Eds.), *Pervasive computing paradigms for mental health: 4th International Symposium, Mind-Care 2014, Revised Selected Papers* (pp. 103–114). New York: Springer.

Natale, V., Drejak, M., Erbacci, A., Tonetti, L., Fabbri, M., & Martoni, M. (2012). Monitoring sleep with a smartphone accelerometer. *Sleep and Biological Rhythms*, *10*, 287–292.

Nesse, R. M. (1990). Evolutionary explanations of emotions. *Human Nature*, *1*, 261–289.

Onnela, J. P., Saramaki, J., Hyvonen, J., Szabo, G., Lazer, D., Kaski, K., Kertesz, J., & Barabasi, A. L. (2007). Structure and tie strengths in mobile communication networks. *Proceedings of the National Academy of Sciences*, *104*, 7332–7336.

Ortony, A., & Turner, T. J. (1990). What's basic about basic emotions? *Psychological Review*, *97*, 315–331.

Osmani, V., Carreras, I., Matic, A., & Saar, P. (2014). An analysis of distance estimation to detect proximity in social interactions. *Journal of Ambient Intelligence and Humanized Computing*, *5*, 297–306.

Oulasvirta, A., Rattenbury, T., Ma, L., & Raita, E. (2012). Habits make smartphone use more pervasive. *Personal and Ubiquitous Computing*, *16*, 105–114.

Ozer, D. J., & Benet-Martinez, V. (2006). Personality and the prediction of consequential outcomes. *Annual Review of Psychology*, *57*, 401–421.

Pan, W., Aharony, N., & Pentland, A. (2011). Composite social network for predicting mobile apps installation. In: *Proceedings of the 25th AAAI Conference on Artificial Intelligence* (pp. 821–827).

Pollick, F. E., Paterson, H. M., Bruderlin, A., & Sanford, A. J. (2001). Perceiving affect from arm movement. *Cognition, 82,* B51–B61.

Portio Research. (2011). Portio Research Mobile Factbook 2011. Chippenham, UK. Available from http://www.telecomsmarketresearch.com/Free_Telecoms_Market_Research/Portio_Research_Mobile_Factbook_2011_DownloadQ.pdf

Quercia, D., Lathia, N., Calabrese, F., Di Lorenzo, G., & Crowcroft, J. (2010). Recommending social events from mobile phone location data. In: *2010 IEEE International Conference on Data Mining* (pp. 971–976). IEEE.

Rachuri, K. K., Musolesi, M., Mascolo, C., Rentfrow, P. J., Longworth, C., & Aucinas, A. (2010). EmotionSense: a mobile phones based adaptive platform for experimental social psychology research. In: *Proceedings of the 12th ACM international conference on Ubiquitous Computing*, Ubicomp (p. 281). New York, NY: ACM Press.

Roberts, B. W., Chernyshenko, O. S., Stark, S., & Goldberg, L. R. (2005). The structure of conscientiousness: an empirical investigation based on seven major personality questionnaires. *Personnel Psychology, 58,* 103–139.

Rotheram-Borus, M. J., le Roux, I. M., Tomlinson, M., Mbewu, N., Comulada, W. S., le Roux, K., Stewart, J., O'Connor, M. J., Hartley, M., Desmond, K., Greco, E., Worthman, C. M., Idemundia, F., & Swendeman, D. (2011). Philani Plus (+): a mentor mother community health worker home visiting program to improve maternal and infants outcomes. *Prevention Science, 12,* 372–388.

Scherer, K. R. (1986). Vocal affect expression: a review and a model for future research. *Psychological Bulletin, 99,* 143–165.

Scherer, K. R. (2005). What are emotions? And how can they be measured? *Social Science Information, 44,* 695–729.

Schiel, R., Kaps, A., Bieber, G., Kramer, G., Seebach, H., & Hoffmeyer, A. (2010). Identification of determinants for weight reduction in overweight and obese children and adolescents. *Journal of Telemedicine and Telecare, 16,* 368–373.

Schiel, R., Thomas, A., Kaps, A., & Bieber, G. (2011). An innovative telemedical support system to measure physical activity in children and adolescents with type 1 diabetes mellitus. *Experimental and Clinical Endocrinology, 119,* 565–568.

Schneiderman, N., Ironson, G., & Siegel, S. D. (2005). Stress and health: psychological, behavioral, and biological determinants. *Annual Review of Clinical Psychology, 1,* 607–628.

Seneviratne, S., Seneviratne, A., Mohapatra, P., & Mahanti, A. (2014). Predicting user traits from a snapshot of apps installed on a smartphone. *ACM SIGMOBILE Mobile Computing and Communications Review, 18,* 1–8.

Shepard, C., Rahmati, A., Tossell, C., Zhong, L., & Kortum, P. (2011). LiveLab: measuring wireless networks and smartphone users in the field. *ACM SIGMETRICS Performance Evaluation Review, 38,* 15–20.

Siedner, M. J., Haberer, J. E., Bwana, M., Ware, N. C., & Bangsberg, D. R. (2012). High acceptability for cell phone text messages to improve communication of laboratory results with HIV-infected patients in rural Uganda: a cross-sectional survey study. *BMC Medical Informatics and Decision Making, 12,* 56.

Song, C., Qu, Z., Blumm, N., & Barabasi, A. L. (2010). Limits of predictability in human mobility. *Science, 327,* 1018–1021.

Stuckey, M. I., Kiviniemi, A. M., & Petrella, R. J. (2013). Diabetes and technology for increased activity study: the effects of exercise and technology on heart rate variability and metabolic syndrome risk factors. *Frontiers in Endocrinology, 4,* 121.

Sweeney, L. (2002). k-Anonymity: a model for protecting privacy. *International Journal of Uncertainty Fuzziness and Knowledge Based Systems, 10,* 557–570.

Tomlinson, M., Rotheram-Borus, M. J., Swartz, L., & Tsai, A. C. (2013). Scaling up mHealth: where is the evidence? *PLoS Medicine, 10,* 1–5.

Tomlinson, M., Solomon, W., Singh, Y., Doherty, T., Chopra, M., Ijumba, P., Tsai, A. C., & Jackson, D. (2009). The use of mobile phones as a data collection tool: a report from a household survey in South Africa. *BMC Medical Informatics and Decision Making, 9,* 51.

Van De Water, A. T. M., Holmes, A., & Hurley, D. A. (2011). Objective measurements of sleep for non-laboratory settings as alternatives to polysomnography—a systematic review. *Journal of Sleep Research, 20,* 183–200.

Versichele, M., Neutens, T., Delafontaine, M., & Van de Weghe, N. (2012). The use of Bluetooth for analysing spatiotemporal dynamics of human movement at mass events: a case study of the Ghent Festivities. *Applied Geography, 32,* 208–220.

Ward, D. S., Evenson, K. R., Vaughn, A., Rodgers, A. B., & Troiano, R. P. (2005). Accelerometer use in physical activity: best practices and research recommendations. In: Medicine and science in sports and exercise, Vol. 37 (pp. S582–S588).

Weppner, J., & Lukowicz, P. (2013). Bluetooth based collaborative crowd density estimation with mobile phones. In: *2013 IEEE International Conference on Pervasive Computing and Communications* (Per-Com), March (pp. 193–200). IEEE.

Wu, W., Dasgupta, S., Ramirez, E. E., Peterson, C., & Norman, G. J. (2012). Classification accuracies of physical activities using smartphone motion sensors. *Journal of Medical Internet Research, 14,* e130.

Yakoub, F., Zein, M., Yasser, K., Adl, A., & Hassanien, A. E. (2015). Predicting personality traits and social context based on mining the smartphones SMS data. In: *Intelligent Data Analysis and Applications, Proceedings of the Second Euro-China Conference on Intelligent Data Analysis and Applications,* ECC 2015 (pp. 511–521). Springer International Publishing.

Zang, H., & Bolot, J. (2011). Anonymization of location data does not work. In: *Proceedings of the 17th annual international conference on Mobile Computing and Networking,* MobiCom (p. 145) New York, NY: ACM Press.

Zhou, G., Hansen, J., & Kaiser, J. (2001). Nonlinear feature based classification of speech under stress. *IEEE Transactions on Speech and Audio Processing, 9,* 201–216.

Intervening Online: Evaluating Methods, Assessing Outcomes, and Signposting Future Directions

E. Sillence*, L. Little*, A. Fielden**

*PaCT Lab, Department of Psychology, Faculty of Health and Life Sciences, Northumbria University, Newcastle, United Kingdom; **School of Psychology, Newcastle University, Newcastle upon Tyne, United Kingdom

INTRODUCTION

Successful behavior change interventions can be seen as the culmination of a process of good planning, careful implementation, and thoughtful appropriate evaluation all underpinned by relevant theory and evidence based behavior change techniques. In fact a great deal of the work around evaluation actually takes place during the design and planning phase of any study. Here questions associated with the target population and the target behavior are discussed and decisions about what to measure, how to measure, and for how long are finalized. In this chapter we discuss some of these issues and highlight how decisions around evaluation are not always straightforward sometimes raising a new set of questions altogether. The intention of the chapter is to provoke thought around key evaluation issues and to look forward to new ways of evaluating behavior change interventions within a technological context. To these ends the chapter is organized as follows: First, we introduce some of the key questions researchers are faced with when deciding upon their evaluation strategy; we point out common practice from a predominantly psychological perspective but highlight issues of contention or variation

Behavior Change Research and Theory. http://dx.doi.org/10.1016/B978-0-12-802690-8.00008-6

among disciplines. We then pick up on a number of these issues and high-light them through two case studies in which we discuss how and why decisions were made, their implications and as such evaluate the eval-uation process. Finally, we spend some time examining the future with respect to evaluation and highlight a number of areas in which technology has a role to play in shaping the nature of such evaluations.

Evaluating Behavior Change Interventions

Recently, a number of authors have written about the importance of evaluating both the outcome of the intervention and the process itself (Abraham, 2015; Craig et al., 2008). In a later section, we have described these different approaches and have summarized the steps involved in Table 8.1.

Evaluations of the outcome primarily focus on whether or not the interven-tion "worked." We might ask questions about whether the target behav-ior increased or decreased across the duration of the intervention, for example, did handwashing rates increase or did the number of cigarettes smoked decrease. If a change in behavior was observed we want to be able to say something meaningful about the efficacy of the intervention. Typically psychologists, along with many other professions, compare the difference between pre- and postintervention scores and seek to reject the null hypothesis and confirm a statistically significant difference between

TABLE 8.1   Summary of Steps Involved in Evaluating Interventions

Measuring outcomes	Measuring process
1. Decide on target behavior 2. Consider the desired behavior change (increase, reduction, uptake, or cessation) 3. Decide on what constitutes an effect. Use statistically significant difference between the two sets of data alongside an estimate of the effect size or alternative, for example, the smallest important effect between pre- and postintervention scores and minimum magnitude based inference 4. Decide on timeline for measurement. In addition to baseline and postintervention measurement, consider appropriate timeline for follow up data collection (e.g., 1 week, 1 month, 6 months)	1. Refer back to study plan 2. Identify variables 3. Evaluate how the behavior change technique was implemented and measured 4. Use qualitative data collection alongside outcome measurement to understand the experience of the process itself and where appropriate how the resource was used and understood by the target users 5. Consider any moderating variables, for example, gender, age, socioeconomic status, technology experience 6. Consider data collection techniques, is self-report acceptable, are there alternatives? How can data be collected objectively and how can technology automate data collection?

the two sets of data alongside an estimate of the effect size. Another approach, used in sport interventions, for example, asks questions about the smallest important effect the researcher wishes to see between the pre and postintervention scores and then uses this value in another form of analysis called minimum magnitude based inference (Barnes, Hopkins, McGuigan, & Kilding, 2015). Clinical significance may also be a more meaningful way of defining change in health based behavior change studies (Jacobson & Truax, 1991). Finally, when examining the outcome of the intervention we might want to evaluate the longevity of intervention effect. During the planning stages a timeline for evaluation will have been formulated. Researchers will have decided when to measure the behavior either at a single point in time or whether to include follow-ups and if so how many and when. Sometimes these decisions are based around practical considerations or may be made in relation to anticipated dropout rates. Typically, studies measure the behavior (or at least intentions) immediately postintervention and then again one or two weeks later. Some researchers have argued for longer timelines to assess the real outcome of the intervention (e.g., in smoking cessation studies). Within a wholly online intervention this should be relatively easy to achieve. Automated prompts can be sent reminding participants to complete follow up measures and this has been successfully used in a number of studies (Sillence, Harris, & Briggs, 2015) although reminders do not guarantee participation and unfortunately, evaluation of outcome of a single point intervention at follow-up often indicates disappointing results with little long-term behavior maintenance.

In evaluating the process we might focus attention on the intervention itself and explore its mechanisms. Specifying the components of behavior change interventions should of course have occurred during the planning section of the project (Michie, Fixsen, Grimshaw, & Eccles, 2009). It should be possible to identify how and why the intervention worked. Here we might refer back to the planning stage to see how the theories and mechanisms of behavior change relate to the behavior in context. We might reflect on the variables in the study, what was manipulated and what was controlled for–was there an adequate control group present? This is important in experimental designs but is typically less so in Randomized Controlled Trials (RCTs) which would typically include a range of potential causal factors. How well were the behavior change techniques implemented and measured? Was more than one behavior change technique employed (Webb, Joseph, Yardley, & Michie, 2010), and is it possible to evaluate the effects of each separately?

In less tightly controlled, more naturalistic settings for interventions the complexity of evaluation might seem a larger task (see, e.g., Maher et al., 2014's review of social network site based interventions). In such studies is it possible to control for other factors? Is this feasible or even desirable to tease apart the different effects? In both RCT style interventions, experimental designs and those conducted within more naturally occurring settings naturalistic settings including a qualitative element to the evaluation would help researchers assess the process itself more clearly (Campbell et al., 2007). In some fields, for example, education, researchers are interested in measuring the process itself. How did the teachers, for instance, make use of the resource provided and did the target group find taking part useful and interesting in and of itself?

We might also want to consider any moderating variables. Here the evaluation centers around the question: Did the intervention work for everyone in the target group and if so to the same degree? If the answer is no then the evaluation needs to think about whether this was a predictable or even intentional aspect of the intervention, or whether it reflects some issue relating to the way in which data was collected, the influence of the recruitment strategy (Smit, Hoving, Cox, & de Vries, 2012), or the setting of the study.

Data collection impacts upon the process itself. Behavior change interventions typically rely upon self-report measures. Participants may be asked to complete self-reports of cigarettes smoked, fruit and vegetables consumed, security practices followed, and electrical devices switched off. Some self-report measures, for example, number of cigarettes smoked, have shown to be accurate in comparison to objective data (McDonald, Perkins, & Walker, 2005) but others may suffer from biases or simply poor grasp of the behavior or the measurement scale itself—understanding a portion of fruit or vegetables or having a real sense of how long you spend online or even what constitutes time online? Although of course issues surrounding the accuracy of self-report will exist at both pre- and postintervention and across experimental and control groups and thus do not prevent the identification of a change in behavior. Finally we might want to reflect on the use of technology across the intervention and specifically in relation to evaluation. Here we might question whether the use of technology within behavior change interventions really is cost effective, and time sensitive (Griffiths, Lindenmeyer, Powell, Lowe, & Thorogood, 2006), whether it is appropriate in order to reach the target population and consider how it could be better used going forward (see Chapter 7 for suggestions of how technology is enhancing the objective collection and measurement of behavioral data).

EVALUATION CASE STUDIES

As a research team working with different target groups we recognize "a one size fits all" approach cannot be adopted when trying to change behavior (Noar, Benac, & Harris, 2007). As we highlighted at the beginning of this chapter key concepts for evaluation need to be discussed and considered during the very earliest planning stages of the research. During the design of the following two case studies decisions around the "target group" for the behavior change were considered vital in terms of signposting subsequent decisions about behavior change theories and techniques. In case study 1, for example, getting teenagers (the target group) to feel involved in the process was an important factor in the decision to use implementation intentions (a technique we felt was readily understandable and flexible enough to allow participants to generate their own plans). In the following two case studies, we present a brief description of the project and then follow-up with a discussion of the key evaluation issues.

Case Study 1: Implementation Intentions and Saving Energy

Background

The *Taking on the Teenagers: Using Adolescent Energy to Reduce Energy Use Project* (Grant EP/I002251/1) targeted adolescents with energy-saving interventions. The study (see Bell, Toth, Little, & Smith, 2015; Toth, Bell, Avramides, Rulton, & Little, 2014, for more detail) aimed to reduce the energy use of teenagers over a prescribed period of time. The entire intervention was carried out online and made use of implementation intentions as the behavior change technique.

The Intervention

The aim of the intervention was to reduce energy consumption in teenagers. The intervention itself was based on implementation intentions (Gollwitzer, 1999). These are precise behavioral plans, identifying the specific behaviors that an individual will perform in specified critical situations (Armitage, 2006; Gollwitzer & Sheeran, 2006). Implementation intentions take the form of an "if–then" plan, wherein individuals create a link within their memory between a critical situation (if…) and a behavioral response (… then …) that fits with their overarching behavior change goal (Armitage, 2006; Gollwitzer & Sheeran, 2006). It has been argued that the key to the success of implementation intentions is based on the specificity of the plans developed. Detailing the "when, where, and how" ensures an individual intends to achieve his or her goal (Gollwitzer & Sheeran, 2006, p. 82).

The Study

The entire study was conducted online. 180 adolescents, aged 13–15 years, were allocated to either the intervention or control condition. All participants recorded their current energy saving behavior and then the intervention group were asked to read through 4 "IF" statements relating to common scenarios, for example, "If I leave a room ..." they were then required to complete the sentences with details of a behavior (the THEN part) they could perform in that scenario to save electrical energy. They could choose from a number of prepared THEN statements or formulate their own, for example, "If I leave the room I will turn off the light."

Evaluating the Study

Participants were asked to self-report their energy saving behavior immediately after the intervention, 5 days later and 6 weeks poststudy on a 5-point Likert-type scale (1 = never, 2 = rarely, 3 = sometimes, 4 = often, and 5 = all the time). The researchers found a significant increase in adolescent's self-reported energy saving behavior.

Discussion

In terms of evaluating the outcome the intervention appeared to work. Overall, participants reported an increase in energy saving behavior. A 6-week follow-up is a useful and practical follow up period but sustained behavior change would need to be examined 3 or 6 months later. In terms of the size of the change what does it mean? The study indicated that on average people moved from an energy saving frequency score of 2.73–3.05 and back to 3.00 over the data collection period (recall that a score of 2 = rarely, 3 = sometimes, and a score of 4 = often). These results are statistically significant but still represent answers that equate to "sometimes" in relation to the frequency of the target behavior. It might be interesting here to consider what the minimum desired change would be and how this might be measured and the value that might be extracted from more observed and objective measures of energy saving, for example, the number of kilowatt per hour saved or equating these savings to monetary value. Furthermore, the introduction of smart thermostats presents opportunities for automatic, objective data collection counteracting the common problem of self-report data within this type of research.

In terms of evaluating the process itself the mechanism of change appeared to be successful with those developing implementation intentions saving energy. We do not know whether crafting your own versus picking predesigned implementation, intentions made a difference and that would be something to investigate further. In trying to understand both these issues a qualitative approach as part of the evaluation process would have proved useful albeit difficult to arrange. Interestingly participants were invited to complete an open ended text box at each time point asking "how are you finding saving energy at home?" although very few responses were recorded.

In terms of moderating effects the researchers noted that some adolescents were more affected by the intervention than others. Having measured participants' readiness to change (Prochaska & DiClemente, 1983) they concluded that adolescents who already actively engaged in energy saving (as identified by their readiness to change prior to the intervention) reported a significant increase in energy-saving behaviors as a consequence of participation in the intervention, whereas those who were not already saving energy did not. Participants that were already saving energy continued to save *more* energy as a result of taking part in the intervention unlike those who were not already saving energy. Thus the intervention was most beneficial for people already performing the desired behavior. Interestingly not all studies have found this effect with John, Yudkin, Neil, and Ziebland (2003) noting that a participant's stage of change may have little bearing on their success with the target behavior. Although the distribution of people to stages was very different. Finally, the setting itself is worth evaluating in relation to the overall process. Asking participants to complete the study in the classroom environment might have heightened their social desirability bias or reduced their sense of anonymity—but permission wise was vital (part of the issue of running studies with under 18 year olds).

Finally, how should we evaluate the role of the technology in this behavior change intervention? The main role of the technology in this case study was to provide a cost effective and quick way of delivering an intervention to a relatively large number of participants. The automatic data collection was straightforward and easy for participants to engage with and speeded up the process of data management and analysis for the researchers. Going forward it is possible to envisage a system that links objective energy saving behavior to an online recording service, feasibly through the use of real time energy monitors.

Case Study 2: Self-Affirmation and Increased Fruit and Vegetable Consumption

Background

This study was concerned with increasing fruit and vegetable consumption among groups at high risk of low intake—namely students and mothers with low social economic status (see Fielden, Sillence, Little, & Harris, 2016, for more details). The entire intervention was carried out online and made use of self-affirmation as the behavior change technique (see the chapter by Schüz et al. in this book for more information on selfaffirmation studies).

The Intervention

The aim of the intervention was to increase fruit and vegetable consumption. The intervention itself was based on self-affirmation—a procedure in which people reflect on cherished values or attributes and which has been shown to have the potential to promote more open minded, balanced appraisal of messages in target audiences (McQueen & Klein, 2006,). Self-affirmation is most commonly achieved by asking participants to complete scales or write about a cherished value, for example, kindness.

The Study

The entire study was conducted online, 85 participants including 26 low SES mothers were recruited to the study. A baseline measure of fruit and vegetable consumption was collected and then participants were either assigned to the self-affirmation condition or a control task in which they completed a personal opinions questionnaire. All participants then viewed online health information about the benefits of fruit and vegetables specifically tailored to their group membership (mothers vs. students).

Evaluating the Study

Self-reported fruit and vegetable consumption was recorded on a daily basis for seven days using an online diary. Participants in the self-affirmed group consumed significantly more portions of fruit and vegetables than those in the control group.

Discussion

The intervention appeared to be successful with participants in the experimental group consuming more fruit and vegetables than those in the control group. The intervention was only assessed for a 7-day period following the intervention so it is difficult to get a sense of whether the intervention has a lasting effect. In terms of the size of the behavior change the authors report that relative to the condition group self-affirmed participants reported consuming eight more portions of fruit and vegetables over the week, which equates to more than one extra portion a day. Again, when we start to think about the minimum effective/desired change, than its right to note that self-affirmed participants in this study still did not meet the "5-a-day" target. However, the authors provide some information about the relevance of even a modest increase, such as the one observed. "Research indicates that an increase in just one portion a day can lead to a 4% reduction in the risk for CHD and a 6% reduction in the risk for stroke" (Joshipura et al., 2001). So this study documents a clinically significant behavior change.

In terms of evaluating the process itself the mechanism of change appeared to be successful with those in the self-affirmed condition consuming an increased amount of fruit and vegetables over the course of the week. The authors performed a manipulation check to ensure that those in the self-affirmation group had indeed affirmed. In trying to unpack why the intervention worked, recent work on self-affirmation has explored the idea that anticipated regret and intentions are serial mediators linking self-affirmation and behavior (van Koningsbruggen et al., 2014) although currently such studies rarely make use of qualitative data either during or poststudy to be able to understand the process further.

In terms of moderating effects, the researchers noted that self-affirmation led to greater increases in fruit and vegetable consumption among lowest baseline consumers. This is in line with other studies that have reported that self-affirmation is most effective for those at high to moderate risk (Armitage, Harris, Hepton, & Napper, 2008; van Koningsbruggen & Das, 2009).

Participants recorded their daily fruit and vegetable consumption using the same online system. They were provided with an automated daily email prompt to do so. While this approach should ensure a more accurate recording of the target behavior it didn't guarantee that all participants completed the study. Dropout rates were slightly higher than in a comparable offline study (Epton & Harris, 2008) although it is worth noting that the two studies differed in their approach in compensating people for their participation. Finally, the setting itself is worth evaluating in relation to the overall process. Here, we note that different samples carried out the intervention in different settings (University vs. local community setting).

So how should we evaluate the role of the technology in this behavior change intervention?

In addition to the cost-savings benefits of using technology to roll out the intervention the technology also prompted daily reminders for diary completion. A key focus for the intervention was the use of tailored web information. This information, developed in participatory workshops, was seen as credible by the participants groups. Future work could build on the possibilities of producing materials that best fits a participant's background and preferences to enhance the outcome of the intervention something that is obviously cost prohibitive in terms of paper based material. Technological solutions to recording data, for example, a photographic analysis of fruit and vegetable consumption, may also increase accuracy of the data collected.

DISCUSSION

The case studies have highlighted a number of issues around the evaluation of both the outcome and the process of the intervention. The main issues are discussed further alongside ideas for the way in which technology can play a role.

Technology to Improve Data Recording and Collection

Having the right data at the right time is important in order to be able to evaluate the outcome of the intervention. A key issue for many interventions is the reliance on self-report data which is prone to biases, errors of recall, and estimation difficulties. Technology offers a number of opportunities for improving data collection measures. Wearable technologies and mobile apps allow users to automatically collect data in relation, for example, to physical activity, heart rate, and calorie consumption (see, e.g., Chapter 7).

Technology also makes it easier to record data and upload results. Participants can record events in real time and synchronize data with researcher. There are also situations in which objective data from sensors external to the participant could also be collected, for example, energy monitoring devices could record energy use over a given period of time. This kind of objective data could also be analyzed alongside self-report data.

Technology to Improve the Tailoring of the Intervention

Recognizing that different people might react differently to the intervention suggests an opportunity for technology in relation to the tailoring of the behavior change intervention. Tailored messages have been used in studies to match up the content with the participant's stage of readiness to change (Spittaels, De Bourdeaudhuij, Brug, & Vandelanotte, 2007). Web designers have also sought to increase engagement with web-based health interventions, for example, through enhancing the credibility of the health message (see Hu & Sundar, 2010). Studies have shown that the gender of the source plays a role in credibility (Flanagin & Metzger, 2003) or that posthoc preference matching relates to increased acceptance of the health message (Sillence et al., 2015). A more embedded use of the technology could see the correctly tailored version of the materials being assigned reactively as each new participant signs into a system and provides details, such as age, gender, and relevant preferences. Other possibilities include using Location Based Services (LBS) to deliver intervention materials in a timely manner, for example, reminders to stop at the gym on the way home. Technology would also allow participants some degree of customization control over their interface with the intervention and this may help to promote overall engagement with the process and reduce dropout rates.

Technology to Maintain Longer Term Engagement in the Intervention

The delivery of any behavior change intervention and especially those targeting public health is at its most effective when the user stays fully engaged with the process in order to receive, in medical terms, the full intervention "dose." High attrition rates are problematic for evaluating interventions and technological responses have focused on two main areas. First, the use of prompts and reminders in order to keep participants engaged. Emails and text reminders are present in a wide range of online intervention studies (Webb et al., 2010) and have been shown to improve engagement.

Second, designers are recognizing the importance of social influence in maintaining engagement with interventions. As the role of peer-to-peer advice and information increases across a number of domains including health, researchers are increasingly considering the role that homophiles may come to play in influencing behavior change. Homophile addresses the extent to which two or more individuals who interact are similar in certain attributes, beliefs, education, social status, and preferences (Rogers, 2003). Certainly homophile appears to increase the source credibility of information (Phua, 2014) and this, in turn, can lead to greater acceptance of persuasive messages (Hovland & Weiss, 1951).

Indeed, patients have been shown to be more willing to trust others, such as themselves, exhibiting homophile in their preferences for health information and advice (Sillence, Hardy, Briggs, & Harris, 2014). Technological solutions to presenting an intervention based around someone like themselves could be seen as advantageous here and over longer term interventions providing better opportunities for social networking (Poirier & Cobb, 2012) may also be beneficial.

A final note of caution, however, is important that we carefully consider the ethical implications of any practice in which we deny the recipient an informed choice about the kinds of messages they might receive, for example, within their social network. The wider context of this kind of work falls under the area of social marketing and behavioral nudging both of which have been challenged on the basis of reduced individual autonomy (Yeung, 2012).

References

Abraham, C. (2015). *A systematic approach to behaviour change intervention design and evaluation*. Presentation to Newcastle University. Available from: http://fuse.ac.uk/media/sites/researchwebsites/fuse/Charles%20Abraham%20Presentation.pdf

Armitage, C. J. (2006). Evidence that implementation intentions promote transitions. Through the stages of change. *Journal of Consulting and Clinical Psychology, 74*, 141–151.

Armitage, C., Harris, P., Hepton, G., & Napper, L. (2008). Self-affirmation increases acceptance of health-risk information among UK adult smokers with low socioeconomic status. *Psychology of Addictive Behaviors, 22*, 88–95.

Barnes, K. R., Hopkins, W. G., McGuigan, M. R., & Kilding, A. E. (2015). Warm-up with a weighted vest improves running performance via leg stiffness and running economy. *Journal of Science and Medicine in Sport, 18*(1), 103–108.

Bell, B. T., Toth, N., Little, L., & Smith, M. A. (2015). Planning to save the planet using an online intervention based on implementation intentions to change adolescent self-reported energy-saving behavior. *Environment and Behavior*, 1–24.

Campbell, N. C., Murray, E., Darbyshire, J., Emery, J., Farmer, A., Griffiths, F., Guthrie, B., Lester, H., Wilson, P., & Kinmouth, A. L. (2007). Designing and evaluating complex interventions to improve health care. *British Medical Journal, 334*(7591), 455.

Craig, P., Dieppe, P., Macintyre, S., Michie, S., Nazareth, I., & Petticrew, M. (2008). Developing and evaluating complex interventions: the new Medical Research Council guidance. *British Medical Journal, 337.*

Epton, T., & Harris, P. R. (2008). Self-affirmation promotes health behavior change. *Health Psychology, 27*(6), 746.

Fielden, A., Sillence, E., Little, L., & Harris, P. (2016). Self- Affirming online promotes increased fruit and vegetable consumption in high-risk populations. *Applied Psychology: Health and Wellbeing, 8*, 3–18.

Flanagin, A. J., & Metzger, M. J. (2003). The perceived credibility of personal Web page information as influenced by the sex of the source. *Computers in Human Behavior, 19*(6), 683–701.

Gollwitzer, P. M. (1999). Implementation intentions: strong effects of simple plans. *American Psychologist, 54*(7), 493.

Gollwitzer, P. M., & Sheeran, P. (2006). Implementation intentions and goal achievement: a meta-analysis of effects and processes. *Advances in Experimental Social Psychology, 38*, 69–119.

Griffiths, F., Lindenmeyer, A., Powell, J., Lowe, P., & Thorogood, M. (2006). Why are health care interventions delivered over the Internet? A systematic review of the published literature. *Journal of Medical Internet Research, 8*(2), e10.

Hovland, C. I., & Weiss, W. (1951). The influence of source credibility on communication effectiveness. *Public Opinion Quarterly, 15*(4), 635–650.

Hu, Y., & Sundar, S. S. (2010). Effects of online health sources on credibility and behavioral intentions. *Communication Research, 37*, 105–132.

Jacobson, N. S., & Truax, P. (1991). Clinical significance: a statistical approach to defining meaningful change in psychotherapy research. *Journal of Consulting and Clinical Psychology, 59*(1), 12.

John, J. H., Yudkin, P. L., Neil, H. A. W., & Ziebland, S. (2003). Does stage of change predict outcome in a primary-care intervention to encourage an increase in fruit and vegetable consumption? *Health Education Research, 18*(4), 429–438.

Joshipura, K. J., Hu, F. B., Manson, J. E., Stampfer, M. J., Rimm, E. B., Speizer, F. E., Colditz, G., Ascherio, A., Rosner, B., Spiegelman, D., & Willett, W. C. (2001). The effect of fruit and vegetable intake on risk for coronary heart disease. *Annals of Internal Medicine, 134*(12), 1106–1114.

Maher, C. A., Lewis, L. K., Ferrar, K., Marshall, S., De Bourdeaudhuij, I., & Vandelanotte, C. (2014). Are health behavior change interventions that use online social networks effective? a systematic review. *Journal of Medical Internet Research, 16*(2), e402014.

McDonald, S. D., Perkins, S. L., & Walker, M. C. (2005). Correlation between self-reported smoking status and serum cotinine during pregnancy. *Addictive Behaviors, 30*(4), 853–857.

McQueen, A., & Klein, W. M. (2006). Experimental manipulations of self-affirmation: a systematic review. *Self and Identity, 5*(4), 289–354.

Michie, S., Fixsen, D., Grimshaw, J. M., & Eccles, M. P. (2009). Specifying and reporting complex behaviour change interventions: the need for a scientific method. *Implementation Science, 4*(40), 1–6.

Noar, S. M., Benac, C. N., & Harris, M. S. (Jul 2007). Does tailoring matter? Meta-analytic review of tailored print health behavior change interventions. *Psychological Bulletin, 133*(4), 673–693.

Phua, J. (2016). The effects of similarity, parasocial identification, and source credibility in obesity public service announcements on diet and exercise self-efficacy. *Journal of Health Psychology, 21*(5), 699–708.

Poirier, J., & Cobb, N. K. (2012). Social influence as a driver of engagement in a web-based health intervention. *Journal of Medical Internet Research, 14*(1), e36.

Prochaska, J. O., & DiClemente, C. C. (1983). Stages and processes of self-change. of smoking: toward an integrative model of change. *Journal of Consulting and Clinical Psychology, 51*, 390–395.

Rogers, E. M. (2003). *Diffusion of innovations*. New York: Free Press.

Sillence, E., Hardy, C., Harris, P.R. & Briggs, P. (2014). Modelling patient engagement in peer-to-peer healthcare. In *Proceedings of WWW'14 Proceedings of the companion publication of the 23rd international conference on World wide web companion*, pp. 481–486.

Sillence, E., Harris, P.R., & Briggs, P. (2015). Assessing patient experience and patient preference when designing web support for smoking cessation. In *Proceedings of the 5th International Conference on Digital Health 2015* (pp. 25–26). ACM.

Smit, E. S., Hoving, C., Cox, V. C. M., & de Vries, H. (2012). Influence of recruitment strategy on the reach and effect of a web-based multiple tailored smoking cessation intervention among Dutch adult smokers. *Health Education Research, 27*(2), 191–199.

Spittaels, H., De Bourdeaudhuij, I., Brug, J., & Vandelanotte, C. (2007). Effectiveness of an online computer-tailored physical activity intervention in a real-life setting. *Health Education Research, 22*(3), 385–396.

Toth, N., Bell, B. T., Avramides, K., Rulton, K., & Little, L. (2014). Is the next generation prepared? Understanding barriers to teenage energy conservation. In S. Reiter (Ed.), *Energy consumption: Impacts of human activity, current and future challenges, environmental and ecological effects* (pp. 117–140). New York, NY: Nova Science.

van Koningsbruggen, G. M., & Das, E. (2009). Don't derogate this message! Self-affirmation promotes online type 2 diabetes risk test taking. *Psychology & Health, 24*, 635–649.

van Koningsbruggen, G. M., Harris, P. R., Smits, A. J., Schüz, B., Scholz, U., & Cooke, R. (2014). Self-affirmation before exposure to health communications promotes intentions and health behavior change by increasing anticipated regret. *Communication Research*, 1–19.

Webb, T., Joseph, J., Yardley, L., & Michie, S. (2010). Using the internet to promote health behavior change: a systematic review and meta-analysis of the impact of theoretical basis, use of behavior change techniques, and mode of delivery on efficacy. *Journal of Medical Internet Research, 12*(1), e4.

Yeung, K. (2012). Nudge as fudge. *The Modern Law Review, 75*(1), 122–148.

BinCam: Evaluating Persuasion at Multiple Scales

R. Comber, A. Thieme

Open Lab, School of Computing Science, Newcastle
University, Newcastle upon Tyne, United Kingdom

OVERVIEW

This chapter describes the lessons learned in the deployment of Bin-Cam, a system designed to persuade people to reduce food waste in domestic settings. This system has been deployed in three separate evaluations, and in this chapter we report on our experiences and findings from the second case study. This case study is particularly interesting not only for the interactions between participants and the system, but how the system was received more widely in the media and in society. We begin with a description of the context in which the BinCam system was designed and the motivations for its particular material configuration. We then detail the various forms of data that we collected throughout the study and outline the materials and participants directly involved. We then outline results from the different scales of change. Finally, drawing on the findings from our deployment we discuss the implications of designing technologies for behavior change across multiple levels of end-user participation

INTRODUCTION

The BinCam project asked what seemed like a relatively simple question: can we improve young adults recycling behavior using social media? The way we went about exploring the topic over three deployments was a little less straightforward, and involved a two-part technology system that integrated provocative and pervasive technologies with online social

Behavior Change Research and Theory. http://dx.doi.org/10.1016/B978-0-12-802690-8.00009-8

media, and has been positioned and understood as an example of a persuasive technology (Thieme et al., 2012), a nudge for habitual behavior (Comber & Thieme, 2012), a disruptive intervention (Poole, Hoonhout and Comber, 2014), and an abomination of privacy invading technologies and solutionism (Vines et al., 2013; Morozov, 2014). While the project ostensibly targeted personal and small group behavior change, it has evoked responses from the media and the public that considered a wider societal impact of what was sometimes perceived to be an overly simplistic and technologically deterministic approach to a significant societal challenge (see Vines et al., 2013). In this chapter, we explore the multiple and sometimes conflicting ways in which we can evaluate behavior change technology and the resultant narratives that surround technology interventions like BinCam. Through the exploration of the BinCam project, we discuss the ways in which we can evaluate the impact of these systems in light of increasing academic and popular discourse on the design of technology to shape behavior. We are concerned in this chapter, with how or if we should delineate our interventions and their assessment from a wider landscape of technology use and discourse. In particular, we are interested to respond to the challenges of understanding behavior change as something that happens across multiple scales and through multiple channels, and which occurs embedded in a history of understanding behavior change.

BACKGROUND

The BinCam project was originally conceived as a response to the growing problem of consumer food waste. It is estimated that approximately 5.3 million tons of food and 4.9 million tons of recyclable packaging are improperly disposed of as waste by UK households alone (WRAP, 2011). Issues are seen to arise from a lack of knowledge on appropriate recycling behaviors (e.g., what is and is not recyclable?), availability of appropriate recycling facilities (e.g., PET recycling), and perceived effort and value (e.g., efficacy of segregated recycling at home). This gap, between knowledge or attitude and action, is even more pronounced for university students, where it has been found that recycling practices established in the parental home are not transferred to university residence (Scott, 2009). Despite significant public messaging in the United Kingdom in relation to recycling over the past 10 years, reports continue to suggest that young adults between the age of 18 and 34 are particularly under-aware of issues of recycling (WRAP, 2011).

The BinCam project was designed as a first step to explore the possibility to connect young adults in relation to issues of sustainability, through the wider discourses on social media. Young adults are typically some of the most digitally enabled populations and reports suggest a continual increase in the daily usage of social media (Pew Internet, http://www.pewinternet. org/fact-sheets/social-networking-fact-sheet/, Hazard Owen, 2015). Social media has become a popular target for behavioral interventions on issues such as sustainability, political engagement, and physical activity, leveraging both its increasing presence in everyday life and the ability to draw together like-minded individuals across society. Social media promises to amplify the impact of behavioral interventions through the establishment and exploitation of social influence, support and capital. Social media has also been seen as a site for the development of social change (Crivellaro, Comber, Bowers, Wright, & Olivier, 2014). Social media is, in this light, a place where the actions and discourse of sustainability are made public. With BinCam we made the actions of waste disposal visible (Ganglbauer, Fitzpatrick, & Molzer, 2012), and hoped to generate a discussion among participants on the ways in which they could act more sustainable.

Across much behavior change research, this focus on raising awareness and visibility has often been undertaken targeting individual change. However, there is a growing recognition of the need to explore the household as a unit of change (Scott, Oates, & Young, 2015). Given the current infrastructures of household and industrial recycling, it is clear that as a unit of waste production, the household has a large appeal for possible reductions. However, despite its apparently natural boundaries, the home is continuously reshaped around bodies, boundaries, and physical and technological buildings (Coughlan, Comber, Mortier, Ploetz, & Mitchell, 2014). Consequently, the sustainable behaviors and practices that we wish to observe in the home often extend far beyond the home (Ganglbauer, Fitzpatrick, & Comber, 2013). We can take both the positive from this position, that behavior change targeted at the individual or collective in the home has the potential to invoke change across society, and the negative, that focusing on the household reinforces a siloed approach to waste reduction (McDonald, 2011).

There is a growing body of research and popular media that suggests the need to look beyond the consumer as the chief actor (or subject) of change (e.g., Morozov, 2014; Dourish, 2010). In this light, the notion of behavior change interventions is tied to the dominant 'market' approach of neoliberalism. Dourish (2010) makes this argument most clearly when he suggests that "by turning the problems of environmentalism into questions of personal moral choice and by turning environmental action into a redirection of consumption patterns, research in HCI for environmental sustainability has systematically ignored important areas for potential action" (p. 8). These areas of action are changes to infrastructure and to ways of conceiving of waste as something other than the by-product of consumption. This is as much about how we talk about what we do with behavior change, as it is about the interventions we design and the impact they have on behavior. This has lead some (e.g., Brynjarsdottir et al., 2012) to question the value of individual-level behavior change techniques in relation to sustainability and to look at a variety of social units (e.g., practices) and scales (e.g., policy, culture).

In this chapter, we examine the impact of the BinCam system across these scales—the individual, the home, the extended social network, and in society. In particular, we examine the way in which the data and discourses that are created through and surround the project, frame the possibility for change to occur across these scales.

METHOD

Design

The studies carried out with the BinCam system follow a case study methodology, using mixed-methods and tools for data collection. Given the novel technology intervention, and the complex configuration of household waste, social media, and individual attitudes and behaviors in the domestic setting, it was decided to focus on a small set of households across deployments of up to 6 weeks. Significant challenges exist in accurately quantifying household food waste at scale, and the case study approach allowed us to examine in detail the change that occurred in the small sample. While many behavior change interventions using novel technologies demonstrate novelty effects, we were particularly interested in how longer deployments could be used to understand engagement with the behavior change intervention.

Materials

The BinCam studies utilized mixed-methods for data collection, and included data collected from the system, from pre- and postintervention questionnaires, and individual and focus group interviews. During the studies, these were intended to reveal changes in how individuals and households thought and talked about recycling and sustainability, and the extent to which they also changed their behavior. Table 9.1 provides an overview of the measures and tools to assess change at various levels. Throughout the deployments we also provided participants with

TABLE 9.1 Levels and Measures of Analysis in the BinCam Project

Level of analysis	Individual	Household	Group	Society
Measures	Attitudes	Behavior	Practices	Discourses
Data source	Questionnaire	BinCam system	Interviews	Media

informational resources, taking inspiration from local government resources, on what could and could not be recycled in their area. This information was intended to reveal some of the infrastructures that support
(or are absent from) waste disposal, but are also used to inform individual
behavior (i.e., to know what is "recyclable").

BinCam System

The BinCam system comprised two parts: a typical household bin
(Fig. 9.1), and an online social media application. The bin was augmented
with a mobile phone in the lid. Through the mobile phone and its in-built
camera and accelerometer images were captured inside the bin whenever
the lid was closed. The images provide a dataset from which we infer the
recycling and food waste behavior of the household. In our initial study,
we used both participants-driven tagging and crowd-sourced tagging
using Amazon Mechanical Turk. Although more recent studies (Lessel,
Altmeyer, & Krüger, 2015) have demonstrated some increased performance in localized crowd-sourced identification of waste, we found the
accuracy of the data to be too low to strongly support claims of changes
in behavior. Up to 75% error was recorded, resulting in poor correlations with participants' behavior and expectations in relation to behavior

FIGURE 9.1   The BinCam system comprises a household refuse bin, with a mobile
phone mounted inside the lid. When the lid closes, an image is taken and uploaded to a
social media site.

change techniques. In our later studies, we employed manual tagging by a researcher with a carefully defined set of heuristics for evaluation.

The images captured through the phone were also sent to an invitation-only application on facebook that shared the image with other users of the BinCam system. Only participants in the study could view and comment on these pictures. The facebook application is intended to support discussion between and among households on the images. In each of three studies, the bins were placed in shared student households in a shared space (i.e., kitchen). Consequently, individually disposed of items were not publically and identifiably associated with an individual. The posted images were processed to record the types of waste captured in the images. This processing afforded the possibility to calculate a metric of recycling performance for each bin and to construct a competitive league between households. These features of the system were most informed by notions of improving the information that participants had about their own waste disposal.

An unexpected consequence of the system implementation was that the camera in the bin emitted a vibration noise after each image had been captured. This postactional cue became a significant discussion point with participants, as it drew attention to the system and to a just-performed behavior (Comber & Thieme, 2012).

Questionnaire

Pre- and postintervention questionnaires were designed to investigate behavior change techniques, including: *awareness raising, competition, coercion, personal informatics, and normative and informational influence* (for more information on the design, see Comber et al., 2013). The pre-/postintervention questionnaire comprised a set of items for evaluating attitudes and self-reported behavior in relation to recycling based on the measurements used by WRAP (2011). Questions included topics such as attitudes to recycling (36 items), and food waste (43 items). Both topics were explored through measures of proenvironmental attitudes, and self-reported behaviors in relation to recycling, food waste, and shopping. Questions related to attitudes toward recycling included, for example, "I recycle because it is good for the environment and saves resources," while self-report questions asked, for example, "I often forget to put the recycling out because I'm not sure of the collection date." Alongside these, we also used preintervention measures of use of social media (11 items, Ellison, Steinfield, & Lampe, 2007) and the perceived social context of the household in general and in relation to the project specifically (48 items, e.g., "There is a feeling of unity and cohesion in our flat."). Both the Facebook Intensity scale and the group cohesion measures we used to assess potential compounding variables within household and individual use of the system.

The postintervention questionnaire repeated the same measures with additional questions posed in relation to the perceptions of privacy among participants. Evaluation in the second study–explored issues raised in the previous study in more depth, such as concerns for privacy, awareness raising through the system, and the impact of changes made to the system (i.e., competition, personal informatics). Privacy was assessed through 6 item Likert scale exploring willingness to share (e.g., "I would not mind if everybody on Facebook could see pictures of our bin," and "I do not want other people to see what we dispose of.") and access (e.g., 'I do not mind that our waste is visible on the BinCam App as long as only participants have access to the pictures'). Measures of user-perception of the system examined the various representations of data (e.g., "I found the statistical presentations about our waste informative") and the perceived use and quality of the competitive and information interfaces (e.g., "I regularly compared how we did in the BinLeague to other households").

Participants

To date, BinCam has been deployed in three studies over 4, 6, and 5 weeks respectively with a total of 93 participants in 16 households. In each study university students have been the target population. For the purposes of this chapter, we outline the participants in our second study. 34 individuals completed the questionnaire for the study. The study sample was aged 18–27 ($\bar{x} = 21.12, SD = 1.935$), of whom 20 were female, 2 were in part-time education, with the remainder in full-time education, 17 were in the first year of their third level education, 3 in the third year of their undergraduate degree, 12 were enrolled in Masters level education, and one undertaking a PhD. One student was an exchange student from an international university. All but one flat had students at different stages of education. Five households had six participants and one household had five participants. Three households were mixed gendered (three female, three male) and three households were single gendered (one household of five males, and two households of six females).

Interviews and Focus Groups

Interviews and focus groups were also conducted with participants to reveal changes that would not be evident in our existing data sets and to further unpick some of the qualities of interaction with the system. Interviews were conducted with one randomly selected participant from each household. Only one participant declined to participate in an individual interview, result in five individual interviews. The remaining participants were invited to participate in per-household focus groups, with all but one participant agreeing to participate, resulting in 6 focus groups with a total of 27 participants. Both interviews and focus groups were open-ended, with the aim of capturing the diverse perspectives of participants on the BinCam system, the impact of social media on their behavior, and concerns on privacy. Audio recordings were transcribed, anonymized, and analyzed using an inductive thematic analysis (Braun & Clarke, 2006).

Media

Finally, an unexpected data source came from the media response to the BinCam project (see Vines et al., 2013 for a full account of this dataset and analysis). In the immediate response to the project this comprised at least 91 responses, including TV, radio, newspaper, and online coverage. Subsequently, the project has been included in 3 exhibitions, a TV show on future domestic technologies, and similar systems have been designed and deployed in academic research (e.g., Lessel et al., 2015; Lim, Yalvac, Funk, Hu, & Rauterberg, 2014) and commercial services. Data in these sources refers primarily to textual accounts of the system, opinion on the merit of technological intervention, and debate on issues of privacy. These accounts support analysis of the impact of the system as part of the discourses on these topics.

RESULTS

Individual Change

Technologies for behavior change often take an explicit focus on changing individual behaviors. With BinCam we hoped to impact on individual behaviors, but focused on the household level for measurement. This was necessary to preserve privacy on individually disposed items, but also as the nature of waste disposal in shared households. To represent change we expected at the individual level, we instead chose to evaluate changes in attitudes and self-perception. We used a questionnaire to explore individual change and potential links to recycling, proenvironmental, shopping, and food waste attitudes and behaviors. We also explored participants' use of social media, and their sense of group cohesion with their flatmates, which could be a useful predictor of the influence of social media. Finally, following the deployments we also enquired about their concerns about privacy and impressions of the system.

Although prior research had suggested that young adults were under-aware of recycling issues (WRAP, 2011), we found our self-selected participants to hold strong positive attitudes toward recycling and sustainability. Consequently, statistical analysis using t-tests showed no significant change between pre- and postintervention responses in reported attitudes or behavior, with only marginal significance found in relation to meal planning (e.g., "I plan what I will eat for each meal of the forthcoming week") and shopping (e.g., "I check several packets of the same product to find the one with the longest expiry date."). We have previously argued that this indicated that issues other than attitudes to sustainability and recycling need closer examination in behavior change for sustainability, including immediate awareness of recycling opportunities and perceived control over recycling opportunities. Indeed, interview data further supported these findings and often suggested that participants knew they should recycle, but either did not know what they could recycle or were not strongly informed about the facilities available to them, presumably because they were in rented accommodation. In some cases, they specifically felt that the facilities were lacking, for instance, for composting.

Household Change

As our data revealed little change in attitudes or self-reported behavior, we turned to our captured data to explore whether any significant change had occurred in what was placed in the bins. In comparison to our initial study, where we had employed crowd sourcing for data tagging, in this instance manual tagging created a richer dataset for analysis. Each item was classified as either appropriate (i.e., nonrecyclable) or inappropriate (i.e., recyclable or food waste) for the landfill bin. In order to make sense of this data, it was necessary to calculate the ratios of correct and inappropriate waste. For each bin we could calculate the relative amount of waste in the bin that should not have been there. This data was also fed back to participants on a weekly basis to inform their own perceptions on recycling behavior. In general, while there was a reduction in overall waste, there were no significant changes to the ratio of appropriate to inappropriate waste. In later interviews, some participants suggested that even when some waste may have appeared to be inappropriate (e.g., cardboard in the landfill bin) it might have been appropriate (e.g., cardboard with food on it).

Group Change

While our quantitative data did not suggest any significant change to waste disposal in the household, participants reported changes to how they went about food planning, shopping, and waste. In fact, one of the most surprising findings was that participants reported to be more actively attempting to reduce waste through sharing food purchasing (e.g., buying loaves of bread together) and reducing waste through, for example, sharing leftovers. As Julia, a participant, suggested:

> I don't like wasting food. Erm... and I'm definitely aware of the amount that I've wasted as the BinCam has been on. Erm... so it's made me just kind of just reduce my portion size and then think about how much stuff I'm throwing away and trying to catch things before they go out of date and stuff like that.

In this sense, the presence of the BinCam system caused participants to reconsider their practices around food consumption. However, the data available within the BinCam system did not, and could not, reflect changes that were specifically undertaken to avoid interaction with the bin.

Societal Change

While the BinCam project engaged with social media as a means to connect individuals and households, it did not originally aim to influence the discussion of sustainability beyond the participating households. Yet, the extensive media coverage of the project was a sign of the potential to engage the public in debate on the role of technology in sustainability. While much of the reporting on BinCam in the media was framed as either negative or saw the project as an academic curiosity (Vines et al., 2013), it also engaged readers in a debate about the nature of technological solutionism—the idea that technology can easily fix complex societal challenges. More so, it engaged a large section of the media in concerns about invasion of privacy, particularly in relation to local government engagement in observation of individuals' behavior, either for corrective punishment (e.g., fining for inappropriate waste) or for surveillance. For instance, with the media response to BinCam many questions were raised about the nature of "shaming" users. Our data never suggested that participants were shamed (by others), but rather that they felt guilty about the disparity of their own (recorded) behavior from their attitudes or perceived self. Nevertheless, the BinCam system can be and has been understood as a paternalistic device—as far as some media coverage was concerned it "knows" what is right. Consequently, the focus on individual change is seen to impinge upon the agency of individuals.

Most interestingly, comments on news articles moved beyond simply reflecting on the BinCam system or research and began to question wider infrastructural issues, such as the extent to which current recycling practices are futile, or the explicit role of technology in enforcing political decisions. While these questions are precisely the forms of change (i.e., infrastructure and policy) that have been suggested are needed beyond individual change (Dourish, 2010), they are also those that are most fervently questioned by public perceptions of behavior change interventions. These arguments are not created by the BinCam project, but their response to the project demonstrates a need to continue to bring to the surface the tensions between technology and societal challenges.

DISCUSSION

When thinking about assessing the impact of BinCam as an intervention, the challenge of understanding the complex variety of factors that shape peoples' behaviors other than the intervention itself deserve attention. This is particularly so when explaining why behaviors might have changed, didn't change, or when we cannot conclude in either direction. As we have seen, the results of our individual and household level intervention suggest modest and anecdotal change. In this way, whether BinCam is understood as a behavior change technology and how successful it was, is a complicated question. Its goal was to invite participants to reflect on and engage in discussion with others around their own and shared recycling behavior, and as a means to support that discussion to create visibility around recycling behavior. With this much of the framing of BinCam and its public perception has been to take a more critical stance of the role of technology in changing behavior. The BinCam system as designed almost asked a question as "What would happen if…?" and the responses we got were both directly from our studies and from the public when people outside the research project also ask "what would happen if…?" From this question, we identify three responses which act as bridges across scales and allow us to evaluate our outcomes when designing and evaluating digital interventions that consider their discursive impact.

System as Bridge Between Mundane and Provocation

The BinCam system as a household bin was designed to "fit into" the home, to be inconspicuous, and thus, not to draw attention to itself. Yet, as an Internet connected gadget and a novelty, it was designed to be conspicuous, to raise awareness. The duality of the system allowed it to be both a part of the fabric of everyday life and a connection to a future, of desired sustainability, or as in the case of much public perception, otherwise. Thus digital systems which bridge between the mundane and the provocative can give rise to new ways of talking about artifacts and practices in the home. Among participants in our studies, this is most evident in the ways in which the sound of the photographs being captured drew attention to the presence of the otherwise "invisible" digital system within the bin. Yet, outside of the study, this bridge gives rise to a number of discussions on the role of surveillance in the home and the problematic nature of digital solutionism. A digital camera in a bin can thus be related to CCTV cameras, and a bin to improve recycling can be equated to a technological determinist perspective on how society works. With the BinCam system, we have learned that by examining the multiple roles of digital systems in the home and in society, we can more carefully design interventions that have the potential to create bridges across scales. At the individual level we might expect this to be a novelty or a curiosity, but it can also have the power to break habits. At the societal level, it can reveal tensions which exist in the ways in which we, as researchers and as a society, use and talk about technology. To evaluate this we must be aware of and analyze the multiple ways in which the systems themselves are talked about as artifacts and should not assume that they have a neutral impact on discourses, even if we are focusing on changing behaviors.

Network as a Bridge for Experiences

The BinCam system was designed to connect a network of households through facebook. Our initial idea was that simply by seeing what other people do and do not dispose of, individuals could reflect on their own behavior. More widely, the network became a channel through which information and experiences could be shared. Such experiential networks can, in and of themselves, be considered as sites for discussion where varied experiences come together and can produce action (Crivellaro et al., 2014). In this project, we have limited the extent to which the network is utilized for information sharing and the network itself is shared only among participants in the study. Yet, even the mere thought of sharing images of waste on a social media site is enough to raise eyebrows and open discussion. We continue to see the social as a significant resource in raising awareness and for supporting reflection. Often it need only be the potential, as much as the reality, of networked sharing which is a successful mechanism to channel discussion. With BinCam, we have learned that it is the possibility for our behaviors to be seen on unexpected scales that raises critical reflection on our behavior.

Media as a Bridge of Discourse

Perhaps the most surprising feedback we have received on the BinCam system has been the public evaluation provided through media coverage. These discourses covered a wide array of issues and perspectives, and became a source of insight on how behavior change technologies can be understood by the public. Consequently, we end up questioning how can we evaluate the impact of our work through the media. Indeed, going further we can ask whether the media can or should be considered part of the "intervention." In this latter sense, we are faced with a problem of how we do or whether we can configure the "persuasion" of media (Vines et al., 2013). As digital systems become embedded in social contexts and histories, as artifacts and channels for discourses, they become subject to increasing numbers of possible interpretations. With BinCam we have seen the project be interpreted in many ways we would not envisage. Here we must also consider the system and the network as sources of discourses that can be adopted by the media. Importantly, we must then consider the role of public discourse in enacting change. Given that the BinCam system set out to raise awareness of recycling issues, can we really consider that "no news is bad news?"

CONCLUSIONS

In this chapter we have discussed the multiple scales from which the BinCam system can be assessed—the individual, the household, the network, and in the wider public arena. In these intertwining discourses the project has had varied successes. Whether these are significant or long-term seems both unlikely and as yet undecided. However, what we have learned from it are the ways in which anticipated and unexpected interconnections of systems, networks, and society, can produce change. We have identified those systems networks, and media as artifacts, channels, and actors in the production of discourses of change where they give rise to new ways to talk about our behaviors and to reflect on the role of technology in our lives.

References

Braun, V., & Clarke, V. (2006). Using thematic analysis in psychology. *Qualitative Research in Psychology*, 3(2), 77–101.

Brynjarsdottir, H., Håkansson, M., Pierce, J., Baumer, E., DiSalvo, C., & Sengers, P. (2012). Sustainably unpersuaded. In: *Proceedings of the 2012 ACM annual conference on Human Factors in Computing Systems - CHI'12* (p. 947). New York, New York, USA: ACM Press.

Comber, R., & Thieme, A. (2012). Designing beyond habit: opening space for improved recycling and food waste behaviors through processes of persuasion, social influence and aversive affect. *Personal and Ubiquitous Computing*, 17(6), 1197–1210.

Comber, R., Thieme, A., Rafiev, A., Taylor, N., Krämer, N., & Olivier, P. (2013). BinCam: designing for engagement with facebook for behavior change. In P. Kotzé, G. Marsden, G. Lindgaard, J. Wesson, & M. Winckler (Eds.), *Human-Computer Interaction—INTERACT 2013 SE-7* (pp. 99–115). (Vol. 8118). Berlin, Heidelberg: Springer.

Coughlan, T., Comber, R., Mortier, R., Ploetz, T., & Mitchell, V. (2014). HomeSys 2014. In: *Proceedings of the 2014 ACM International Joint Conference on Pervasive and Ubiquitous Computing Adjunct Publication—UbiComp'14 Adjunct* (pp. 879–885). New York, New York, USA: ACM Press.

Crivellaro, C., Comber, R., Bowers, J., Wright, P.C., & Olivier, P. (2014). A pool of dreams: facebook, politics and the emergence of a social movement. In: *Proceedings of the 32nd annual ACM conference on Human factors in computing systems—CHI '14* (pp. 3573–3582). New York, New York, USA: ACM Press.

Dourish, P. (2010). HCI and environmental sustainability. In: *Proceedings of the 8th ACM Conference on Designing Interactive Systems—DIS'10* (p. 1). New York, New York, USA: ACM Press.

Ellison, N. B., Steinfield, C., & Lampe, C. (2007). The benefits of Facebook "friends:" social capital and college students use of online social network sites. *Journal of Computer-Mediated Communication, 12*, 1143–1168.

Ganglbauer, E., Fitzpatrick, G., & Molzer, G. (2012). Creating visibility. In: *Proceedings of the 11th International Conference on Mobile and Ubiquitous Multimedia—MUM'12* (p. 1). New York, New York, USA: ACM Press.

Ganglbauer, E., Fitzpatrick, G., & Comber, R. (2013). Negotiating food waste: using a practice lens to inform design. *ACM Transactions on Computer-Human Interaction (TOCHI), 20*(2), 11.

Hazard Owen, L. (2015). Messaging and chat apps continue their rise in popularity, especially among young people. Nieman Labs. Available from: http://www.niemanlab.org/2015/08/messaging-and-chat-apps-continue-their-rise-in-popularity-especially-among-young-people/

Lessel, P., Altmeyer, M., & Krüger, A. (2015). Analysis of recycling capabilities of individuals and crowds to encourage and educate people to separate their garbage playfully. In: *Proceedings of the 33rd Annual ACM Conference on Human Factors in Computing Systems—CHI'15* (pp. 1095–1104). New York, New York, USA: ACM Press.

Lim, V., Yalvac, F., Funk, M., Hu, J., & Rauterberg, M. (2014). Can we reduce waste and waist together through EUPHORIA? In: *2014 IEEE International Conference on Pervasive Computing and Communication Workshops (PERCOM WORKSHOPS)* (pp. 382–387). IEEE.

McDonald, S. (2011). Green behaviour: differences in recycling behaviour between the home and the workplace. In D. Bartlett (Ed.), *Going green: the psychology of sustainability in the workplace* (pp. 59–64). Leicester, UK: The British Psychological Society.

Morozov, E. (2014). *To save everything, click here: technology, solutionism, and the urge to fix problems that don't exist*. New York: PublicAffairs.

Poole, E. S., Comber, R., & Hoonhout, J. (2014). Disruption as a research method for studying technology use in homes. *Interacting with Computers, 27*(1), 13–20.

Scott, A.K. (2009). Towards sustainable consumption: Understanding the adoption and practice of environmental actions in households. Unpublished PhD thesis, University of Sheffield.

Scott, A., Oates, C., & Young, W. (2015). A conceptual framework of the adoption and practice of environmental actions in households. *Sustainability, 7*(5), 5793–5818.

Thieme, A., Comber, R., Miebach, J., Weeden, J., Kraemer, N., Lawson, S., & Olivier, P. (2012). "We've bin watching you." In: *Proceedings of the 2012 ACM annual conference on Human Factors in Computing Systems—CHI'12* (p. 2337). New York, New York, USA: ACM Press.

Vines, J., Thieme, A., Comber, R., Blythe, M., Wright, P.C., & Olivier, P. (2013). HCI in the press: online public reactions to mass media portrayals of HCI research. In: *Proceedings of the SIGCHI conference on human factors in computing systems—CHI'13* (p. 1873). New York, New York, USA: ACM Press.

WRAP. (2011). Research Guidance: Monitoring and evaluation guidance (Annex 3). Available from: www.wrap.org.uk/local_authorities/research_guidance

Conclusion

A. Joinson*, E. Sillence**, L. Little**

*School of Management, University of Bath, Bath, United Kingdom;
**PaCT Lab, Department of Psychology, Faculty of Health and Life
Sciences, Northumbria University, Newcastle, United Kingdom

ALIGNING DIGITAL BEHAVIOR CHANGE

In the first chapter of this book, we define digital behavior change as a "behavior change that makes use of technology to either: (1) promote the delivery of the intervention; (2) enhance the environment through which the intervention occurs; or (3) encourage specific patterns of interaction that underpin the intervention." As we have seen through the chapters that followed, there are a variety of techniques and opportunities to use technology in support of behavior change, ranging from its use as a medium for the transmission of a behavior change intervention or message to the potential for mobile phone sensor data to provide diagnostic data and just-in-time intervention.

Across the fields of behavior change and human–computer interaction, there are a number of promising approaches to the *alignment* of behavior change and technology. In his pioneering work on persuasive technology, Fogg (2002) proposes that the persuasive uses of technology can be grouped into a "functional triad." This "triad" comprises technology as a tool for persuasion, as a medium for the conveying of persuasive messages, or technology as a social actor that persuades by exploiting norms of social interaction. More recently, Joinson and Piwek (2016) argued that technology can change behavior in three main ways. The first is by *extending* our capabilities as humans, a notion first proposed by McLuhan (1964). This extension can take various forms, including an extension of our physical capabilities (e.g., to travel distances at speed, to view into the distance), as well as our cognitive abilities (e.g., to remember, to compare alternatives, to conduct calculations). In the case of behavior change, this extension may take the form of the ability to collect, process, and analyze data about our own behavior. The second way is through *amplification* of existing or known social effects. For instance, we know substantial amounts about the impact of many forms of influence on behavior change, ranging from the effectiveness of self-monitoring (Harkin et al., 2015) to social norms and herding behavior (Cialdini, 2001, see also Briggs et al., Chapter 6 in this book). Technology can be used to amplify these effects,

Behavior Change Research and Theory. http://dx.doi.org/10.1016/B978-0-12-802690-8.00014-1

for instance, by providing evidence of herding and social norms through simple mechanisms such as the number of "likes," "retweets," or "up votes" (all of which are ideal for algorithmic analysis and presentation to users). Finally, Joinson and Piwek suggest that technology can *shape* behavior through the use of defaults, rewards, or constraints on behavior. In combination, they claim that technology can be transformative in its impact on behavior. They argue that

> When the outcomes of extension, amplification and shaping combine ... then we can start to think about technology as transformative in that it no longer becomes an extension of human behaviour and capabilities, but it in turn begins to exert a widely felt effect on societal values and more general human behaviour. (*Joinson & Piwek, 2016,* p. 163)

As noted earlier, the key to successful digital behavior change is the alignment between the technology used and the behavior change technique or approach adopted. As noted by Abraham and Dunlop in Chapter 2, successful behavior change interventions require careful and systematic planning. The original UK National Centre for Health and Care Excellence (NICE) guidelines for behavior change state (2007):

> ...it is important to specify three things with respect to any intervention that aims to change behaviour. First, be as specific as possible about its content. Second, spell out what is done, to whom, in what social and economic context, and in what way. Third, make it clear which underlying theories will help make explicit the key causal links between actions and outcomes. (*NICE, 2007,* 2.12)

The 2014 revision of the NICE guidelines suggest that an intervention mapping approach (Bartholomew et al., 2011) can aid in the planning for behavior change interventions. The six stages are shown diagrammatically in Fig. 1.

In terms of the alignment of the technology and behavior, we suggest that technology choice needs to reflect the different intervention stages, rather than simply be considered during the fourth (delivery) stage. For instance, various target populations will have different access rates to technologies, and some technologies will be more acceptable than others to different target populations. The first stage, then, should be to consider potential technologies from the perspective of access and usage patterns in the target population.

During the second stage of intervention mapping (when the primary and secondary goals of the intervention are described), we propose digital behavior change interventions should begin an initial scoping of potential technologies that could be utilized in the intervention.

The third stage in intervention mapping is to conduct an in-depth, evidence-based analysis of the causes of the behavior to be changed, and the potential ways they can be addressed by an intervention. This stage

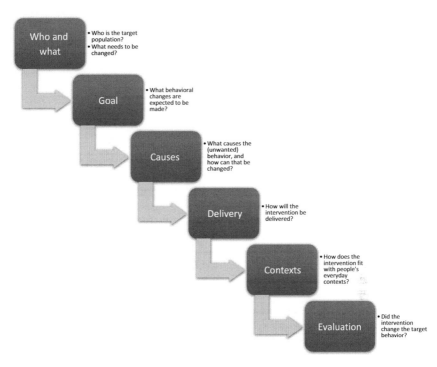

FIGURE 1   **Intervention mapping stages.** *Source: Adapted from NICE. (2014). Behaviour change: individual approaches. Available from https://www.nice.org.uk/guidance/ph49*

reflects the approach of Michie, van Stralen, and West (2011) toward understanding the causes of a behavior and how those relate to possible intervention techniques. At this stage, digital behavior change designers should be also able to evaluate the way in which the proposed digital behavior change intervention will extend, amplify, or shape behavior. Further, the relations between the affordances of the technology and the desired outcome need to be explored and explicitly stated. In more traditional research parlance, this would be akin to fully describing one's research model before conducting data collection. For instance, just as one might predict a mediation or moderation effect when designing a study, so digital behavior change needs to explain the features of the technology relate to the behavior under consideration. For instance, an intervention using a smartphone to track activity levels and provide feedback operates at multiple layers. First, it provides an extension of capability (Fogg's "tool" within the functional triad) by using GPS and the gyroscope to record movement. It then may seek to amplify the effect of self-monitoring on behavior by providing activity level goals, a history function, on-going feedback, and so on. The digital behavior change designers might also plan to shape behavior through either competition/gamification, or perhaps by

CONCLUSION

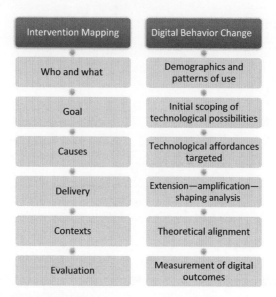

FIGURE 2   Aligning behavior change and technology choice.

encouraging users to make a public commitment or set implementation intentions. These are shown as steps three and four in Fig. 2.

The fifth stage we propose is that, alongside a consideration of the social context in which an intervention will be conducted (the "contexts" stage in intervention mapping), there should also be appreciation of the technological context, and designers should be in a position to align the intervention mapping to the choice of technology, affordances it provides, and the way in which it will support the proposed intervention. For instance, if the theoretical rationale for an intervention is to encourage public commitment, then the theoretical alignment stage is used to explicate how the chosen technology supports this theoretical mechanism, and potential contraindications.

In the final, sixth stage, designers need to be able to identify the measures that will not only be used to evaluate the impact of the intervention on the targeted behavior, but also any "within technology" measures. We propose that evaluation should not just be focused on the desired behavior (outcome evaluation), but there should also be an attempt to measure how people are engaging with the technology (process evaluation), and if the technology is acting as more than simply a messenger for a persuasive communication, whether or not use led to changes in that explanatory variable. For instance, one might argue that providing information about the behavior of peers might lead to behavior change based on people's understanding of descriptive social norms. In this case, rather than simply measuring the outcome behavior, we would also propose that digital behavior change designers also investigate whether using the technology led to changes in people's beliefs about social norms (and how any changes relate to the intensity of use of the technology).

In conclusion, the key to successful digital behavior change lies in the alignment between the technology used and the behavior change technique or approach adopted. The chapters in this book illustrate examples of this alignment in action and the six-step alignment framework presented previously offers behavior change designers a practical tool for developing successful digital behavior interventions.

References

Bartholomew, L. K., Parcel, G. S., Kok, G., et al. (2011). *Planning health promotion programs: An intervention mapping approach* (3rd ed.). San Francisco: Jossey-Bass.

Cialdini, R. B. (2001). *Influence: Science and practice* (4th ed.). Boston: Allyn & Bacon.

Fogg, B. J. (2002). *Persuasive technology: Using computers to change what we think and do*. San Francisco, CA: Morgan Kaufmann.

Harkin, B., Webb, T. L., Chang, B. P. I., Prestwich, A., Conner, M., Kellar, I., Benn, Y., & Sheeran, P. (2015). Does monitoring goal progress promote goal attainment? A meta-analysis of the experimental evidence. *Psychological Bulletin*. Advance online publication.

Joinson, A. N., & Piwek, L. (2016). Technology and the formation of socially positive behaviours. In F. Spotswood (Ed.), *Beyond behaviour change: Perspectives from a diverse field* (pp. 157–176). Bristol: Policy Press.

McLuhan, M. (1964). *Understanding media: The extensions of man*. New York, NY: McGraw Hill (Reissued MIT Press, 1995).

Michie, S., van Stralen, M. M., & West, R. (2011). The behaviour change wheel: a new method for characterising and designing behaviour change interventions. *Implementation Science, 6*(1), 1.

NICE. (2007). Behaviour change: General approaches. Available from https://www.nice.org.uk/guidance/ph6

NICE. (2014). Behaviour change: individual approaches. Available from https://www.nice.org.uk/guidance/ph49

Index